REGULATING DANGER

REGULATING

BY JAMES WHITESIDE

DANGER

The Struggle for Mine
Safety in the Rocky
Mountain Coal Industry

UNIVERSITY OF NEBRASKA PRESS
LINCOLN AND LONDON

Acknowledgments for the use of previously
published material appear on page xv.

The paper in this book meets
the minimum requirements of
American National Standard for
Information Sciences—Permanence
of Paper for Printed Library
Materials, ANSI Z39.48–1984.

**Library of Congress
Cataloging-in-Publication Data**
Whiteside, James, 1950–
    Regulating danger : the struggle for
mine safety in the Rocky Mountain
coal industry / James Whiteside.
        p.   cm.
    Includes bibliographical references.
    ISBN 0-8032-4752-4 (alk. paper)
    1. Mine safety—Rocky Mountains
Region—History. 2. Coal mines
and mining—Rocky Mountains Region—History.
3. Mine safety—Law and legislation—
Rocky Mountains Region.   I. Title.
TN295.W43   1990
363.11′9622′0978—dc20   89–39702
                                                    CIP

FOR MARY ANN

Contents

Illustrations

The first mine rescue car
Interior of the rescue car
A mine rescue team practices
rescue techniques
John D. Rockefeller, Jr.
Company-sponsored first-aid contest
Rock dusting
Dust barriers for flame suppression
A punching machine
A cutting machine
A Jeffrey trolley motor
A Jeffrey L-600 loading machine
A Joy Continuous Miner

Maps

Preface

Ludlow lies in the heart of what once was southern Colorado's Kingdom of Coal. Located a few miles north of Trinidad, near the
Colorado-New Mexico border, Ludlow was a depot of the Colorado
and Southern Railroad. Nearby, the Colorado Fuel and Iron Company and the Victor-American Fuel Company operated several large
coal mines. Little remains to recall the days when thousands of coal
miners worked there and at dozens of other coal camps in the Rocky
Mountain West, taking fuel from the earth to power the region's
economic growth. Today an old filling station and store command the
interchange on Interstate 25. If you leave the highway and follow the
dirt road for a short distance, you will come on a strange sight. There,
where one of the many foothills canyons opens out onto the plains,
stands a monument, a large corniced column with the granite figures
of a man, woman, and child at its base. The Ludlow monument
commemorates the worst episode in Colorado's turbulent, sometimes violent history of industrial labor relations. Here, on 20 April
1914, fighting broke out between a detachment of the Colorado
National Guard and striking miners who, with their families, had
established a tent colony. When the shooting stopped, the smolder-
ing wreckage of the colony yielded nearly a score of dead, mostly
women and children. Their names—Tikas, Fyler, Bartolotti, Costa,
Rubino, Valdez, Petrucci, Snyder, Pedregone—offered a roster of

the family of nations that filled the mines and camps of the West's coal-fields.

The central issue dividing strikers and coal operators in 1913–14 was the question of the miners' right to organize and bargain collectively. The strikers also demanded enforcement of the state's coal-mining laws. On this count the coal miners had much to complain about, since from 1884, when the state began keeping records, until the time of Ludlow more than seventeen hundred men were killed in Colorado's coal mines. Sometimes they died by the dozens, or even the hundreds, in fires and explosions. At those times newspapers were filled with expressions of shock and anger. Soon, however, the press and the public forgot the scenes of horror and grief acted out at the mine portal. More often, coal miners died alone or in twos and threes, crushed by collapsing roofs of tunnels and rooms, mutilated by runaway mine cars, or blown up or burned to death by a misfired shot. News of these deaths rarely spread beyond the boundaries of the coal camp. The widows and children buried their dead and moved on.

Colorado, and the rest of the coal-producing West, paid a terrible price in blood to bring coal out of the depths of the earth. In this hazardous industry the mines of Colorado were, for many decades, among the most dangerous in the nation, with fatalities surpassing national rates two, three, or more times. Similar rates were common in neighboring Wyoming, Utah, New Mexico, and Montana. From the 1880s to the 1980s more than eighty-two hundred workers died as the result of coal-mining accidents in the Rocky Mountain states.

Labor historians and old-timers in coal-mining communities often point an accusing finger at rapacious "Coal Barons" who, in their single-minded pursuit of profit, ruthlessly exploited and killed miners, giving no thought to the safety and welfare of either workers or their families. Every coal camp had its tales of owners or superintendents who showed more concern for the well-being of company mules than for company employees. However satisfying ideologically, the image of the ruthless coal baron is not an adequate explanation of the causes of danger in the mines. Indeed, it only oversimplifies and enflames a complicated industrial issue.

Operators and miners alike worked in a setting conditioned by many factors: economic self-interest and fierce competition, whether for markets or for jobs; physical isolation; technological change affecting the nature and organization of work in the mines; evolving social and political attitudes; and racial and ethnic prejudice. Thus, although coal companies ultimately bore responsibility for work conditions, it is to the total industrial environment—economic, technical, institutional, social, political, and legal—that we must look for meaningful answers about safety and death in the mines.

This is a study of work, death, and regulation in the Rocky Mountain coal-mining industry. Though much of the focus is on Colorado, the book also deals extensively with the situation in New Mexico, Utah, Wyoming, and Montana. In showing that western coal mines were extremely hazardous, it also takes up complex questions: why was work in the mines so dangerous? What did operators, miners, and government do to improve conditions in the mines? Answers require the study of work relations in the industry: the physical, technological, and institutional setting of work; the economic interests of operators and miners in implementing or delaying changes in the work environment; and evolving industrial, political, and legal attitudes on the issues of responsibility for safety in the mines and the proper role of government in regulating industrial work conditions. Finally, how were all these factors reflected in the enactment and enforcement of coal-mining laws?

Beginning in the 1880s, legislatures in the Rocky Mountain states enacted laws to improve conditions in the mines and reduce the industry's extremely high death rate. For the most part well-intentioned, these laws failed, mainly because they did not effectively address the major causes of death in the mines or the underlying contributing conditions in the relations of work. The same may be said of federal efforts to regulate safety conditions in the mines.

Reform of coal-mining laws often followed some especially terrible disaster. Operators, labor leaders, newspaper editors, and government officials all would agree that something had to be done about mine safety. Time and again the results were laws aimed primarily at preventing major disasters and therein lay their fundamental weakness. Laws requiring better ventilation and measures to control coal dust may have reduced the risk of devastating explosions, but they did not fundamentally alter the relations of work which contributed to the vast majority of coal-mine deaths.

Over the years, as coal-mine fatality rates improved, it became clear that safer conditions owed as much to changes in the industry as to laws and regulations. Especially important were unionization and mechanization and their altering of the physical, technical, and human environment in which coal miners worked.

As the industry changed, so too did the locus of primary regulatory authority. Since 1941 the federal government has increased its commitment to regulating and inspecting the nation's coal mines. As it did so, the role of the states declined. The federal takeover did not occur, however, without resistance from both state governments and the industry.

Throughout this study reference is made to rates of death in the coal mines of the Rocky Mountain states and the United States. These rates are expressed in terms of deaths per thousand employed. In recent years government and industry have adopted as the standard of measurement an exposure rate of incidents per million man-hours of work. However, for many of the decades covered here there is no way of calculating with any acceptable accuracy the number of man-hours worked. Until well into the twentieth century, in fact, the standard measure was deaths or injuries per thousand, or some other measure such as deaths per million tons produced. Colorado, for example, did not report fatalities in terms of exposure until the 1960s. The use of deaths per thousand employed provides a consistent measure of rates over the entire century with which this study is concerned. All fatality data used in this study are taken from state and territorial coal-mine inspectors' reports and from U.S. Bureau of Mines publications.

In researching and writing this book, I have enjoyed the help of institutions and individuals from all over the Rocky Mountain region. Especially important were the staff members of the Colorado Division of State Archives and Public Records; the Colorado Historical Society; the Denver Public Library; the Western Historical Collections and the Coal Project at the University of Colorado at Boulder; the CF&I Steel Corporation; the New Mexico State Records Center and Archives; the Museum of New Mexico; the Utah State Archives and Records Service; the Utah State Historical Society; the Wyoming State Archives, Museums and Historical Department; the American Heritage Center at the University of Wyoming; and the Montana Historical Society.

Lee Scamehorn introduced me to the subject of coal mining in the West. He has shared with me his knowledge, his enthusiasm for history, and, I hope, his commitment to excellence. Patricia Nelson Limerick read an early version of the manuscript and offered invaluable criticisms and editing. My friend Ruth Helm endured too many long lunches listening to me talk about the mines and the miners.

More than anyone, Mary Ann Whiteside sustained me through years of research and writing. I have dedicated this book to her, my cherished friend and partner.

Some material in chapters 1 through 7 has previously appeared in *Essays and Monographs in Colorado History* and *New Mexico Historical Review*. Permission has generously been given to use material published in two articles, "Protecting the Life and Limb of Our Workmen: Coal Mining Regulation in Colorado, 1883–1920" (*Essays and Monographs in Colorado History*, No.4, 1986) and "Coal Mining, Safety, and Regulation in New Mexico: 1882–1933" (*New Mexico Historical Review*, April 1989).

Finally, the coal miners and their families—ordinary people who lived, worked, and sometimes fought and died in extraordinary circumstances—were a constant source of inspiration to me. I hope that this book honors their lives and their work.

Chapter 1

The Industrial Setting

Mention the subject of mining in the Rocky Mountain West and very likely a variety of colorful images comes to mind: rugged and reclusive prospectors; wild and wooly mining camps with saloons, gambling halls, and red-light districts; bonanza kings and their ladies; tales of fortunes won and lost at the turn of a card. The rough and ready days of the Rocky Mountain hard-rock mining industry had all the stuff of history and legend. But the days of the sourdough and his loyal, if obstinate, mule and of the uproarious mining camps were short. Soon corporations replaced bonanza kings, and engineers and skilled workers displaced the prospectors as mines followed veins of ore deep into the earth. Up top, rough camps turned into towns and cities with most, if not all, of the trappings of society and law.

None of this was possible without fuel to run the mines, mills, smelters, and railroads. Photographs of mining camps in their heyday often reveal an environment stripped of trees, for local lumber supplies quickly were consumed for fuel and construction. What nature did not provide in abundance on the surface, though, was available in vast quantities not far below in the enormous deposits of coal found throughout the Rocky Mountain West. Coal fueled the economic growth of the West by providing power and heat not only for mines, smelters, and railroads but for homes, shops, farms, and ranches.

Seeming to lack much of the color and excitement of the hard-rock mining industry, coal mining has been treated as a poor second cousin in the history of the Rocky Mountain West. Histories of the region and of western mining commonly take little note of, or overlook entirely, the coal-mining industry and its place in the West's growth. In fact, in terms of dollar value produced, not to mention its role in making everything else go, coal's direct contribution to the western economy far surpasses that of the more glamorous precious-metals industry.

The history of coal mining in the Rocky Mountain region reveals certain basic characteristics. For example, railroads played a vital role in organizing coal mining and creating markets, as well as carrying the fuel. Rapid consolidation, often under railroad parent companies, enabled a few operators to dominate the industry. The economic importance of coal and consolidation of the industry gave coal operators great political influence in statehouses and courthouses. Operators also dominated life in the coal camps. That, in turn, created the setting for the turbulent, sometimes violent relations between operators and organized labor which color much of the history of coal mining. Finally, coal mining has always been vulnerable to external trends, especially depressions and the introduction of alternate fuels, making for cycles of boom and bust, overcapacity, and intense competition.

The presence of coal in the Rocky Mountain region was well known by the time extensive American settlement began. Native inhabitants and Spanish and Mexican settlers doubtless noted surface outcroppings of coal in what is now New Mexico and Colorado. Americans first heard of the presence of coal in the West through the reports of fur trappers and military explorers. Lewis and Clark, for example, sighted coal outcroppings during their explorations of the upper Missouri and Yellowstone rivers. One claim has it that Americans first discovered coal in Wyoming as early as 1834. In the early 1840s Rufus Sage noted coal deposits in three places: near the "Cimarone" River in present-day northeast New Mexico, a bit north on a tributary of the Arkansas River, and near "the headwaters of the Platt" in present-day Wyoming. A decade later territorial governor William Carr Lane described coal deposits around Raton Mountain and near Taos and Las Vegas in northeastern New Mexico. Military and geological surveys, including the Frémont expedition in 1843–

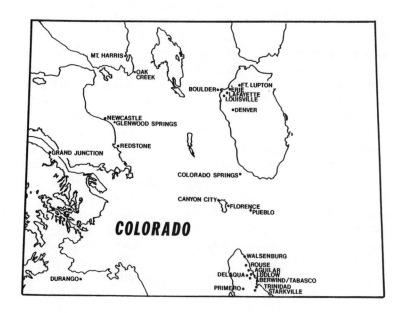

Major Coalfields in Colorado

44, the Gunnison-Beckwith railroad survey in 1853, and the Hayden survey in 1871, all noted the availability of coal in the region.[1] However, knowledge of the actual extent of the coalfields of the Rocky Mountain area awaited systematic exploration and development stimulated by the demands of fuel-hungry industries and towns.

Colorado led the Rocky Mountain region in coal production until well into the twentieth century. Coal occurs throughout much of Colorado in eight major and minor fields covering approximately one-fourth of the state. The major producing fields lie in three general zones: the eastern, park, and western. In the east the fields of the Denver Region stretch from Weld and Larimer counties in the north to El Paso County in the south, and from Boulder and Jefferson counties in the west almost to the eastern boundaries of Adams, Arapahoe, and Elbert counties. Known as the northern field, this area produces a grade of sub-bituminous, or black lignite, coal used for domestic and industrial burning. To the south, in Las Animas and Huerfano counties, is the southern field, part of the Raton Mesa Region, which extends into New Mexico. Long the heart of the coal-mining industry in Colorado, the southern field produces high-grade bituminous coals with excellent coking characteristics. Between and slightly west of the northern and southern fields is the small Canon City field with its bituminous coal. West of the northern field lie the North Park field of Grand and Jackson counties and the South Park field in Park County, which produce mainly low-grade bituminous and sub-bituminous coals. On the west slope of the Colorado Rockies are found three major coal regions, the Green River, the Uinta, and the San Juan River. The Green River Region, lying in Moffat and Routt counties, produces low-grade bituminous coals, as does the extensive Uinta Region, lying in the west-central counties of Rio Blanco, Garfield, Mesa, Gunnison, and Pitkin. Metallurgical-grade bituminous and a small amount of anthracite are found in the eastern end of the Uinta region, around Crested Butte. Beginning just south of the Uinta region in Mesa County and extending south through Delta, Montrose, Ouray, San Miguel, Dolores, Montezuma, and Archuleta counties is the San Juan River region, which contains high-grade bituminous coals.

Early settlers probably took coal from surface outcroppings in Boulder County almost as soon as settlement began in 1859. The first reliable reports of commercial coal mining in Colorado came in 1863, when Joseph W. Marshall's mines near Boulder produced a more-or-less regular supply of fuel for his pig-iron furnace and for local customers. The following year Colorado's coal mines produced five hundred tons, most of it from "wagon" mines in the northern field (small, one- or two-man operations not served by a railroad). From these beginnings coal mining in the northern field grew rapidly, stimulated by and providing fuel for "the mining excitements and the rapid growth of Denver and adjoining mining towns" which soon had the mines working to capacity.[2] As demand and the scale of operations grew, so too did production. From the five hundred tons produced in 1864, output from the northern field increased to more than one hundred thousand tons in 1876. Growth continued throughout the 1870s, encouraged by construction of the Boulder Valley, Denver Pacific, and Golden, Boulder and Caribou railroads. With increased demand and more ready access to markets, mines opened in the Erie and Louisville areas and at Canfield in the eastern end of Boulder County. By 1884 nine companies operated twelve mines in the field. The northern field provided most of Colorado's coal supplies until surpassed by the development of extensive operations in the south. Though the presence of coal in the Trinidad area was well known to potential developers early on, the remoteness of the field from the major areas of settlement and mining activity discouraged development until the entry of the railroads. In the 1870s, however, the availability of fuel on the approaches to Raton Pass, the gateway to New Mexico and the rest of the Southwest, attracted railroads to the area. The Rio Grande's William Jackson Palmer, for example, in 1874 learned that there was not "a more valuable deposit of coal west of the anthracite region of Pennsylvania."[3] Both the Denver and Rio Grande and the Atchison, Topeka and Santa Fe lines arrived in the vicinity of Trinidad in 1876. Ultimately, the Atchison, Topeka and Santa Fe won the race to Raton Pass and pushed its line into New Mexico. Both railroads, however, participated in developing coal mining in the Trinidad area.

With the entry of the railroads, coal mining near Trinidad grew rapidly and, with its more abundant and higher-quality coal, soon displaced the northern field as Colorado's major coal-producing center. By 1884 approximately three-quarters of the state's coal production came from the southern field.

Growing apace with the development of coal mining in these early years was coal's role in Colorado's economic growth. As early as 1866 the operators of a mine in Boulder County noted the need for greater supplies of coal to fill the "daily growing scarcity" of wood to fuel ore processing and iron manufacturing and to meet domestic demand by "the inhabitants of Denver, Central and other cities," who relied increasingly on the coal mines of the Boulder area for their fuel. Even though production grew rapidly in the early years, operators were hard pressed to keep up with demand. In the winter of 1881–82, for example, when production approached one million tons, the Denver *Republican* worried that the city was "in immediate danger of a coal famine."[4]

Along with the impressive growth of coal mining came signs of the volatility and intense competition that would characterize the industry throughout most of its history. Prices fluctuated wildly in the early days. For example, in September 1859 coal sold in Denver for twenty-five dollars a ton; the following summer, as the gold boom got underway, the price soared to forty dollars a ton, then fell by September 1860 to five dollars.

Competition among some early operators became downright nasty and destructive. In one case in 1869, vandals knocked down props and set fire to a Boulder County mine. "The object of this vandalism," said the *Boulder County News*, "is to stop the working of these banks, so that the proprietors of some other mine may have a monopoly of the market."[5]

Coal famines, price instability, and fierce competition underscored the role of coal in Colorado's economic development. Governor Frederick Pitkin in 1881 predicted that coal would be the foundation for the state's industrial development, providing employment for skilled workers in manufacturing establishments that would turn out all the machinery needed in the gold and silver mines. "Around such establishments healthy and prosperous communities" would grow up, attracting "the best class of emigration." Eventually, Pitkin believed, manufacturing plants, such as the steel mill then being built at Pueblo, would make Colorado "as well known for her manufactures as for her productions of gold and silver."[6]

The Pueblo steel mill of which Governor Pitkin spoke was part of an industrial empire being forged by William Jackson Palmer, founder of the Denver and Rio Grande Railway, the company largely responsible for the opening of the southern field to coal production. The great western railroad companies played a central role in taking western coal mining beyond the wagon-mine stage. Coal provided the basic source of fuel for steam locomotives, as well as income from freight and sales as railroads and subsidiary coal companies supplied coal for domestic and metallurgical consumers in the region. The Rio Grande, an indirect forebear of Colorado's coal and steel giant, the Colorado Fuel and Iron Company, mined and transported coal in Colorado, New Mexico, and Utah. In Wyoming and Utah, and briefly in northern Colorado, the Union Pacific and its Union Pacific Coal Company were important forces in the industry. To the south, in New Mexico, the Santa Fe opened mines or contracted with local operators as the line progressed across the territory from Raton in the northeast to Gallup in the west. In Montana the Northern Pacific, Great Northern, and Milwaukee Road developed important coal-mining operations.

By the early 1880s the railroads had become the largest producers and consumers of coal in Colorado. Companies affiliated with the Rio Grande operated seven mines, six in the southern field and one near Crested Butte; the Santa Fe, with mines at Rockvale, in Fremont County, and at Trinidad, challenged the Rio Grande in southern Colorado; and the Union Pacific owned five mines in northern and western Colorado. By the middle of the decade railroad-controlled mines accounted for about 85 percent of Colorado's coal production.

The mid-1880s proved to be the heyday for direct railroad involvement in coal mining in Colorado. Soon the lines began to divest their coal operations, preferring to secure coal supplies and traffic from other large operators or, in the case of the Union Pacific, to rely on mines in Wyoming. The brief direct role of the railroads in Colorado's coal industry, however, transformed coal mining from the small wagon-mine business of the 1860s and 1870s to an industry dominated by large-scale operations owned and managed by corporations. The railroads, in short, industrialized coal mining in Colorado and the rest of the Rocky Mountain region.

Industrialization also meant consolidation. William J. Palmer envisioned an industrial empire in which his narrow-gauge railroad would be only a part. Palmer aimed to create an integrated industrial complex based on steel manufacturing, and "from its very inception, provision was made for Colorado's steel industry to be self-contained, dependent on no outside sources for its raw materials," including coal. Palmer had some acquaintance with coal mining, having written, in 1855–56, a series of articles for the Pottsville, Pennsylvania, *Miners' Journal* describing English mines and mining methods.[7] His dream of a western industrial complex was achieved, by his successors, with the founding in 1892 of the Colorado Fuel and Iron Company.

The Colorado Fuel and Iron Company (CF&I) was the product of the merger of the Colorado Coal and Iron Company and the Colorado Fuel Company. Colorado Coal and Iron was itself created in 1880 by the merger of three Denver and Rio Grande subsidiaries, the Southern Colorado Coal and Town Company, the Colorado Coal and Steel Works Company, and the Central Colorado Improvement Company. Palmer and his associates intended, in this merger, to bring under a single management all the materials and processes of steel-making. When organized, the Colorado Coal and Iron Company owned more than thirteen thousand acres of coal land around Trinidad, Walsenburg, and Canon City and immediately became the largest coal producer in the southern field.

John C. Osgood, a man who loomed large in the Colorado coal industry for decades, in 1883 organized the Colorado Fuel Company, the other immediate predecessor of CF&I. Osgood had come to Colorado as an agent of the Chicago, Burlington and Quincy Railroad. His mission was to assess the potential of the state's coal resources. Osgood was impressed with what he found and organized the Colorado Fuel Company to supply fuel for the railroad. The company soon had mining properties and operations on the west slope and in the northern field around Erie. In the late 1880s Colorado Fuel expanded into the southern field and, by 1892, with some thirty-four thousand acres of coal land, seven mines, and two coking plants, overtook Colorado Coal and Iron as Colorado's largest coal and coke producer.

Managers of the two companies worried that competition might prove ruinous to both and so in 1892 agreed to merge them. With some sixty-nine thousand acres, fourteen mines, and four coking plants with eight hundred ovens, the new Colorado Fuel and Iron Company became, and for decades remained, the dominant force in Colorado's coal industry. At the time of the merger CF&I accounted for approximately 75 percent of the coal produced in Colorado, the majority of it from the company's mines in the southern field. CF&I strengthened its commanding position in the industry in 1896 when it leased three of the Santa Fe Railroad's coal operations in Colorado.

The Colorado Fuel and Iron Company was born and rose to dominance in the western coal industry during an era of hostility toward large corporations. All over the country reformers attacked trusts and demanded laws and regulatory agencies to supervise big business. In Colorado the Populist platform in 1892 called for the state to take over the coal mines. By the end of the century the United States Industrial Commission had begun its studies of the impact of industrial consolidation on American business and society. Asked to discuss the impact of consolidation on coal mining in Colorado, D. C. Beaman, CF&I's secretary-treasurer, assured the commission that consolidation had not destroyed competition in Colorado, but only eliminated its potentially destructive aspects. Because of that, he said, industry, labor, and consumers alike benefited from a healthier coal industry providing stable prices and wages. Healthy or not, Colorado Fuel and Iron's consolidation made it a force to be reckoned with. By 1906 the *Engineering and Mining Journal* estimated that 10 percent of Colorado's wage earners depended on CF&I for their livelihood.[8]

Because of its unique position in the region's economy, CF&I attracted the attention not only of industrial critics but of financial speculators. The growing and powerful enterprise made a tempting target for a takeover bid, and the opportunity came in 1901 when the company issued securities and bonds to finance a modernization program for its Pueblo steelworks. In a financial and legal struggle lasting nearly two years, CF&I management, led by John C. Osgood, thwarted a bid by John W. "Bet-a-Million" Gates to take control of the company. However, Osgood's victory proved to be pyrrhic. The struggle against Gates and the costs of the modernization program left the company on the edge of bankruptcy. To save the company, Osgood agreed in June 1903 to relinquish control to John D. Rockefeller and railroad financier George Jay Gould. Within weeks the Rockefeller-Gould interests took over management of CF&I and its subsidiary companies. CF&I remained part of the Rockefeller empire until 1944.

Osgood's departure from the Colorado Fuel and Iron Company by no means signaled his exit from the coal industry. In 1900, while still with CF&I, Osgood organized the Victor Fuel Company, with operations in Las Animas and Huerfano counties, and the American Fuel Company, with mines in the Gallup, New Mexico, area. After leaving CF&I, he concentrated his energies on expanding these operations and in 1909 decided to merge them. The new Victor-American Fuel Company became the number-two producer in the southern field and Colorado Fuel and Iron's chief competitor in Colorado and New Mexico.

In Colorado's northern field numerous independent mines shared production with the Union Pacific Railroad's subsidiaries, the Union Coal Company and its successor, the Union Pacific Coal Company. During the 1890s the Union Pacific began to curtail its Colorado coal-mining interests and ceased operations entirely by 1902. Following the railroad company's exit from northern Colorado, leadership fell first to the Northern Coal and Coke Company and in 1911 to the Rocky Mountain Fuel Company, when it acquired the properties of Northern Coal and Coke.

Coal mining in the other western states grew much as it did in Colorado, with extensive development awaiting the entry of the railroads. And as in Colorado, a few major operators soon dominated coal mining in New Mexico, Utah, Wyoming, and Montana.

Most of New Mexico's extensive coal resources are located in the fields of the San Juan and Raton regions. By far the largest coal area in the state, the New Mexico portion of the San Juan Basin underlies most of San Juan and McKinley counties and portions of five others making up the state's northwest quadrant. The coals here are bituminous and sub-bituminous. The first workings, opened in the early 1880s, were in the Gallup area. The mines of the Gallup field, serving the east-west railroad route and a limited domestic market, took an early lead in New Mexico's young coal industry, but they soon were eclipsed by competitors in the Raton field. Because much of the San Juan region's coal lay in remote areas far from railroad lines, the area was not fully developed until recent times.

More important in the history of coal mining in New Mexico is the Raton field in Colfax County, along the route of the Atchison, Topeka and Santa Fe Railroad as it enters the state over Raton Pass. With the railroad serving as a ready outlet for its high-quality steam and coking coals, the Raton field by the turn of the century had emerged as the heart of the coal industry in New Mexico.

A third, but much smaller, area is the Cerrillos field, located a few miles southwest of Santa Fe. The Cerrillos field is unique in the West because it produces both bituminous and anthracite coals. Other minor fields are located in south-central New Mexico in Socorro and Lincoln counties. Though small, the Carthage field in Socorro County contains valuable coking coal.

Coal may have been mined by settlers living in the Cerrillos area as early as 1835, but the earliest reliable reports of commercial mining date to 1846, when contractors hauled fuel to nearby Santa Fe for the American army. Small mines opened near Madrid and Carthage in the 1860s produced only a few hundred tons per year.

By the 1870s territorial boosters were hard at work promoting their vision of New Mexico's future as an industrial center. With New Mexico's vast coal resources, they said, businessmen would find a

Major Coalfields in Mew Mexico

ready and inexpensive source of fuel for railroads and gold and silver mining. In the early 1880s town boosters in Raton predicted the growth of an industrial complex of railroads, coal mining, and manufacturing that would make their town the "Pittsburgh of New Mexico." Concern that the entry of railroad companies, particularly the Atchison, Topeka and Santa Fe, might discourage other potential coal-mining investors prompted no less an authority than territorial chief justice L. Bradford Prince to declare that "there is still room for plenty of private enterprise in this direction."[9]

Large-scale commercial coal mining in New Mexico began with the railroads' arrival in the territory. The Atchison, Topeka and Santa

Fe became the first when it beat the Rio Grande to Raton Pass and drove its line into New Mexico in 1878–79. Initially, the Santa Fe relied on coal from its mine at Trinidad, but the costs of hauling fuel over the pass from Colorado soon became too high. To secure more convenient and less expensive fuel supplies for its New Mexico operations, the Santa Fe in December 1880 joined with the Maxwell Land Grant Company to form the Raton Coal and Coke Company. By the following summer some one hundred fifty men were at work in mines in the Raton area, and the company had plans for a work force of one thousand by the spring of 1882. Many of these miners were recruited from as far away as Pennsylvania, with the Santa Fe offering free transportation from Kansas City, Kansas.

Large-scale production from the Raton mines began in 1882, and by February 1884 more than nine thousand tons were being shipped per month. By 1887 production from Santa Fe–controlled mines in Raton and Cerrillos had grown to more than two hundred thousand tons, most of it used by the Santa Fe and other railroads in New Mexico. In addition to the operations of the Raton Coal and Coke Company, the Santa Fe also opened mines in the Madrid area operated by the Cerrillos Coal Railroad Company and in the Carthage area operated by the San Pedro Coal and Coke Company.

The Santa Fe Railroad also played a part in opening the Gallup field when, in 1879, the company sent engineers into the area to prospect for coal. Mining in the field began in 1881, when the Atlantic and Pacific Railroad drove through the Gallup area. Production from the Gallup field expanded rapidly, increasing from thirty-three thousand tons in 1882 to almost a quarter million tons a decade later. The Gallup field's rapid growth quickly made it the leading producing field in the territory, a position it held until 1903.

By the twentieth century the continuing development of coal mining in New Mexico had ensured the industry's place as a vital part of the territory's economy and made New Mexico itself an important coal producer for the entire region. By 1892, the first year for which U.S. government mine inspectors provided reliable reports, New Mexico's mines produced almost six hundred thousand tons of coal annually; they nearly doubled that amount at the turn of the century.

With adequate supplies of coal assured, the railroads began to shift control of coal mining in New Mexico to independent operators. The Atchison, Topeka and Santa Fe in 1904 conveyed its share of the

Raton Coal and Coke Company to the Maxwell Land Grant Company. The following year, the Land Grant Company sold all of its coal-mining interests to the Saint Louis, Rocky Mountain and Pacific Company. Continued growth of the railroads; mining booms in gold, silver, and copper; and settlement in neighboring west Texas and Oklahoma quickly increased demand for the company's high-quality steam and coking coals. Saint Louis, Rocky Mountain and Pacific in 1905 owned 189,470 acres of coal land and held coal and surface rights to another 125,000 acres, as well as mines at Blossburg and Van Houten and a coke plant at Gardiner. A decade later the company worked thirteen mines with an annual capacity of three million tons. It remained a major New Mexico coal operator until 1955, when it sold its properties to the Kaiser Steel Company.

Saint Louis, Rocky Mountain and Pacific shared control of the Raton Field with another large operator, the Phelps-Dodge Company. Phelps-Dodge also had major copper-mining and smelting operations at Bisbee, Arizona. By 1885 the company's smelters had consumed the timber resources around Bisbee, forcing it to look elsewhere for fuel supplies. Phelps-Dodge temporarily solved its fuel problem by buying from the Colorado Fuel and Iron Company. Preferring to control its own fuel resources, however, the company in 1905 seized the opportunity to acquire the Dawson Fuel Company from the El Paso and Northeastern Railway Company. Reorganized in 1908 as the Stag Canon Fuel Company and headquartered at Dawson, a few miles southwest of Raton, the Phelps-Dodge operation included nearly 39,000 acres of coal land and mining rights to an additional 17,500 acres, six mines with a capacity of 120,000 tons per month, and a coking plant with 550 ovens. With this capacity, Phelps-Dodge became an important fuel supplier for railroads and other customers in the Southwest. Phelps-Dodge maintained its operations at Dawson until 1950, when because of declining demand the company closed and dismantled the camp.

The Colorado Fuel and Iron Company also became, for a time, a major force in the New Mexico coal industry. Through a series of business arrangements made between 1899 and 1902, CF&I acted as marketing agent for the Raton Coal and Coke Company, the Cerrillos Coal Railroad Company, and other, smaller New Mexico operations; managed the properties of American Fuel; and acquired those of the Crescent Coal Company in the Gallup area. In 1899 CF&I took over

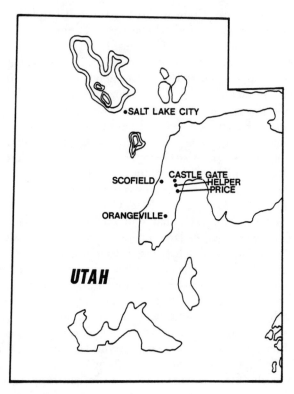

Major Coalfields in Utah

the Atchison, Topeka and Santa Fe Railroad's coal mines and coke ovens near Madrid, which it operated until 1905. CF&I in 1906 leased its operations in the Cerrillos area to the Albuquerque and Cerrillos Coal Company. In 1902, when CF&I's penetration of the New Mexico industry was greatest, the company controlled five mines employing 1,032 men.

Another major operator in early-twentieth-century New Mexico was John C. Osgood's Victor-American Fuel Company. After the merger of Victor Fuel and American Fuel in 1909, the company became the largest producer in the Gallup field, providing fuel for the Atchison, Topeka and Santa Fe as well as supplying domestic and commercial customers in New Mexico, Arizona, and California until 1917, when it sold its Gallup properties.

Utah's coalfields cover some fifteen thousand square miles, extending from Morgan and Summit counties near the Wyoming border, through much of the eastern and central part of the state, and across the southern tier of counties. By far the largest area is that portion of the Uintah Region covering parts of Uintah, Duchesne, Wasatch, Utah, Sanpete, Sevier, Emery, Grand, and Carbon counties. With a band of high-grade bituminous coal stretching from Sevier County northeast across Sanpete, Emery, and Carbon counties, this area became the heart of Utah's coal-mining industry. Carbon County was especially important, accounting for more than 90 percent of production and employment by 1901. The fields of south-central Utah contain high- and low-grade bituminous coal, but because of their remote location, they were not commercially developed until recent decades.

Brigham Young and his followers wasted no time in beginning efforts to supplement the sparse timber resources within reach of the Salt Lake Valley. Soon after the first Mormon settlers arrived in the summer of 1847, the colony's leaders sent out groups to search for coal for the growing settlement. What coal they found was too little and too far away to alleviate the colony's mounting fuel problems. By 1854 the situation in Salt Lake City had become serious enough to prompt the legislature to offer a one-thousand-dollar bounty to anyone "who would open a vein of coal not less than 18 inches thick within forty miles" of the town. Some development occurred in the 1850s in Sanpete and Summit counties, but the coals were of low quality and very costly to freight. Not until 1863 did a mine open within forty miles of Salt Lake City, in the Coalville area in Summit County. This mine offered coal at forty dollars per ton.[10]

The arrival of the Union Pacific Railroad in 1870 finally solved Utah's fuel problems, or at least the problem of supply. In June the railroad brought the first carload of coal into Salt Lake City from a mine at Coalville. Although a few small operations appeared in the Carbon County area in the 1870s, the Union Pacific enjoyed an effective monopoly over the coal market in Utah, a monopoly it tightened by discriminating against Utah operators in favor of coal hauled from its own mines in Wyoming. Utahans accused the railroad not only of rate discrimination against local coal operators, but of limiting the flow of coal from Wyoming in order to force up prices. As the 1880s began, however, events in Colorado spelled the doom of the Union Pacific's dominance.

When the Atchison, Topeka and Santa Fe beat William J. Palmer's Denver and Rio Grande to Raton Pass, it dashed his hopes of driving his line south to Mexico. Palmer thus turned his attention and his railroad westward up the Arkansas River, over the mountains, and ultimately into Utah. He aimed his tracks toward Salt Lake, taking them directly through coal-rich Carbon County.

News of the approach of the Denver and Rio Grande Western and the promise of access to Utah's own coal prompted the *Daily Herald* of Salt Lake City to declare that the territory soon would reap the benefits of lower fuel prices and industrial growth, "instead of being compelled to keep men at work in another and rival territory, and to burn foreign coal, while we have equally as good an article here."[11] The Rio Grande's Utah Fuel Company soon replaced the Union Pacific as the dominant force in the Utah coal market. In 1900, when Utah's coal output topped one million tons, the Utah Fuel Company accounted for 90 percent.

The fuel demands by Utah's population and growing hard-rock mining industry soon encouraged other operators, including the Independent Coal and Coke Company, the Standard Coal Company, and the Spring Canyon Coal Company, to challenge Utah Fuel's dominance. To resist its competitors, Utah Fuel resorted to rate discrimination, price cutting, and the use of gunmen to control public coal lands. The independents held on, however, and by 1916 Utah Fuel's share of the market had been cut to only 40 percent.

The story of coal mining in Wyoming is closely linked to that of the Union Pacific Railroad. Wyoming's coalfields lie in two major zones spread across the northern plains and mountain regions. The most important are located along the southern tier of counties in the Hanna field (part of the Green River Region, which extends into northwestern Colorado) and in the Hams Fork Region. The Union Pacific drove its main line directly through these fields, and the existence of large quantities of bituminous and sub-bituminous coal suitable for steam use was an important factor in locating the route. The second major coal area in Wyoming is the Powder River Basin, extending from the east-central counties of Natrona, Converse, and

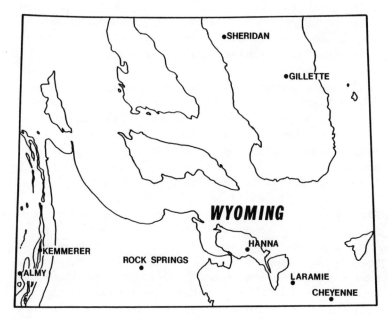

Major Coalfields in Wyoming

Niobrara northward along the base of the Rockies into Montana. Other areas, containing less desirable formations, are found in the Wind River Basin, the Bighorn Basin, the Jackson Hole field, the Rock Creek field, and the Goshen Hole field.

As it pushed its track across Wyoming, the Union Pacific opened mines at Carbon, Rock Springs, and Almy. For a brief time outside managers ran the railroad's mines. Later the road's own fuel department took over. Finally, in 1890, the Union Pacific transferred operation of its mines to a new subsidiary, the Union Pacific Coal Company. By the late 1890s the coal company was operating seven of Wyoming's eighteen commercial mines, making it by far the leading producer in the state. In 1900 Union Pacific mines produced 45 percent of Wyoming's nearly 3.8 million tons of coal. Wyoming coal mines not only provided a reliable supply of fuel for Union Pacific locomotives but also became an important source of freight and revenue for the company, which supplied customers between Omaha and the West Coast. The Union Pacific held its dominant position in the Wyoming coal industry until the 1950s, when the railroad company decided to convert its engines to diesel fuel. As a result, in the early 1960s the last of the Union Pacific Coal Company's mines closed and the company dissolved.

The Union Pacific had little interest in Wyoming's northern plains fields and left development of that area to others. By the early twentieth century two producers, the Sheridan Coal Company and the Wyoming Company, dominated the northern plains fields. In 1903 the Peabody Coal Company took over the Wyoming Coal Company, and in 1919 the Sheridan Coal Company and five other operators merged to form the Sheridan-Wyoming Coal Company. The Chicago, Burlington, and Quincy railroad and smelting operations in South Dakota were important early consumers of coal and coke produced from the Sheridan and Cambria fields.

Since the 1970s coal mining in Montana has centered on the enormous lignite and sub-bituminous fields of the eastern and southeastern areas of the state, especially in Rosebud and Musselshell counties. Strip mining operations there began on a small scale in the 1920s, but major development awaited the energy crisis of the seventies. Commercial coal mining in Montana began in the 1860s and 1870s in the bituminous and sub-bituminous fields around Bozeman, Red Lodge, Great Falls, and Roundup. Colonel James D. Chestnut, a Bozeman businessman, in 1868 opened the territory's first commercial-scale coal mine, located east of Bozeman in Rocky Canyon. Chestnut's mine and other small operations in the territory supplied domestic and metallurgical fuels during the gold and silver excitements of the 1860s and 1870s.

The arrival of the Northern Pacific in the early 1880s inaugurated Montana's first coal-mining boom as the railroad took control of the Bozeman field and developed new operations in the Red Lodge area. Soon Northern Pacific mines supplied metallurgical customers, including the smelters at Butte and Anaconda, and domestic consumers in Montana and as far away as Minnesota and Washington. The Anaconda smelter and James J. Hill's St. Paul, Minneapolis, and Manitoba Railroad stimulated coal mining in the Great Falls field in the 1880s and 1890s. The Chicago, Milwaukee, and St. Paul Railroad in the early years of the twentieth century developed the Roundup field in the Bull Mountains of central Montana.

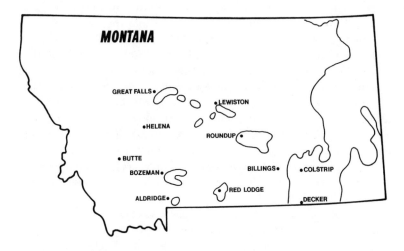

Major Coalfields in Montana

By the early twentieth century the railroads had established their dominance over Montana's coal industry. Under their control, production reached half a million tons in 1890, 1.6 million tons in 1900, 2.9 million tons in 1910, and peaked at 4.5 million tons in 1918. After World War I, reduced metallurgical demand, rising labor costs, improved combustion technology, and the development of large earth-moving machines encouraged the railroads and their coal-mining companies to turn their attention to eastern Montana's sub-bituminous and lignite fields. The Northern Pacific's Northwestern Improvement Company in 1924 began strip mining at Colstrip, in Rosebud County. By the 1930s the Colstrip operation was producing 40 percent of Montana's coal.

As major employers and producers of a commodity vital to the Rocky Mountain region's economic growth, coal operators wielded significant influence in territorial, state, and local politics. The operators exercised their greatest power in local affairs in the coalfields. On the other hand, though potent, they apparently did not usually control state legislatures. Instead, they were but one of a complex of interests whose needs and influence colored politics and law in the West.

Nevertheless, in the early twentieth century many Coloradans believed that the Colorado Fuel and Iron Company, because of its economic power and because the Rockefellers controlled it, ran the Colorado statehouse. During Colorado's greatest labor upheaval, the "coalfield war" of 1913–14, large segments of the press and public in Colorado and around the country viewed the governor as a CF&I errand boy and the state militia as mine guards in uniform. Critics also complained that the company controlled the legislature. In 1909, for example, the Colorado State Bureau of Labor Statistics charged that the company had blocked a bill to require better ventilation and dust control in the mines. [12] Two years later labor leaders and government officials blamed CF&I for sabotaging a reform of the state coal-mining law.

The Colorado Fuel and Iron Company was not insensitive to its reputation as a sometimes-abusive power in Colorado. CF&I chairman L. M. Bowers, in a 1913 letter to John D. Rockefeller's personal secretary, conceded that in the past the company had the reputation of being "the political dictator of southern Colorado" and "a mighty power in the entire State"; that it "voted every man and woman in [its] employ, without any regard to their being naturalized or not, and even their mules, it used to be remarked, we registered, if they were fortunate enough to possess names." Bowers admitted that in the past the company operated a political department, "at heavy expense," but maintained that during his tenure "not a nickel has been paid to any politician or political party." In something of an exaggeration Bowers claimed that even old enemies no longer had any political criticisms of CF&I. [13] Despite its confessional tone, Bowers's defense of CF&I's political reputation overlooked the question of whether a company that directly or indirectly supported 10 percent of the state's wage earners needed to vote its mules or flex bulging political muscles in other such crude ways.

In New Mexico, in the early years of the industry, the territorial legislature protected the interests of coal operators, particularly those controlled by the Atchison, Topeka and Santa Fe Railroad. The territory's original coal-mining law neatly exempted most mines in the state from its flimsy provisions and otherwise provided no means of inspection and enforcement. There is no evidence, however, that the legislature bowed to the desires of the great railroad company in enacting this law or that the Santa Fe was a dominant force in New Mexican politics.

By the late 1880s, in fact, "rings" of local businessmen-politicians controlled politics and government in New Mexico. Territorial governor Edmund G. Ross in 1887 complained of "Cattle Rings, Public Land Stealing Rings, Mining Rings, Treasury Rings, and rings of almost every description." The most potent was the "Santa Fe Ring," which based its power and wealth on control of the huge Maxwell Land Grant, a vast empire of land in northeastern New Mexico, including the Raton field. Prominent figures in the Santa Fe Ring were Thomas Benton Catron, a Santa Fe attorney and small coal operator with property in the Rio Arriba area, and Stephen B. Elkins, who, after his New Mexican sojourn, settled in West Virginia to become a coal baron and U.S. senator. By the late 1880s the Santa Fe Ring had become so powerful that it "dictated at will the legislation and general conduct of affairs in the Territory."[14]

In Utah the Mormon hierarchy and the territorial assembly actively promoted the coal industry in order to meet the fuel needs of settlers. Thus although railroad and coal companies did not dominate politics and government, friendly church and political leaders, anxious to build up Utah's economy, looked after their interests.

The Union Pacific Railroad, and its subsidiary coal operations, was for many years the largest single taxpayer and employer in Wyoming. Nevertheless, Wyoming legislatures, dominated by hard-rock mining and ranching interests, enacted personal and property injury laws and measures protecting railroad workers and coal miners. Much the same situation prevailed in Montana, where stockmen, railroads, and hardrock mining interests had great power.

In sum, even where coal operators and their parent railroad companies did not dominate politics and government, legislatures and governors concerned with providing a legal environment conducive to business and economic growth willingly protected the coal industry's interests. Thus, in its early years the western coal industry grew up largely free of restrictive regulation.

If the coal operators' influence in the statehouses was limited, their power in the coalfields was, at times, nearly absolute. This was particularly true in Colorado's southern field, where CF&I dominated local life and politics. In Huerfano County during the first two decades of the twentieth century, Sheriff Jefferson Farr ran things to the company's liking. Known as the "King of Huerfano," Farr was especially zealous in his efforts to protect his county from the influence of union organizers, telling them, "If you want to do any of your dirty work, you gonna have to do it someplace else. Not in this county while I am sheriff." Old-timers recalled that it was not safe to be a Democrat in Walsenburg and that if the Republicans could not muster enough votes to win elections they would vote the names of company mules.[15]

Coroners' juries also protected the coal operators by shielding them from the economic consequences of mine accidents and disasters. In Huerfano County between 1904 and 1914, coroners' juries ruled that eighty-five of ninety-five coal-mining fatalities resulted from the deceased's own negligence. In only one case did a jury fix any blame on mine management. The Colorado State Bureau of Labor Statistics in 1910 criticized the Las Animas County coroner and coroner's jury for their hasty ruling that the cause of an explosion that killed seventy-five miners at Colorado Fuel and Iron's Primero mine was unknown. In their haste to "protect the interests of the company against the widows, mothers, and surviving relatives of the dead" the jury ruled only five days after the disaster, "without making any kind of an investigation that would determine the cause." Colorado state coal mine inspector James Dalrymple in 1914 criticized the Las Animas County coroner for finding "in case after case where a miner has been killed—'no inquest necessary.'" County coroners' records sometimes reflect a callous attitude toward the victims of mine accidents. The Las Animas County coroner's death record of coal miner Wyatt Buckner reads, "Accident; fall of rock in mine; internal injuries; pelvic region; no relatives and damn few friends."[16]

Even mining-industry journals found much to criticize in the conduct of coroners' juries, nationally as well as in the West. *Coal Age*, the organ of American coal operators, condemned as "the blackest stain on the coal industry" the "deceit and perjuries accompanying accident investigations." *Engineering and Mining Journal* described coroners' inquests as "laughable comedies, where no one but the dead are held responsible, and where the defendants suggest the questions put to themselves," and as "useless mockeries," with conclusions framed "according to the quality of the cigars furnished by the operating company."[17]

The western coal operators' dominance of local politics and government was not unique to Colorado. *Engineering and Mining Journal,* for example, described Price, Utah, as a "coal operator's town" and noted of Rock Springs, Wyoming, that "although it was never company owned the Union Pacific controlled it in almost every way."[18]

Influential as they may have been in county courthouses, it was in the coal camps that the operators' power over the lives of miners and their families was greatest. Operators built and owned most of the camps, providing housing, water and other utilities, stores, medical and hospital services, and even churches, saloons, and other recreational facilities. This enabled them to exercise almost total control over their employees' working and social lives. Though some companies exercised this power benevolently, if paternalistically, many others were more interested in profits than in the quality of life in the camps.

Some camps, such as Colorado Fuel and Iron's Redstone, built in 1902 along the Crystal River in western Colorado, stood out as models of corporate benevolence. John C. Osgood intended Redstone, with its attractive bungalows, modern health services, and social activities, to be something of a workers' utopia. His own home, a great Tudor-style mansion, commanded the scene like a baronial manor house. From there, he proudly controlled life in his fiefdom. Though Redstone's workers and their families enjoyed a fairly high standard of living, all knew to whom they owed their good fortune.

The Colorado Fuel and Iron Company took great pride in the accomplishments of its Sociological Department in upgrading the physical and social condition of its camps. Established in 1901 in response to a coal miners' strike and a report by the Colorado legislature critical of CF&I's labor policies and conditions in the company's camps, the Sociological Department administered educational, health, and recreational services for employees and their families and worked to improve housing in the company's camps. The widespread abuse of alcohol by miners especially worried company officials. Not only a social problem, drunkenness could also adversely affect the miner's performance on the job, creating safety problems and impeding production. Thus, the Sociological Department went to great lengths to try to stem the flow of alcohol in the camps. Because the miners often answered outright prohibition with bootlegging, most camps permitted the sale of alcohol under closely regulated conditions. The Sociological Department tried to tempt the men away from drink by offering "soft drink clubs," reading rooms, lecture programs, and other elevating activities. Within a few years the Sociological Department had earned praise for leading the company's seventeen thousand workers and their families "from conditions of drunkenness and dirt to well-ordered living" and for "doing everything possible to make the men and their families contented and happy."[19]

Other western operators undertook similar, but less sweeping, efforts. In Wyoming the state coal-mine inspector in 1919 reported that "progressive" operators were installing bathhouses, modern dwellings, and amusement halls for "the health and entertainment of workmen and their families." New Mexico's mine inspector asserted that the living conditions of the average coal miner were "equal, if not superior, to the living conditions of the working man in our large towns" and "far ahead of anything that New Mexico has to offer in its country districts."[20]

Too often, though, poor and abusive physical and social conditions prevailed in the camps. Miners' houses sometimes were little more than makeshift tarpaper or adobe shacks; water supplies often were inadequate and unsanitary; company stores were notorious for charging extortionate prices for goods; and miners sometimes were paid in illegal scrip redeemable only at company stores for merchandise or for discounted currency. Company superintendents wielded absolute authority within the confines of the camps. They barred union organizers and other undesirables and unceremoniously ran off those bold enough to enter. Superintendents also decided what newspapers, magazines, and books to allow in the camp. When they discharged a miner, they usually also immediately evicted the man and his family from their home and sent them packing "down the canyon."

Even activities intended to improve the quality of life for the miners aimed also to strengthen the company's control over their lives. During the depression of the 1930s, at the Albuquerque and Cerrillos Coal Company's camp at Madrid, New Mexico, an employees' social organization sponsored entertainments at major holidays (including the camp's famous display of Christmas lights) and fielded a respected baseball team. However, in establishing the social organization, the camp superintendent also hoped to promote "the intangible benefits of keeping our employees satisfied by keeping their minds occupied with wholesome entertainment" instead of dwelling on their economic troubles and, perhaps, attempting to organize.[21]

Miners had few means of resisting the operators' power over their lives. One alternative was to quit and move on to another job in another camp. Another was to organize. The first at best offered only marginal improvement and did not challenge the operators' power; the second promised better wages, better conditions in the mines and in the camps, and a real voice in the industry. Operators did not often care if a man quit to look for a better job, but they fiercely resisted efforts by the miners to organize unions.

During the last quarter of the nineteenth century scores of strikes occurred in the western coalfields. Most were over wage issues and usually affected only one or two operators. Occasionally, though, other issues were at stake, including ethnic and personal animosities. In Wyoming in 1885, whites who feared losing their jobs to Asians hired by the Union Pacific Coal Company attacked Chinese miners at Rock Springs, killing twenty-eight. Sympathetic miners at Louisville, Colorado, struck to protest the presence of the Chinese in Rock Springs. Ethnic minorities were not always on the receiving end of labor disorders, however. In 1886 Italian miners at the Raton Coal and Coke Company's mine at Blossburg, New Mexico, shut down the mine and escorted the superintendent and outside boss out of town on a rail because the two officials opposed the efforts of a "clique," rumored to be associated with the Knights of Labor, trying to impose its will on the company. And in 1893 two hundred Finnish miners at Hanna, Wyoming, marched on the Union Pacific Coal Company's office to notify the superintendent that they would hang their abusive mine boss if he did not leave town within twenty-four hours. Although local lawmen promised him protection, the mine boss immediately "left for parts unknown."[22]

In spite of the volatility of the labor situation in the western coalfields, major unions made only sporadic organizing efforts until late in the nineteenth century. Large-scale organizing drives, and some of the most dramatic episodes in American labor history, awaited the entry of the United Mine Workers of America (UMWA) into the West.

One of the earliest appearances by the UMWA in the Rocky Mountain region came in New Mexico in 1900, when the union organized a strike in the Gallup area. Two years later the union was at work in the Raton field, at Blossburg and Gardiner. By 1910 the union had chartered new locals at Allison, Gallup, and Madrid. These early union efforts in New Mexico met with a hostile reception from the territorial government. Governor Miguel Otero in 1905 declared that he would tolerate no interference with the rights of capital and labor, that "riotous demonstrations would not be suffered to take place and . . . the right of the laboring man to work for whomever and at what terms he pleased would be respected and protected."[23]

Utah's first experience with the UMWA came in 1903, when the miners of Carbon County struck for union recognition. That strike collapsed when the state militia intervened on behalf of the Utah Fuel Company. Another major strike, in 1922, also ended when the state intervened.

The UMWA enjoyed its greatest early successes in the West in Wyoming and Montana. The union organized Montana's coal miners in 1903 and Wyoming's Sheridan field miners in 1903–4. Despite the Union Pacific Company's resistance, the southern fields, where two-thirds of Wyoming's coal miners worked, were organized in 1907 when operators and the UMWA signed a contract covering the entire state.

Union activity, and an era of industrial conflict, began in the Colorado coalfields in 1901. From January through April miners in Louisville, El Paso County, and Fremont County struck for wage concessions and recognition of the union. The strike was strongest in the northern areas, where small operators quickly agreed to the union's terms. The Northern Coal and Coke Company, the largest producer in the field, held out for four months until it, too, granted a wage increase and agreed to work with miners' committees, but not the union, to resolve disputes.

Coal miners in Colorado struck again in 1903, seeking higher wages, better working conditions, and recognition of the union. In the north operators negotiated with representatives from the various mines and agreed to a contract embodying many of the strikers' demands, except formal recognition of the union. In the south the outcome was quite different, as the Colorado Fuel and Iron Company and Victor-American refused to deal even indirectly with the union through miners' committees. The strike collapsed when Governor James Peabody declared martial law and sent in troops to harass the strikers and deport union leaders.

For the next few years the union pinned its hopes on the northern field, where it had had some limited success. In July 1908 a major breakthrough seemed at hand when seventeen northern operators signed a two-year contract with the UMWA recognizing the union and providing for an eight-hour day, safety and ventilation standards, and grievance procedures. These gains were shortlived, however, and in 1910 the operators refused to renew the contract with the United Mine Workers. In April the miners began a strike that lasted for more than three years. The strike swept the entire state in September 1913, when the union led ten to twelve thousand miners and their families out of the camps of the southern field.

Violence soon flared among strikers, strikebreakers, and company guards, prompting Governor Elias Ammons to send in the National Guard to maintain order. The striking miners, hoping for protection from company gunmen, initially welcomed the troops but soon came to see them, too, as hired guns working for the operators. Even though Governor Ammons did not declare martial law, the guard's commander, General John Chase, imposed military rule and initiated a campaign of arrests and harassment of strikers and union leaders.

During the winter and early spring of 1914 relations between the guard and the strikers deteriorated as it became apparent that company guards, many of them professional strikebreakers hired from the infamous Baldwin-Felts detective agency, had penetrated the ranks of the National Guard. In March troops sacked a strikers' tent colony at Forbes, near Trinidad, in retaliation for the supposed murder of a nonunion miner. Then, on 20 April 1914, fighting broke out between strikers and a detachment of the guard at the Ludlow tent colony. Throughout the day guard members directed machine gunfire into the camp, forcing strikers and their families to try to flee or to seek shelter in pits dug below their tents. Eleven of Ludlow's nineteen dead were found in one such pit, suffocated by smoke from their burned tent.

The Ludlow Massacre touched off ten days of fighting in the southern field as enraged strikers occupied towns, attacked mine guards, and destroyed mine facilities. The violence ended only when President Woodrow Wilson sent federal troops into the field. The coalfield war loosed a storm of public and editorial protest, in Colorado and across the nation, directed at Governor Ammons, General Chase and the guard, and especially the Rockefeller family, who controlled CF&I. Despite this support, the strike collapsed. The long strike in the northern fields, the costs of supporting thousands in tent colonies in the south, and the fighting stretched union resources to the limit. In December 1914 the union called off the strike and retreated from Colorado.

In the aftermath of the coalfield war many, including John D. Rockefeller, Jr., realized that a simple return to the status quo antebellum was not possible. Though he never acknowledged any personal or corporate responsibility for the strike and the deaths at Ludlow, Rockefeller was appalled by the violence in Colorado and set out to try to meet the miners' demands for a voice in the industry, short of recognizing the union. To do this, Rockefeller instituted in the mines and steel operations of the Colorado Fuel and Iron Company an employee representation plan devised by Canadian labor expert W. MacKenzie King. This experiment in industrial paternalism, called the Colorado Industrial Plan, or Rockefeller Plan, permitted employees to elect representatives to joint worker-management committees. The job of the committees was to formulate recommendations regarding working conditions and practices, camp life, health services, and other matters concerning employees' working and living conditions. In addition, the plan included a formal grievance procedure allowing employees to air complaints with committees and company officers. However, authority to decide on committee recommendations and employee grievances remained firmly in the hands of company officials.

A 1924 study by the Russell Sage Foundation noted that the Rockefeller Plan intended to bridge "the mental and economic separation" of labor and management and thereby "to restore personal relationships" in the industrial environment.[24] Nonetheless, desirable as good personal relations among workers, managers, and employers are, in the complex setting of modern industry organized power is what matters. Under the Rockefeller Plan CF&I's miners remained unorganized and under the dominance of the company. That dominance was challenged by renewed efforts, led by radical unions, to organize coal miners in the West and ended with the collapse of the American economy in the 1930s.

Renewed labor agitation in the late 1920s and early 1930s and the impact of the Great Depression opened the way for the triumph of the United Mine Workers in the coalfields of the West. The relative peace in labor relations enjoyed during most of the 1920s, a peace that owed much to antiradicalism and right-to-work laws, ended in 1927 when the Industrial Workers of the World (IWW, or Wobblies) led Colorado coal miners out on strike. The strike was strongest in the northern field, where miners protested the lack of union representation, wage cuts, short weights, intimidation of miners by company officials, noncompliance with safety and ventilation laws, and loss of income due to delays in delivering supplies and cars.

The strike turned ugly on 21 November 1927 when state policemen guarding the Rocky Mountain Fuel Company's Columbine Mine, in Lafayette, opened fire on demonstrating strikers, killing six. Once again state intervention threatened to crush union activity. The situation changed, however, when John Roche, one of the principal owners of Rocky Mountain Fuel, died. Soon Roche's daughter, Josephine, a woman already well known for her support of progressive reforms, won control of the company. Sympathetic to the miners' grievances and shocked by the "Columbine Massacre," Roche decided to deal with the miners and in 1928 signed a contract with the UMWA. Other operators opposed Roche's move and held out against the union for another five years.

Much the same pattern occurred in New Mexico and Utah when the radical National Miners Union (NMU) led miners in those states out on strike. In both cases, after violence and state intervention, the operators agreed to contracts with the more conservative United Mine Workers.

Indeed, there is evidence that the UMWA encouraged state governments to intervene against the radical unions. During the 1927–28 Wobbly strike in Colorado, for example, a UMWA organizer advised the governor's office on tactics to break the strike. In Utah in 1933 the UMWA helped operators and Carbon County authorities break the NMU strike by providing strikebreakers and harassing NMU organizers.

The New Deal lifted the last roadblocks to union organization in the coal industry. With the passage in 1933 of the National Industrial Recovery Act, guaranteeing American workers the right to organize and bargain collectively, UMWA organizers, using the slogan "The

President Wants You to Organize," fanned out across the country. In Colorado the union breached the largest obstacle to organization when, on 30 October 1933, the Colorado Fuel and Iron Company's miners voted to abandon the Rockefeller Plan.

In other policies and programs the Roosevelt administration sought not only to protect the rights of miners to organize and bargain collectively, but to bring a measure of economic stability to the highly competitive coal industry. The Guffey-Snyder Act (1935) and the Guffey-Vinson Act (1937) aimed to stabilize supplies and prices through industry-wide production quotas and wage and price agreements. One important goal was to end the cycle of boom and bust that had plagued the industry since the nineteenth century.

In the Rocky Mountain states hard-rock mining and related industries, the railroads, and population increase made for a period of growth in the coal industry lasting through the first two decades of the twentieth century. In Colorado output peaked in 1910 at just over twelve million tons produced by nearly fifteen thousand workers. New Mexico, Wyoming, and Montana reached production highs in 1918, and Utah in 1920. After World War I, decreasing industrial activity and competition from petroleum, natural gas, and hydroelectric power caused two decades of decline in the western coal industry. By 1935 total production in the five states had fallen to 18.1 million tons. World War II caused a "boomlet" in the western coalfields, but the general decline resumed in the postwar years. Beginning in the 1960s, however, the Rocky Mountain coal industry enjoyed a new period of sustained growth stimulated by fuel demands of other regions and the West's own economic and population growth. Much of the new demand for coal comes from the huge, coal-fired electrical plants built since the 1960s in the Four Corners area and in the northern plains. The energy crisis of the 1970s also helped by encouraging industry and utility companies all over the United States to convert from fuel oil to coal.

By the time this new boom had begun, many of the old leaders in the western coal industry had disappeared. Though the names are different, consolidation in the industry has, if anything, increased. Today companies such as Consolidation, Peabody, Pittsburg and Midway, and Mid-Continent, as well as electric utility and oil companies, dominate the industry. Indeed, the growing role of oil companies, including Gulf, Exxon, and Atlantic-Richfield, underscores the future importance of the region's coal resources. Predicting that the American West will be the Saudi Arabia of the twenty-first century, economist Kenneth Boulding has observed that "what we have in the Rocky Mountain states is the largest reserve of fossil fuel in the world. When everything else is gone, we're going to have it."[25]

The new boom not only led to growth in the industry, but also dramatically altered the character of coal mining itself. By the 1970s underground coal mining had all but disappeared from the West as operators sought more efficient methods of extracting coal from the earth. Huge earth-moving machines now strip away the overburden to expose whole coal seams—seams that miners once would have followed into the earth.

In the decades of the late nineteenth and early twentieth centuries, coal operators in the Rocky Mountain region created an industrial environment dominated by a small number of companies. From their position of control in an industry crucial to the region's economic growth, operators wielded significant power not only in legislatures and executive chambers, but over local affairs and the daily lives of their employees. That industrial setting, in turn, influenced the physical and social environment inside the mines where men actually worked and, too often, died.

Chapter 2

Work in the Hand-Mining and Early Machine Era

In 1881 a group of tourists traveling in the Arkansas Valley region of Colorado visited a coal mine near Canon City. One of the tourists recorded a description of the adventure evoking Dantesque images of a hellish underworld. In a coal car pulled by a blind mule, the tourists went on "a weird ride . . . into the inky bowels of the earth" where they saw "not the forms of the men, their faces, nor their hands, only the lampwicks sickly flaring from the unseen hats." On the way in they passed through a heavy oak door, there to preserve "the little of wholesome air left in the drift." As the door closed behind them, it seemed as if it barred them "forevermore from the world behind." These visitors, no doubt, were glad when their underground tour was over. "The ride in appears an age," the diarist wrote, and "the ride out of but a moment's time in comparison."[1] What to the casual visitor seemed a hellish place, tolerable only for a short visit, was to the miners a daily workplace.

A coal seam is a pool of organic matter compressed and solidified over time by heat and the weight of overlying strata deposited by the earth's violent self-transformations. If this subterranean mass cannot be exposed and mined by removing the overburden of soil and rock, it must be extracted underground. For the coal operator, this presents the problem of organizing capital, managers and engineers, equipment and a work force to bring out the coal. For the coal miners, working underground means earning a living in a dark and dangerous environment and coming out alive at the end of the day.

Two basic operating systems are used in underground coal mining: the longwall method and the room-and-pillar method. In both systems the coal seam is opened by a drift, slope, or shaft. If the coal is exposed on the surface, it can be opened by a drift driven directly into the seam, or if the coal is known to lie close to the surface, the seam may be approached by a sloping shaft driven to it. When the coal is too deep for a slope, a vertical shaft is sunk from the surface to the seam.

In longwall mining a large block of coal, up to seven hundred feet wide and several thousand feet long, is laid out between parallel entry tunnels. The coal then is sheared off the seam in long retreating rows. Portable jacks support the roof in the work area to protect men and machinery from falling material. As production proceeds, the jacks are removed and the overburden collapses into the void left by mining the coal. Because it is especially suited to the use of continuous mining machines, which cut the coal and load it into cars or onto conveyor belts, longwall mining came into wide use only in recent times.

The room-and-pillar system is the traditional method of mining coal. A map of a room-and-pillar mine looks very much like a city map, with main thoroughfares and side streets, blocks, and residences. In a coal mine the main entry is the principal passageway for moving men, equipment, and coal into and out of the mine. Branching off from the main entry are side entries that define the blocks of coal under development. These side entries always are driven in pairs in order to allow air to circulate through the mine and carry off noxious gases and dust. Turned off from the side entries are openings to a number of rooms that usually are about twenty feet wide at the face of the coal seam. The room is the coal miners' workplace. Here the miners use picks or machinery to cut into the face of the coal until they come to another entry, the seam "pinches out," or they reach the boundary of the property. As adjoining rooms advance, crosscuts are made between them at regular intervals to provide for ventilation. The "pillars" of coal standing between rooms and crosscuts remain in place to support the overburden. When the area is mined out, the miners "pull" these pillars, allowing the roof to collapse.

Geological conditions vary among, and even within, the coalfields

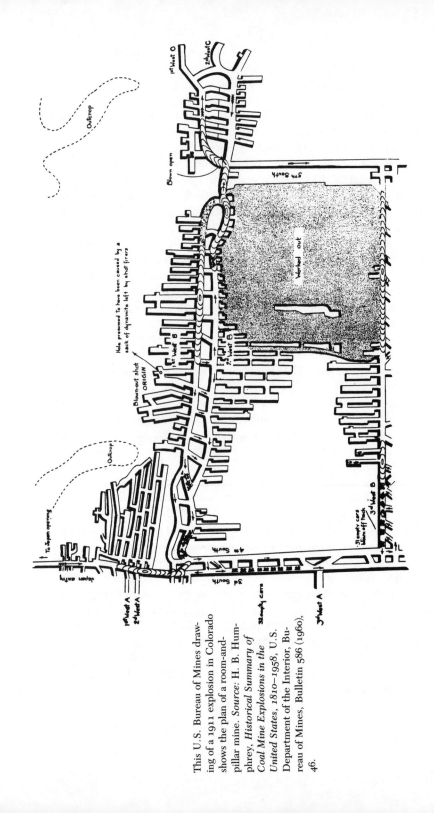

This U.S. Bureau of Mines drawing of a 1911 explosion in Colorado shows the plan of a room-and-pillar mine. *Source:* H. B. Humphrey, *Historical Summary of Coal Mine Explosions in the United States, 1810–1958,* U.S. Department of the Interior, Bureau of Mines, Bulletin 586 (1960), 46.

of the West. In the northern field of Colorado most seams are quite level, though a few are pitched and even nearly vertical. In the southern field the seams, though generally level, often are "broken" by wedges or layers of "bony," which is slate or other material. Coal seams also vary considerably in height. A seam five to eight feet is ideal for underground mining, though seams of good coking coal as thin as two feet are mined. At the other extreme, seams as high as thirty feet exist in western Colorado and Utah.

The amount of gas and dust also varies from field to field. Though coal dust is a common problem throughout the West, some mines contain enough moisture to keep it down, whereas others require extensive sprinkling systems. Gas, especially explosive methane, or "fire-damp," is also found throughout the West, though in the northern field of Colorado some mines were essentially gas-free. In Las Animas County, in the southern field, a local newspaper in the early 1880s maintained that the mines were free of gas and that "such a thing as a coal gas explosion will never be known," a claim tragically disproven in time.[2]

Although different specific geological conditions created different specific problems for miners, certain basic work patterns and hazards were common. Before the advent of effective eight-hour laws and operators' acceptance of the principle of portal-to-portal time, coal miners worked a long day. As one old-timer described it, "we had the eight-hour day—eight hours before dinner and eight hours after."[3] In fact, it was not unusual for twelve or fourteen hours to pass from the time a man left home in the morning till his return at night. Employers commonly expected the miner to be in his room and ready to work at seven o'clock, which meant arriving at the mine in time to walk in or wait in line for a man-trip or a cage. At midmorning, work might stop for a light lunch, a needed break for men who had had their breakfasts at four or five in the morning. Work stopped again at noon for dinner and then resumed until quitting time at five o'clock. If the men could not simply walk out of the mine they again had to wait their turn on a man-trip or a cage. If any coal cars remained to be taken out, they had priority, further delaying the men's exit from the mine.

In the pick-mining and hand-loading days the coal miner's basic task was to break down a quantity of coal from the seam and load it into a car for transport to the surface. That rather straightforward productive goal belies the complexity of the miner's work and working environment. Before (and even after) the intrusion of machinery the coal miners considered themselves skilled tradesmen. Inside their rooms they performed all, or nearly all, of the tasks necessary for producing coal. Each task required different skills and involved different risks of injury or death on the job.

Getting the coal out of the seams required blasting it free with explosives. One method, called "shooting off the solid," involved drilling holes into the face of the coal, loading explosive charges, and firing them. However, miners and operators generally disfavored this method, because it required large amounts of explosives, which tended to pulverize the coal, weakened roofs, and produced excessive amounts of smoke, dust, and fumes.

Miners usually preferred undermining the coal to prepare it for blasting. Kneeling or lying on one side, the miner used his pick to cut into the bottom of the coal. This was uncomfortable and dangerous work. The floor of the room might be covered with water and mud; the miner had to swing his pick in a confined area; and he had to be alert to the condition of the coal. Since he drove the undercut from three to as much as six feet, he had to work beneath the coal. If the coal seemed unstable or if the cut was deep, the miner used short sturdy posts, called "sprags," to support the undermined coal until he completed the undercut.

Next, the miner drilled holes for the explosive charges that would bring the coal down. Using a long auger turned by a hand crank and set up on a jack-and-post or braced against his body, he drilled a series of holes near the top of the seam, driven at a slight upward angle so that the force of the charge would push the coal downward into the undercut. Correct placement and drilling of holes was important to ensure that all the undercut coal came down.

After drilling the holes, the miner prepared and placed the explosive charges, or shots. First, he made a cartridge, or "dummy," by wrapping paper around a pick handle or a stick and sealing it with saliva. He then filled this paper cylinder with blasting powder, closed the ends, and pushed it into the hole with a wooden tamping bar. The miner then inserted a long copper or iron needle into the shot. Next he "stemmed" the hole by packing in dirt, mud, clay, or some other noncombustible material and carefully withdrew the needle, leaving a channel into the powder. Before the invention of reliable fuses, the miner used a "squib," a small tube of paper with powder in one end inserted into the channel left by the needle, to set off the shot. He then lit the empty end of the squib and ran for the safety of a crosscut or entry.

Until the employment of shot firers, whose sole job was to set off explosives after all other workers left the mine, miners fired their shots as soon as they were set, a practice that kept the mines filled with smoke and dust. One old-timer recalled that "sometimes the smoke would be so thick in the mines . . . that you couldn't, if you was drivin' the mule, you couldn't see the head of the mule from the front end of your car. They shot anytime they wanted to."[4]

When the smoke, fumes, and dust cleared, the miner reentered the room and began loading the broken coal into cars. Since he needed to get as much coal as possible onto each car, loading was something of an art. First, he placed the largest lumps on the car and filled the spaces between them with smaller pieces. Then, using a miner's "banjo," he shoveled coal into the car. As he filled the car, he used any remaining larger pieces of coal to build walls so that he could pile coal above the sides of the car. A well-loaded, or "chunked-up," car could carry two to three thousand pounds of coal piled several feet higher than the car itself. Some miners took special pride in their loading techniques. A man who was especially fast with his shovel or who could toss a shovelful of coal against the side or roof and ricochet it into the car could save much time and effort and, more important, load more coal.

When he finished loading his car, the miner pushed it out to the entry, where a driver picked it up to haul to a gathering point in the main entry. From there the cars went to the surface, on cages in shaft mines and in continuous-rope or electric trolley "trips" in drift and slope mines. On the surface each car passed over a scale, where the weigh-boss recorded the weight of the coal and credited it to the miner whose "check," a small metal disk inscribed with a number, hung on the car. From the scale house the cars went to the tipple, where the coal was dumped and sorted by screening devices into lump, pea, and slack sizes.

If the cycle of undermining, drilling, shooting, and loading was all there was to the coal miner's job, his workday might have been short. However, he also had to complete some secondary tasks as part of his regular duties. As he advanced his room, the miner removed, or "brushed," the rock and slate above and below the seam so that men, cars, and, later, machinery could approach the face. Then he had to remove the refuse from brushing and mining and store it in "gobs," or worked-out areas of mine. After brushing the floor of his room up to the face, the miner laid track so that he could push cars in close.

An extremely important part of the miner's work was taking care of the roof in his room. As the room advanced, and after each round of shots, the men used their picks to "sound" the roof to detect any loose rock and shale, which they pried down and stored in the gob. Suspicious-looking areas, or areas too large to take down safely, they supported by installing heavy timbers. Timbering might involve simply setting a single prop and small cap piece or putting up two or more timbers spanned by large cross-pieces.

Although tonnage rates supposedly included brushing, track-laying, and timbering, miners resented the long hours they devoted to this "deadwork." The question of deadwork pay was a persistent irritant in labor relations as miners claimed that tonnage rates did not adequately compensate them for their efforts.

In time, changes in the organization of work and in technology altered the cycle of work in the room. By the second decade of the twentieth century most mines employed shot firers, a change inspired by safety concerns. When the miners arrived for work in mines using shot firers, their first task—after inspecting their rooms for bad roof, setting new props if needed, and repairing any other damage from the night's blasting—was loading their coal. Then they began the work of undercutting, drilling, and placing shots.

Undercutting was the first part of the miner's job taken over by machines. Limited use of cutting machines in western coal mines began in the 1880s. The Union Pacific introduced coal cutters in its Number 4 mine at Rock Springs, Wyoming, in 1882. By 1885 cutting machines were being used in Colorado in some Colorado Coal and Iron Company mines and at Marshall. From such sporadic beginnings mechanized undercutting grew steadily until, by 1930, machine-cut coal exceeded pick-mined coal in four of the five states.

The most common undercutting machines were the "puncher" and the "chain-breast" machines. Punchers were hammering devices, usually powered by compressed air. Working like jackhammers, punching machines pulverized the coal as they moved across the face. Some punchers were mounted on a platform, which operators had to move several times to complete the cut. Others, such as the Sullivan Post Puncher, were mounted on a post and could be swiveled across the face in an arc. Chain-breast cutters were essentially large chain saws with cutters mounted either on the chain itself or on a chain-driven cutter bar. These machines, though larger and less maneuverable, were faster and made a wider cut than punchers. Because of their size, however, they were most suitable for mines with thick seams and level entries. Moving from room to room, the undercutting machine and its operator relieved the miners of the tedious and dangerous work of undermining the coal. Machines performed in minutes work that could take a man hours to do by hand, speeding up the cycle of work and increasing productivity. Because he performed a basic part of the miner's work, the machine operator received a tonnage rate for his work.

Machine operators were one of several types of workers, in addition to the pick miners, employed in the mines. Others, known as company men, or day men, did all the work outside of the rooms and were paid by the day or according to the task. Many boys began their careers helping older relatives or friends in the rooms; others started out as "trappers" or "nippers." Trappers opened and closed doors, placed in the entries to direct ventilation currents, as mine trips passed through. Nippers helped mule drivers and rope-riders (men who assembled coal-trips in the main entry and escorted them to the surface) gather coal cars and keep the trips under control. One of the nipper's most important jobs was spragging the wheels of coal cars. This involved thrusting a sprag into the spokes of the moving wheel in order to slow the car on downgrades.

Other company men were kept busy driving new entries, laying track, setting timbers, and otherwise maintaining the entries. In shaft mines cagers spent the day loading and unloading cars on hoists, and the hoist engineer operated the lift carrying men and coal to and from the surface. On the surface men and boys worked in the tipple grading and sorting the coal, operated the mine's ventilating fan, or worked in shops maintaining and repairing equipment. Especially important was the blacksmith, who sharpened picks and drills and kept coal cars in repair.

Probably the most important and colorful employee, besides the miner, was the mule driver. Before diesel and electric locomotives displaced them, these men and their mules acquired almost legendary status. With nicknames such as "Jimmy the Dog," "Willie the Crow," and "Wedding Bells," mule drivers defied easy, or even coherent, description. Tom Allen, long-time state coal-mine inspector in Colorado, once described them as "reckless, indifferent men" who were morally and physically clean, "excepting that they drank and they spent their money, and just had one hell of a time."[5]

Normally, a driver might be responsible for serving miners in as many as ten rooms. The driver brought cars to the room, took the loaded cars away, and delivered supplies of timber and rails to the miners. Because he provided crucial services, the mule driver was in a position to demand tips or other favors from the miners and could withhold a turn of cars if gratuities were not forthcoming.

The mules spent most of their lives underground and probably knew their way around the mine better than most of the men. Intelligent animals, they might refuse to move if the driver tried to hitch up more than the accustomed number of cars, and they seemed to know when it was quitting time. From his perch on the front of a coal car, the driver handled his animals with only voice commands— "gee" and "haw" (left and right)—and a whip or sprag to convince a balky mule to move. The best speed for a mule trip was all-out, going "to beat the devil down hill so they could get up the other hill without stopping." If a trip got out of control or jumped the tracks, the driver was in real danger of injury, for in the narrow entries there usually was no place to jump to safety. In order to slow his trip the driver, or his nipper, thrust sprags into the wheels of the cars. This caused the wheels to slide on the tracks, eventually creating flat spots. Tom Allen once said that coal mining was "the only industry where the octagon was used for the shape of a wheel rather than a circle."[6]

Mules played an important role in the mines, and they were expensive. Thus, even though a balky animal might sorely provoke him, a driver was well advised not to abuse it. In fact, abusing a mule was a quick way to get "sent down the canyon." The Colorado Fuel and Iron Company, for example, had a strict policy on the subject, requiring not only the discharge of abusive drivers but circulation of their names and descriptions to all company camps. The company thus blacklisted a man who injured or killed a mule.

Electric and diesel engines began to replace mules in western coal mines before the end of the nineteenth century. However, it was not uncommon to find them at work well into the twentieth century, especially in gassy mines where machinery raised the risk of explosion. For example, most mines in Utah still used mule trips in 1926, and some small mines in northern New Mexico used them as late as 1970. Mules, one operator claimed, "are more dependable and a damn sight cheaper than power," and unlike diesel equipment, they never quit running in wintertime. "Just shovel hay to them and they never stop."[7]

A coal mine with its full complement of miners and day men was a complex industrial environment that made for a complex management problem. In most mines four supervisory positions, the superintendent, the foreman, the fireboss, and the shot firer, were of special importance. Together, these officials formed not so much a chain of command as divisions of authority in the operation of the mine, divisions materially affecting the environment, including safety conditions, in which miners worked.

The superintendent had overall responsibility for management of mine and camp. As business manager, he supervised the other officials, had general charge over mine personnel, oversaw operation of camp stores and saloons, allotted housing to miners, prepared payrolls, and saw to it that mine equipment and supplies were adequately maintained. Although the superintendent had general authority, his practical authority usually stopped at the mine portal. Underground, the foreman, or mine boss, had authority over hiring and firing, allotment of rooms, assignment of deadwork, supervision of day men, and all other aspects of work in the mine.

The fireboss was the official most directly responsible for safety conditions in the mine. Usually, firebosses had many years of experience in coal mining and, by the early twentieth century, had to pass examinations and be certified by state mine inspectors. Every morning before the miners reported for work, the fireboss inspected all working areas of the mine for hazardous conditions, particularly gas pockets and bad roof. After inspecting each room, the fireboss chalked his initials on the side, or rib, of the room entry to show that he had been there. The fireboss reported any defects or hazards to the foreman, who in turn ordered the miners to correct them before they did any other work. If he discovered any particularly dangerous conditions, the fireboss could close the room or entry concerned until miners or day men corrected the hazard.

The shot-firer's job also was safety-related. He inspected the placement and loading of all shots and detonated them at the end of the day after all other workers left the mine. The shot firer also had authority to condemn any shot and refuse to fire it. As in the case of firebosses, state governments eventually required examination and certification of shot firers.

Miners, and all the other underground employees and supervisors, worked in an environment in which danger was a constant fact of life. The very process of mining coal created a deadly atmosphere. Coal is partially decomposed organic matter; a by-product of that decomposition is explosive methane gas trapped in the coal. Opening the seam and mining the coal released that gas into the atmosphere of the mine. Odorless and colorless, methane, or "fire-damp," could be detected only by a flame safety lamp, a device constructed with a fine screen or baffles allowing only a small quantity of air, or gas, to contact the flame. If fire-damp was present, the flame flared, harmlessly, warning the miner or the fireboss to increase ventilation in the area. If ventilation currents were not adequate to dilute and carry the gas away, the open flame of a miner's lamp, a "blown-out shot" (which occurred when the force and flame of a shot fired out of the hole, usually the result of improper stemming), or even a spark from a pick striking rock could detonate pockets of fire-damp. One old-timer claimed that "half the mules in the mines had their ears burned off" by small explosions of gas touched off by sparks from car wheels.[8]

Local explosions of fire damp usually did little harm to men and equipment; however, when exploding methane mixed with coal dust, the result too often was disaster. Once ignited, an explosion of coal dust seemed to set the very air on fire. Survivors of gas and dust explosions sometimes described a tongue of flame racing through the mine. On the surface the report of an explosion might sound like a gigantic cannon or be felt, more than heard, as a muffled shudder. As often as not, more men died of suffocation than from the actual flame and concussion of an explosion. As a blast moved through a mine it consumed all the oxygen and left behind a deadly mixture of carbon monoxide ("white-damp") and carbon dioxide ("black-damp"), known to miners as "after-damp." Men caught in the after-damp lost consciousness in a few seconds and usually died in a few minutes. Rescuers would find them sitting with tools, or even with food and drink, in their hands; kneeling as if in prayer; or lying down as though they had just gone to sleep.

Mine explosions in which scores, even hundreds, of men died always drew the attention of press and public. Sometimes the heart-breaking stories of gruesome disaster scenes and of the vigil of families at the portal led to efforts to reform and strengthen coal-mine regulation. Explosions, however, actually accounted for only a minority of coal-mine deaths. Falls of roof, sides, and coal caused half or more of all coal-mine fatalities. Other major killers included mine cars, electricity, mining machinery, cages and shafts, fire, animals, and, on the surface, tipple equipment and railroad cars.

Efficient production in an industrial setting, whether in a coal mine or in a factory, depends on the performance of all the actors in the process. In coal mining, in the pick-mining and early machine period, miners depended on drivers to pick up and deliver cars, machine men to undercut their coal, firebosses to inspect rooms and entries properly, and mine bosses to see to procurement and delivery of timbers and rails. If anyone failed, deliberately or not, to do his job, miners could lose production and pay. Examination of this complex setting, with its layers of authority and interdependent workers, reveals much about coal miners and their work relations and how those relations helped to shape safety conditions in the mines.

In the struggle for control over work, miners had some advantages over their supervisors. One was the almost proprietary attitude miners held toward their rooms. Once a man went to work in a room, he expected to work in it until it was mined out or until he quit or was fired. Because of this feeling of proprietorship, it was the custom of miners not to work in another man's room, and the practice of mine bosses to hold a man's room for him if illness, injury, or some other reason caused him to miss work. This custom was not just a matter of respecting territory, for real economic and safety concerns were at stake. The United States Coal Commission in 1923 noted that a substitute working in another man's room "might get paid for work done by his predecessor" or by leaving the room in bad condition "might involve the original miner in an undue amount of 'non-productive' work." Moreover, the commission noted, "since the worker is responsible for the safety of his working place one worker might be unduly endangered by careless work of others."[9] Because of these concerns and the miner's feeling about his room, fellow workers and mine officials hesitated to challenge his control there.

The miner's perception of himself as a skilled tradesman was a source of both control and conflict in the workplace. Labor leader John Brophy, who learned coal mining at his father's side in the mines of western Pennsylvania, recalled that a man's skill in undercutting and his judgment in drilling and placing shots affected his prestige among fellow workers. Thus, a man who missed his turn of cars because of poor workmanship might lose face.[10] Proud of their skills and jealous of their control in their rooms, many miners did not take well to supervision, criticism, or advice by mine bosses. That resistance to supervision became a source of disagreement and recrimination among miners, operators, and supervisors in controversies over mine safety in the nineteenth and early twentieth centuries.

Sheer numbers and the extensive physical setting of the mine freed miners from close supervision by mine bosses. A boss in a large mine with, perhaps, one or two assistants might be responsible for supervising a work force numbering in the hundreds and spread over many miles. Tom Allen, who had experience as a mine boss and superintendent in Wyoming and Colorado before joining the Colorado coal-mine inspection department, recalled that, "in the old days, the supervision of a mine was generally delegated to one man and you had to fight like the devil to get an assistant where you had maybe a couple hundred men, you ran miles."[11]

Territoriality, the skilled nature of the work, scattered workplaces, and lack of close supervision gave miners a degree of control over the pace of work and even the length of the workday. On the other hand, the introduction of machines, reliance on other workers, the miners' transience, and, for many years, the lack of strong social and organizational cohesiveness weakened that control and reinforced the authority of mine bosses and superintendents.

Mechanization relieved miners of the tedious and dangerous work of undercutting, but machines imposed new requirements on them, altered their relations with managers and with other workers, and ultimately changed the nature of coal mining itself. In the mid-1920s the impact of mechanization prompted Colorado's chief coal-mine inspector to remark that, "where the individual skills of the miner once determined his daily output, a man's tonnage is now largely a question of how much he knows in regard to the use, handling and operation of improved machines." Miners now had to open their rooms wider, set timbers to allow machines to maneuver, and lay tracks right up to the face. That meant more brushing, timbering, and other types of deadwork. The pace and productivity of work also changed, as miners had to wait for machine operators to undercut their coal and depended on them to do it properly. In effect, machine operators wielded a new, if informal, kind of authority in the mine. George Parker, a miner from Dacono, Colorado, in 1927 told the Colorado Industrial Commission that, if a miner complained about a machine man's work, the machine man "has that advantage there that he can say 'If you don't like the work here the way I cut it, you know what you can do.'"[12]

Mechanization also gave foremen and superintendents a new kind of leverage in mine management and labor relations. One way to dispose of troublemakers or to reduce payrolls by eliminating higher-priced pick miners was to put them on a machine. "If they wanted to get rid of you, they'd say, 'There's your machine, you're supposed to be a miner, get in there and cut it.'" Without proper training on the machine the miner was helpless or even in danger. "You couldn't do it," recalled one old-timer. "You didn't know how to run the machine or nothing. You'd hurt yourself, kill yourself probably." If the miner complained, the mine boss could say, "That's all we have so good-bye." One industry analyst in 1894 noted that the mining machine was advantageous to operators "not so much for its saving in direct cost as for the indirect economy in having to control a fewer number of men for the same output," and because it gave operators a "weapon with which to meet organized labor and their unreasonable demands."[13]

Mechanization also devalued the miner's skills. Increasingly, men worked to serve the needs of machines, largely in preparing the rooms for them. One retired miner from the northern field of Colorado recalled that "they picked us guys that make the conditions for the machines to work. . . . These machines won't work any place you put them. You got to have timber, and you got to make room." With the declining importance of miners' skills, machine men displaced pick miners as the leading category of mine employees. In Colorado in 1917 there were 5,448 pick miners and 2,138 machine miners; in

1925, 4,485 pick miners and 3,761 machine miners; and in 1931, 2,565 pick miners and 3,394 machine miners. This displacement of skilled miners by machine men occurred throughout the Rocky Mountain region in the late nineteenth and early twentieth centuries, earlier in Wyoming and somewhat later in Utah. In New Mexico the United States mine inspector, noting the progress of mechanization, in 1901 declared that mining machines promised to solve the territory's perennial labor shortage.[14]

Mechanization not only altered work relations but also created new hazards in the mines. Machine vibration, noise, electricity, inadequate timbering, and increased dust contributed to more frequent roof falls and explosions. As machine cutters tore into the face, vibrations weakened and destabilized roofs and sides, thus increasing the danger of rock falls. The noisy machines also made it difficult for miners to detect bad rock when "sounding" the roof or to hear the distinctive grinding and cracking sounds that often preceded a fall. One man recalled that "when them damn machines are in there growling and smoking and belching . . . you can be working there running that machine and something behind you caving to beat hell and you don't know it till it's too late."[15]

Greater spacing between or removal of timbers to accommodate machinery also added to the danger of falls. Colorado's coal-mine inspector, James Dalrymple, in 1929 reported that "in some of the mines, the mine foremen insist upon the loaders timbering their places to suit the mining machines, instead of timbering them to protect themselves." Dalrymple insisted that, if a machine man removed any timbers in order to get his machine into a room, it was his duty to replace them when done.[16] However, state inspectors, and even foremen, could not realistically be expected to enforce such a policy.

Coal-mining machines also generated enormous quantities of dust, increasing the explosion risk in the mines and the incidence of respiratory ailments among the miners. "Oh, are they dusty sonsofbitches," said one man; "dust in suspension all day long, it never lets down."[17] Adding to the danger of explosion was the use of electricity to power mining machines. Sparks from frayed cables coming into contact with rails, or given off as cables were connected or disconnected, could set off small pockets of gas which in turn could ignite the dust.

Fearing loss of jobs and diminished status, miners attempted to resist the intrusion of machines. Since unorganized miners had little hope of convincing operators not to use machines, they sometimes resorted to sabotage to keep them out. This strategy led to serious conflicts that operators, backed by the power of the state, almost invariably won. In 1886, for example, Colorado attorney general Theodore Thomas told Governor Benjamin Eaton that a Boulder County company could hire armed guards to protect machinery from miners bent on keeping it out of the mine and, further, that the company, "in preventing the destruction by violence of its property . . . can use all the force and arms necessary to accomplish such an end."[18] Ultimately, men yielded to technology, and as noted, by the 1930s machine men outnumbered skilled pick miners.

Transience was another factor limiting the miner's control over work. Coal mining traditionally was a seasonal occupation, with employment rising in the fall and winter months when demand was highest. In the summer many mines shut down or sharply curtailed operation. Captive mines such as those owned by the Colorado Fuel and Iron Company or the Union Pacific offered steadier employment, but they, too, were vulnerable to seasonal and economic fluctuations. Irregular employment created a floating population of mine workers moving from camp to camp and state to state in search of work. Bad luck in room and work assignments also encouraged men to quit their jobs and move on. Noting that "all coal mines have what are termed bad places," a committee of the Colorado legislature studying coal-mining conditions in 1901 found that a miner, "after a few ineffectual attempts to make a living wage" in a bad room, "draws his time and starts to look for work in another district."[19]

Transience also undermined social cohesiveness in the coal camps and reinforced the dominance of operators and superintendents. This situation contributed much to the difficulty of organizing mine workers into effective unions and prevented them from attempting to assert control over work through collective bargaining and strikes. By the time miners organized, in the 1930s, machines had already taken over much of their work, reduced their numbers, and weakened their control over work.

Changing ethnic composition also inhibited cohesiveness in the camps. In the early years of the industry most western coal miners were of Welsh and English stock, many coming by way of Pennsylvania and Ohio. During the 1880s southern and eastern European immigrants began to arrive in the West, brought in as contract laborers or as strikebreakers. Hiring agents recruited many immigrants in the East and in Europe, and others came on their own, lured by the promise of jobs and security. Coal mining attracted not only those immigrants who had worked in the mines in Europe but also, as the U.S. Industrial Commission reported, "many unskilled laborers from European farms" who found "in the American coal mines their introduction to American industry." The arrival of thousands of Italian, Greek, Polish, Slavic, and Mexican immigrants transformed the ethnic composition of the western coalfields during the first decade and a half of the twentieth century. In 1903, for example, the Colorado Fuel and Iron Company found thirty "nationalities" among its work force. By 1912 some 61 percent of Colorado's coal miners were immigrants of nonwestern European origin, and in 1913 coal-mine inspector James Dalrymple reported that twenty-five languages were spoken in the mines.[20]

Similar changes occurred in Utah, Wyoming, and Montana, where Greek, Finnish, Italian, Slavic, Irish, and Asian immigrants made up half or more of the work force in the coal mines. In Wyoming the violent hostility of American-born coal miners to foreign intrusion, evidenced by the anti-Chinese riots of 1885, only delayed the inevitable. In 1915 the Wyoming coal-mine inspector reported that "the majority of men employed in the mines are foreigners."[21]

In New Mexico the pattern was somewhat different. Like the other states, New Mexico experienced an influx of European immigrants in the late nineteenth and early twentieth centuries. The Colorado Fuel and Iron Company in 1902 found Austrians, Italians, Swedes, and Germans, as well as Mexicans, blacks, Navajos, and Japanese, in its New Mexican camps. In contrast to the other states, however, in New Mexico European immigrants did not become predominant in the coal mines. For example, the foreign-born population of Colfax County peaked at about 30 percent in 1910. After 1910 the flow of Europeans into New Mexico slowed, and by 1920 many had drifted away from the mines and were replaced by "Spanish-speaking natives of New Mexico and natives of Mexico," whom the state coal-mine inspector described as "less turbulent by nature than the European."[22]

Ethnic diversity helped to strengthen the operators' and superintendents' control in the camps and mines. Even though the various immigrant groups socialized, they nonetheless tended to segregate themselves in camp housing. Moreover, language barriers and lingering group hostilities, whether transferred from Europe or stemming from operators' use of successive immigrant groups as strikebreakers, hindered union organizing efforts. Ethnic diversity also affected work relations. As ethnic composition changed, a hierarchy emerged, with the old English and Welsh stock miners moving into and dominating management positions in the mines and camps. Operators and mine officials often used ethnic hostilities and language barriers to try to control the work force and prevent organized dissent. A United Mine Workers organizer explained that an Italian would be placed with a Greek, a Croatian with an Austrian, "and so on down the line of 22 or 23 different nationalities" so that "no two of them shall get together and discuss their grievances."[23] Ethnicity not only was a factor in work relations, but also became a matter of concern to persons worried about rising casualty rates in the industry. By the early twentieth century, industry and government officials were commonly blaming ignorant, unskilled foreigners for going into the mines and recklessly killing themselves.

Mechanization, transience, ethnic diversity, and lack of cohesiveness among the miners strengthened the hand of superintendents and mine bosses—with their authority to hire and fire, allot rooms, assign deadwork, control the flow of mine cars, and set pay rates—in controlling working conditions in the mines. Inside, the authority of the mine boss was virtually absolute, a situation that could become abusive. Miners sometimes claimed that mine bosses and superintendents used their positions to extort bribes or other favors from miners in exchange for good rooms or an extra turn of cars. One man, from southern Colorado, recalled that "lots of places was sold in these coal mines through the bosses . . . and superintendents." Another said that if you were a friend of the "super," or brought him a jug of whiskey, "or let him sleep with your wife . . . you get a good place in the mine where you could really make a living." However, if superintendents or mine bosses disliked a man, they could see to it that he got a bad place or no cars. Retired miner Jack Miller, from northern Colorado, claimed that in one mine the foreman ordered a driver to "pass him up every chance" he could and to take extra cars to another man more in favor with the mine boss.[24]

Stories like this are disturbing, and such incidents may have been common; however, the ability—or inability—of managers to provide basic services and supplies when needed was more likely to affect the miner's productivity. In its study of coal-industry problems in the 1920s, the U.S. Coal Commission found that "good service" by management in providing enough timber and cars, explosives, and adequate ventilation to the men at the face was crucial to efficient production and good labor relations. Failure by management to provide the miner "the services necessary for him to produce" meant idleness and lost wages. Dave Hammond, a miner who worked for Victor-American around 1910, complained that "time and again" miners lost hours when props, stored far from the mine, did not arrive when needed because the foreman "could not stop hauling coal to haul these props over to the mine." With no props to secure the roofs of their rooms the men left work and lost pay. "It was not safe for them in the mine in their working place to stay in there," Hammond said; "they had to go home." Hammond claimed that he had had the same experience in other mines, too. Another miner, employed by the Wootton Land and Fuel Company in southern Colorado, told of losing hours, even days, waiting for timbers.[25]

What miners saw as deliberate harassment or lack of concern for mine safety on the part of management may very well have been the result of incompetence. That, however, did not lessen its impact on miners' productivity and wages. Moreover, until coal miners were effectively organized, they could do little about it. A miner had two basic responses to discrimination in assignment of rooms and cars or to management failures: make a "kick" or quit. If a man complained about working conditions, a well-intentioned mine boss might try to accommodate him with a better room or more timbers. However, if the mine boss disliked the man, "kicking" invited retaliation in the form of even worse conditions or discharge.

Ultimately, the coal miner enjoyed little autonomy in his job or in his workplace. Instead, he worked in an environment conditioned by layers or divisions of function and authority which directly affected his ability to work and produce. Fellow workers, the drivers and the machine men, and mine officials could determine whether or not the miner could dig and load his coal. Nevertheless, the assumption that the coal miner was an independent craftsman contracting as an equal with the operator conditioned work relations in the pick-mining and early machine era. That assumption, in turn, colored the attitudes of operators, managers, government officials, and even miners themselves on the issues of safety and death in the mines.

As contractors, miners at the face were paid according to their production. Most often, each miner received a tonnage rate for his coal, though sometimes operators calculated wages on the basis of total mine production, or "run of mine." Reflecting the industry's vulnerability to changing economic conditions, wages for western coal miners were highly unstable. For example, in Fremont County, Colorado, wages dropped from $1.50 per ton in 1872 to $0.75 in 1877 and rose to $1.00 in 1879. The Colorado state coal-mine inspector in 1890 reported that wages ranged from $0.50 to $1.12½ per ton, with an average of $0.76¼.

Operators expected tonnage men to make as much or more than day men. Basic daily wages paid to CF&I workers at Crested Butte, Colorado, in the mid-1890s were $2.24 to $2.75; by 1914 they had risen to between $3.00 and $4.00. A peak in wages came in 1923 when the Colorado Fuel and Iron Company, whose policy by then was to match prevailing union scales, paid the so-called "Jacksonville Scale" of $7.75 per day, agreed to by the United Mine Workers of America and the operators of the Central Competitive Field (Illinois, Indiana, Ohio, and western Pennsylvania). Other Colorado operators soon followed CF&I's lead. From that high point, though, wages declined through the rest of the 1920s, a slide accelerated by the Great Depression. By 1933 wages in the now-unionized northern field of Colorado were $3.40 to $5.55 for day men and $0.70 to $0.76 per ton for pick miners.

Irregular work compounded the fluctuation of wages. A committee of the Colorado legislature in 1901 reported that, even though prevailing wage scales suggested that "some men were able to make wages at the rate of three dollars per day," the fact was that "they were unable to get in many full days' work." Thus, although a man might earn sixty dollars one month, layoffs might reduce his earnings to only twenty dollars the next month. The committee found that most miners at the time earned three to five hundred dollars per year, with a few men, particularly machine operators, making somewhat more.[26]

Various charges for work-related services and supplies also reduced the miners' take-home pay. From their wages miners paid for blacksmithing, blasting powder, oil or carbide for their lamps, and doctors' fees. In 1901 operators deducted approximately seven dollars per month for these expenses.

Whether straight tonnage or run of mine, wages supposedly included compensation for deadwork. Faced with fluctuating tonnage rates and believing that they paid for everything used in production except their own sweat, miners devoted as little time as possible to timbering, brushing, and other types of deadwork. As a result, deadwork became a source of friction between operators and miners. Operators insisted that deadwork was part of the work necessary for producing coal and was taken into consideration in setting tonnage rates. "The coal miner is a contractor," said John C. Osgood; "he is given a certain place in the mine" and "he is paid for the result of his labor," not for the hours he works or for the specific tasks he performs. Thus, Osgood claimed, "it is simply a quibble to say that he does a lot of work that isn't paid for."[27]

Osgood's assertion may have been valid for some ideal mine in which the foreman always arranged for prompt delivery of adequate supplies of timber and in which bad roof was not excessive. Miners, however, maintained that deadwork often went beyond that required for normal room maintenance and production work. Especially common were complaints about having to carry rails and ties into rooms. Miner David Jones, from Fremont County, Colorado, told of going "as far as a quarter of a mile to carry a rail, and when I made a complaint to the bosses, they told me that if I didn't like it . . . I could go to the office and get my time." Another man claimed that in the Walsenburg area, in order to get ties and rails, men had to go into abandoned entries and rooms, "unsafe places for rats much less God's people," remove fallen slate, and drag the ties and rails to their rooms.[28]

Another complaint concerned rock falls and timbering. UMWA district leader John McLennan maintained that "in some cases a man will have a fall in his room [and] it will take a half-day or a whole day to clean up and he would not get paid for it." A miner who had worked for Rocky Mountain Fuel, Victor-American, and CF&I said none of the companies paid for rock and timber work, carrying rails, or other deadwork. "When a man goes in and he does probably $2 or $3 worth of work a day for nothing he will begin to think he has got a little grievance of some kind coming to him."[29]

Whether deadwork was a legitimate grievance or a "quibble," the system of paying miners on the basis of production put great pressure on them to produce and load as much coal as possible, as fast as possible. Thus the miners had a built-in incentive to try to avoid deadwork. As one man summarized it, "All the dead work you done, you done on your own. . . . If you didn't get the tonnage out, you didn't get anything." That meant the miners sometimes had to choose between safety and wages. Time spent setting a prop under a suspicious area of roof was time not spent loading coal, and miners often ran the risk that the roof would hold until they finished loading their coal. To delay loading might mean losing a turn of cars and part of a day's pay; delaying deadwork might mean injury or death. "The miner naturally looks to his own self-preservation, but he considers also his wages," the U.S. Coal Commission noted. "When a tonnage or contract worker puts in an extra timber or takes an extra safety precaution he cuts down his earning power." "Naturally," said Colorado coal-mine inspector Tom Allen, "a man being paid so much per car or so much per ton would give more attention to producing coal than to his own personal safety" and delay setting up a timber. Or as one old-timer described the reason miners failed to set enough timbers, "you put them up on your own time and there was lots of times a fellow was . . . in a hurry . . . they got to hurry to load that car, see, get that loaded and get another one and that's the reason so many men was hurt."[30]

In addition to this incentive to produce, superintendents and mine bosses, anxious to show their employers good production numbers, pressured miners to dig more coal, even at the expense of safety. The *United Mine Workers Journal* in 1914 insisted that mine bosses and superintendents, "hard driven by the knowledge that their jobs depend on their ability to produce coal cheaply," and realizing the powerlessness of miners to protest, "take chances with human life that result in the deplorable percentages of casualties the statistics reveal." The U.S. Coal Commission agreed with this assessment, classifying as a "moral hazard" of coal mining "the disregard for safety that is caused by a continual pressure on a coal-mine superintendent to increase his output, regardless of dangerous conditions."[31]

Clearly, the image of the coal miner as an independent contractor was irrelevant to actual work relations in the mines. The miner

Chapter 3

Early Coal-Mining Legislation in the Rocky Mountain West

When Josephine Roche was a child she sometimes accompanied her father, an officer and major stockholder of the Rocky Mountain Fuel Company, on visits to the company's properties. Once, when she was about twelve years old, Josephine asked her father for permission to go into one of the mines. When the elder Roche refused, saying that it would be too dangerous for her, Josephine is said to have replied, "Then how is it safe for the miners?"[1] John Roche's answer is not known, but he might have told his daughter that the miners knew how to look out for mine hazards and to protect themselves. Knowledgeable about the ways of the mine, the men expected to assume the risks of their work. In addition, the company took pains to see that the mine was well ventilated and company men kept the entries safe and well maintained. Roche might also have noted that laws regulating working conditions and practices protected mine workers.

Indeed, by the turn of the century, laws governing coal mining were on the books in all coal-producing states and territories in the United States. However, these laws proved to be ineffective in preventing high rates of death in the mines. This weakness reflected, in part, the fear of operators and legislators that stringent regulation might retard economic growth. Like operators everywhere, Rocky Mountain coal men worried that strong state or, worse, federal regulation might create competitive disadvantages. Typical of this concern is the comment of D. C. Beaman, a Colorado Fuel and Iron Company official, who maintained that industry efforts to influence or block regulation were purely self-defensive, "to prevent hostile legislation by demagogues for holdup purposes."[2]

Colorado's earliest mining laws evolved from the practices and rules governing placer and lode claims in the gold and silver camps. As the population of the camps grew, miners organized themselves into mining districts, elected officers, and formulated rules regarding the making and perfecting of claims and the resolution of claim disputes. Clearly, the emphasis here was on protecting property rights, not on regulating working conditions. In the early days the miner most likely worked in the relative safety of his placer diggings. The greatest risks he usually faced were bad weather, ornery mules, claim jumpers, and Saturday night in town.

Only when mining moved underground and the sourdough gave way to the corporation did working conditions and safety become a concern to government, industry, and miners. Hard-rock miners faced the same kinds of hazards that coal miners encountered; cave-ins, explosions, machinery accidents, and noxious gases all took their toll. However, because the hard-rock miner, like the coal miner, was considered a skilled craftsman responsible for his own work and safety, and because powerful metal-mining interests held sway in the legislature, serious regulation of working conditions in the hard-rock mines did not occur until the early years of the twentieth century.

The earliest attempt to regulate mine safety and working conditions in Colorado came in 1877 with the passage of a law establishing the office of commissioner of mines with authority to inspect both hard-rock and coal mines. The law authorized the commissioner to visit "the principal coal mines being worked" in the state and examine them as to the safety of the workings, condition of the air inside, methods of ventilation, and to determine if operators employed any children under the age of fourteen. The 1877 law required mine operators to maintain accurate, up-to-date maps and to allow the commissioner access to their mines. Refusal by operators to permit inspection, failure to keep accurate maps, or employment of children under the age of fourteen were misdemeanors punishable by fines up to five hundred dollars or imprisonment up to one year.[3]

This law was weak, at best. It did not provide for regular inspections and contained no effective standards governing mine ventilation or other important safety and working conditions. Moreover, the commissioner had no enforcement authority and, therefore, could not require mine operators to remedy dangerous conditions or shut down extremely hazardous mines.

Apparently, even this measure was too much for Colorado's hard-rock mining interests, for the legislature in 1881 repealed it on the grounds that it was, in Governor Frederick Pitkin's words, an "unjust burden upon the mine owners." Pitkin, an ardent supporter of industrial development, later tried to show himself to be no enemy of mine-safety regulation by claiming that he "reluctantly allowed the repeal of the law, because of its many defects, thinking that thereby the enactment of a proper law . . . would be more speedily secured."[4] Nevertheless, the metal-mining industry in Colorado avoided meaningful regulation until the twentieth century.

Regulation of safety and work conditions in Colorado's coal mines began with the passage in 1883 of a law providing for regular inspections and setting standards for ventilation and other crucial aspects of coal-mine operations. Because no major coal-mine disaster had recently occurred, creating a climate of opinion in favor of regulation, passage of this measure defied a pattern that would emerge in the West and nationwide. A mine explosion had occurred at Crested Butte in January 1883, but no one died in the blast. (One year later fifty-nine men died in another explosion there.)

Why Colorado's legislators chose to enact a coal-mining law in 1883 is something of a mystery. It is possible that the legislature acted in response to rising accident rates in the mining industry and that the state's hard-rock mining interests, wielding more influence than coal operators, were able to focus attention on coal mines only. Labor agitation may have been a factor, too. Late in 1882 coal miners at Louisville, in the northern field, demanded passage of a coal-mine ventilation law. However, miners on strike in 1882 and 1883 were more concerned with demands for better wages and the right to station checkweighmen on tipples than with lobbying for safety regulation. In fact, contemporary opinion suggests that labor upheaval may have retarded mine-safety regulation. The Trinidad *Daily News* in January 1883 asserted that if, "instead of striking against . . . a reduction of a cent a ton," miners had been more concerned with the value of their lives, "means possibly would have been secured by this time for the prevention of loss of life by explosions."[5]

Another explanation may be found by looking beyond the boundaries of Colorado. During the 1870s and 1880s the leading coal-producing states of the East and the Midwest enacted coal-mining regulatory measures. Pennsylvania in 1869 passed the first coal-mining law in the United States. That law, however, applied only to mines in Schuylkill County, in the anthracite region, and its existence was due to "the more harmonious relations between the men and the coal mine operators in that county than in the rest of the anthracite field." The following year, in the aftermath of the Avondale disaster, in which 179 men died, Pennsylvania's legislators set ventilation standards and required inspection of all anthracite mines. Pennsylvania extended regulation to its bituminous mines in 1877, five years after Ohio and Illinois imposed regulation and inspection measures. By the early 1880s seven states—Pennsylvania, Ohio, Illinois, Maryland, Indiana, West Virgina, and Iowa—had coal-mining laws in effect.[6]

Although no organized campaign by labor unions or mine engineering and safety experts occurred in Colorado, as happened in some other states, the trend among coal-producing states to impose regulation and inspection on their coal mines influenced developments there. In his January 1883 message to the state legislature Governor Frederick Pitkin noted that "all coal mining nations have laws for the official supervision of their mines, as have also all the States of this country in which coal mining is extensively carried on." Coal mining, the governor said, was "fast becoming one of the chief industries of this state . . . and the miners are entitled to a just and judicious protection of their lives and health." Pitkin concluded that, were the legislature to enact a law providing for proper ventilation of the mines and greater safety for coal miners, "and at the same time impose no unjust burdens upon the mine owners, it would be an act both of humanity and justice towards the miners."[7] Pitkin, whose personal fortune came from metal mining, did not discuss the need for more stringent regulation of the hard-rock industry.

A few days later Pitkin's successor, Governor James B. Grant, who as a smelter operator also owed his living to the metal-mining industry, seconded the call for a coal-mine safety law. Noting that "the occupation of mining is inseparably connected with many hazards and dangers," Grant told the legislature that many accidents might nonetheless be prevented by the passage of a law. The governor appealed to the legislators' political instincts, too, by pointing out that such a law would "confer a great service to a large class" of their constituents. One such legislator was Fremont County representative B. F. Rockafellow (a distant relative of John D. Rockefeller). Rockafellow, a merchant and coal-mine operator from the Canon City area, was elected to the legislature on the strength of a strong showing among "Coal Camp Republicans." With the cooperation of other "well posted coal miners," Rockafellow framed and sponsored a coal-mining bill.[8]

Considering the growing importance of the industry, debate over the coal-mining bill was surprisingly limited. In fact, a proposal to regulate railroads and the election of U.S. senators attracted much more attention in the press. Still, the question of mine regulation did receive some notice. Speaking to the issue of mine regulation in general, the *Leadville Democrat* called for the creation of a state mining bureau to promote the industry and to "regulate work and assure the safety of miners." The paper noted that efficient, safe operations would be burdensome only to those mines worked in an unsafe manner and those with managers who "from ignorance are unable to look out for their own and their employes' welfare." Specifically addressing the problem of safety in the coal mines, the *Rocky Mountain News* declared that "operators of coal mines in this state should be compelled by law to provide proper means for ventilation and efficient safeguards against the accidents incident to the business of coal mining."[9]

Colorado's legislature unanimously passed the state's first coal-mining law in February 1883. Representative Rockafellow declared that the act "combines the best features of the laws of the older states." With its passage, he said, Colorado would "not be behind any of the states of the old or new world in liberal laws for the mutual protection of operators and operatives."[10]

Based largely on Ohio's coal-mining law, the act established the office of state inspector of coal mines and made mines employing twelve or more men underground subject to provisions concerning ventilation, equipment, and supervision. The main goal was to prevent explosions by requiring adequate ventilation of mines. The act called for operators to provide at least one hundred cubic feet of air per person per minute, and more if ordered by the state inspector. Nonetheless, the law was deficient because it contained no provi-

sions for regulating the use of explosives or the presence of combustibles in the mines or for controlling coal dust (though not all experts
yet agreed that dust was an explosion hazard). The act made mine
bosses responsible for supervising mine ventilation and drainage,
seeing that loose rock in entries was taken down or securely timbered, providing adequate supplies of timber for the miners, and
seeing that miners properly cleaned and timbered their roofs. In
addition, mine bosses were to inspect all working areas daily for the
presence of explosive gas. In large mines the law required escape
shafts or slopes allowing egress in the event that main entries were
blocked by explosion, fire, or cave-in. Miners or other persons who
deliberately damaged mine plant or equipment or who, through
willful negligence, created hazards or disobeyed orders to carry out
provisions of the law were subject to criminal penalties.[11]

The statute gave the state coal-mine inspector general responsibility for examining the coal mines in the state and enforcing the
provisions of the act. However, only those mines employing twenty
or more men were subject to quarterly inspections. Since in 1883 the
average coal mine's work force was fewer than four men, many mines
did not come under the jurisdiction of the state inspector or of the
law.[12] Apparently to compensate for the lack of inspections in smaller
mines, the act authorized miners to appoint committees to inspect
the mines in which they worked.

The 1883 law's emphasis on ventilation and explosion hazards is
readily explained. Mine explosions can be highly destructive, not
only of life but of property. In 1908 Inspector John Jones noted that
"the additional expense thrown upon mine owners through explosions is sometimes enormous and often exceeds the cost of equipment and maintaining a first-class system of ventilation."[13] Ruined
entries, rooms, and equipment could force lengthy, even permanent, shutdowns. Preventing explosions, in short, could be less
expensive than restoring a damaged mine to operation. On the other
hand, accidents caused by falling rock or coal, or involving machinery and mine cars, did not tend to have serious consequences for the
total mine operation, only for individual miners.

The record of operator compliance with the law was a source
of great satisfaction to Colorado's first coal-mine inspector, John
McNeil, and his successors. McNeil, a native of Scotland who went
to work in the coal pits at the age of ten and who had worked in

Colorado Coal and Iron Company and Santa Fe Railroad mines in Colorado, in 1883 stated that the mines had "hitherto been worked in a rude, miserable and even reckless manner." By 1886, however, McNeil was pleased to report that, with only one exception, whenever he had suggested improvements the operators had complied. In 1898 Inspector David Griffiths, who later became a superintendent for the Colorado Fuel and Iron Company, thanked the state's operators for "their courtesies, especially for their promptness in complying with the law, and in many instances, adopting measures for the safety and welfare of our miners" not required by law.[14] Such ready compliance was more typical of large, rather than small, operators. Small operators, fearing that the costs of compliance would put them out of business, long resisted regulation.

The willingness of many operators to comply with the law was especially commendable since inadequate staffing of the inspector's office and the cumbersome procedures prescribed by the statute made the law virtually unenforceable. In his first report McNeil complained that he found it "next to impossible to accomplish the entire routine" of his duties because he had to work alone, lacking even clerical help. Whether adequate staffing would have improved mine safety is problematic since the inspector had no immediate enforcement powers. In practice his ability to enforce the law depended on the concern of local district attorneys and judges, often men who, as one scholar noted, did not care "to incur the enmity of the coal operators."[15] That reluctance was especially strong in the southern districts, where CF&I and Victor-American dominated political life. When he discovered an operator disregarding provisions of the law, the inspector had to apply to the courts for an injunction to halt operations in the offending mine until the operator brought it into conformity with the law. In the meantime, the mine remained open. Moreover, penalties for refusal to obey the law were mild since violations were merely misdemeanors punishable by fines.

The inspectors' claims of cooperation notwithstanding, the mild penalties and the cumbersome judicial process involved in enforcing the 1883 law encouraged some operators and mine officials to ignore it. This was especially true of small operators, who cut corners in order to reduce expenses and stay competitive with larger operators. Sometimes this left the miner caught in the middle of a dispute between his boss and the state inspector, as in an incident related by

George Clark, a Louisville miner, to the U.S. Industrial Commission. The inspector, finding a room to be unsafe, asked the superintendent to remove two miners from the area and see to needed repairs. However, the superintendent refused either to repair the area or to give the miners another, safer workplace. Since the inspector had no authority to order the men out of the dangerous workplace, or to close the mine, his only recourse was to seek an injunction from the courts. Meanwhile, the miners had the choice of working in an unsafe area or, if they refused, losing their jobs and perhaps being blacklisted.[16]

Influenced as it was by the laws of other states, Colorado's coal-mining law did not differ dramatically from them in its emphasis on explosion prevention or in inspection procedures and enforcement. The same, however, was not the case in New Mexico, where the territorial legislature passed a coal-mining law in March 1882. Covering fewer than three pages in the *Session Laws* for 1882, the act purported to set minimum ventilation standards and requirements for mine bosses. Coal-mine operators were to provide ventilation at the rate of fifty-five cubic feet per second, or thirty-three hundred cubic feet per minute, for each fifty workers. Mine bosses were responsible for supervising ventilation, seeing to the maintenance of entries and hoists, overseeing timbering in the rooms, and conducting daily inspections for gas in mines known to generate explosive gas.[17]

New Mexico's law of 1882 might charitably be called a weak measure. It was, in fact, a fraud. Though there is no evidence that New Mexico's most important coal operator at the time, the Atchison, Topeka and Santa Fe Railroad, dictated its terms, the statute reflected the concern of legislators to encourage and protect business investment in the territory. Not only did the law omit penalties against operators, mine bosses, and miners for infractions and negligence, it provided no means whatever for enforcement of its few regulations. It did not provide a mine inspector for the territory, nor did it grant the right of inspection to anyone else. Even mine employees were allowed to inspect only mine maps, not the mines themselves. Most surprisingly, section eleven of the law provided that "this act shall not apply to the opening of new coal mines." This ambiguous wording might be construed as waiving the provisions of the law during the process of driving entries and installing equipment in new mines. In actuality, operators and government officials took it to mean that, just as New Mexico's coal industry was entering its first period of major expansion, mines opened after the effective date of the law, 1 June 1882, were exempted from its provisions.[18]

Coal mines in New Mexico were regulated, or not regulated, by this nonlaw for a decade, though the legislature in 1889 considered a bill providing for the appointment of a mine inspector. One worried mine owner wrote to Governor Edmund G. Ross to express the concern of operators that such a law might be "injurious and malicious" and that they might be "compelled to submit to being blackmailed out of a fee" each time the inspector paid them a visit. Perhaps most revealing of the operators' fears, though, was the assertion that "we do not think that we in our infancy and weak state as mine operators should be subject to the rigid and severe restriction of older and more firmly established localities."[19] Coal operators in New Mexico, in short, feared that regulation of working conditions in the mines might put their young industry at a competitive disadvantage.

Finally, the U.S. Congress in 1891 enacted a measure for the "Protection of the Lives of Miners in the Territories." Originally intended to regulate all mining, the House Committee on Mines and Mining revised the bill to apply only to coal mines because it feared that "too stringent regulation must have the direct effect of retarding the development of mining interests" in the territories. However, because "the dangers of life are far greater in coal mines . . . and of a better defined and more clearly recognized character" than in hard-rock mines, it was deemed practical to limit the proposed law to coal mines.[20]

Congress passed this first federal coal-mining law in March 1891 with surprisingly little debate. In one brief exchange in the House of Representatives, Joseph G. Cannon of Illinois, an important coal-mining state, said that, although he had "every sympathy with any legislation which will protect human life," he was nonetheless suspicious of any law creating new offices and did not "see that the necessity is apparent in this case." (A decade later, Cannon, as Speaker of the House, worked hard to block Theodore Roosevelt's progressive reform measures.) Representative Henry Stockbridge, of Maryland, chairman of the House Committee on Mines and Mining, replied that he and his committee "thought it wise to close the stable door before the horse was out." That is, Congress should impose regulation on coal mining in the territories before, not after, some great disaster occurred. Some congressmen and senators were concerned that a federal coal-mining act would usurp the prerogatives of territorial legislatures. But as one of the bill's supporters explained, it was "very similar to regulations provided in the various States" and "only applies where there are no regulations."[21] Since all of the territories except Indian Territory already had their own coal-mining laws, the effect of this new federal measure would, apparently, be minimal.

Where it applied, the new federal coal-mining law required an annual inspection of every mine by a territorial mine inspector who would examine ventilation and safety equipment, see that clean air reached all working areas in proper quantities, and ensure that all mines had the required secondary shafts for emergency exit. The act required mine operators to provide thirty-three hundred cubic feet of air per minute for every fifty men, or sixty-six cubic feet per minute for each man, so that all working areas remained free of gas. However, it did not require daily inspection of the mines for gas or other hazards. The statute held company superintendents and other officials personally responsible for compliance with its provisions. Failure to comply with the act, or with orders to correct defects, was a misdemeanor punishable by fines.

The act's enforcement procedures were extremely cumbersome. When the territorial mine inspector discovered unsafe conditions in a mine, he was to report them to the secretary of the interior, who then would give notice to the operator specifying the needed repairs or additions to plant or machinery and setting a period of time for compliance. If the operator failed to comply with this notice within the time allowed, it was unlawful for him to continue to operate the mine. But to close a dangerous mine the territorial mine inspector, with the support of the secretary of the interior or the governor of the territory, had to apply to the courts for an injunction prohibiting operation of that mine until needed repairs were made. So unwieldy was this procedure that, during the two decades the federal act was in force in New Mexico, it was used only once. In that case, involving an order to open a second shaft, the territorial mine inspector reported that final compliance took two years.[22]

Because Congress intended the federal statute to apply only in territories with no laws protecting coal miners, it was not clear that it would apply in New Mexico, where the act of 1882 was in force. The first territorial mine inspector, John C. Spears, did not receive his commission and take up his duties until 29 August 1892, eighteen months after the federal law was enacted. Even then, it was uncertain whether the federal or the New Mexican law would prevail. One month prior to assuming his duties, Spears warned Governor L. Bradford Prince that "some of Santa Fe's business men who are interested in coal lands" would resist his appointment on the grounds that the federal law did not apply to New Mexico because of the existence of the 1882 territorial law. Spears reminded Prince that the New Mexico law made "no provision for an Inspector to enforce what law we have on the subject," meaning that the territorial law could not effectively protect coal miners and, thus, must be superseded by the federal act.[23]

Finally, late in 1892, territorial officials resolved the issue in favor of the federal statute. Solicitor General Edward L. Bartlett gave his opinion that the 1882 law did not provide for the safe operation of coal mines in New Mexico because it did not make provisions for a mine inspector to enforce it or for any penalties for its violation, "by reason of which failure the law is practically a dead letter, [and] has never been operative or enforced." Following Bartlett's advice, Acting Governor Silas Alexander informed the secretary of the interior that the act of 1882 did not provide for the safe operation of coal mines in New Mexico, meaning that the federal statute would supersede it. Governor L. Bradford Prince followed up by telling the territorial assembly that the 1882 law, because it did not provide for inspection and enforcement, "had little or no effect." Prince noted that a United States mine inspector for the territory had already been appointed by the president and had taken up his duties, even though it had "been held by some that the existence of our law of 1882 rendered the U.S. law inoperative." "It is certain," Prince said, "that the miners should be fully protected in some way" and that mine owners "are too apt to neglect proper precautions which may be expensive." The governor concluded that the 1882 statute should be "made fully effective by proper amendments, or should be repealed so as not to interfere with the benefits now secured to us under the U.S. statute."[24]

The legislature neither amended nor repealed the 1882 law, but it was a dead letter. By 1895 mine inspector John Fleming could report that "as there are no Territorial laws governing the working of coal mines I have been guided wholly by the act of Congress." Once the issue of the applicability of the federal law was settled, U.S. mine inspectors reported that most New Mexico coal operators cooperated in its implementation and that conditions in the territory's coal mines steadily improved.[25]

Unlike regulation in Colorado and New Mexico, Wyoming's first coal-mining law was prompted by a disaster. On 12 January 1886 an explosion ripped through the Union Pacific Coal Company's Number Four mine at Almy. The blast, probably touched off when a miner's open light came in contact with gas, killed thirteen men. The explosion was so powerful that the mine's pillars were badly weakened, forcing the company, after two years of effort to restore the mine, to close it down. This was not the first such disaster at Almy. Five years earlier, gas ignited by a gob fire had killed thirty-eight men, mostly Chinese, in the Rocky Mountain Coal and Iron Company's Number Two mine.

Unlike the earlier explosion, the 1886 disaster touched off a wave of public protest and agitation by coal miners that reached into the Wyoming territorial legislature. Just six weeks after the Almy disaster, Governor Francis E. Warren signed into law a bill, based on the laws of Pennsylvania, Ohio, and Colorado, providing for inspection and regulation of coal mines in Wyoming. The link between the Almy disaster and the Wyoming coal-mining law is unmistakable and distinguishes its genesis from those of Colorado and New Mexico. Wyoming mine inspector C. G. Epperson referred to the Almy blast as "the immediate cause of the passage of the Mining Law . . . as the 9th general assembly was in session on its occurrence, and the bill was introduced and passed, but a few days later."[26]

The Wyoming law provided for a mine inspector who was to examine all mines subject to the provisions of the act at least every three months. Mines employing more than ten men were subject to regulations pertaining mainly to ventilation and supervision. The act required operators to provide one hundred cubic feet of air per man per minute. Firebosses were to inspect daily all working areas and other areas known to generate explosive gas. Operators were to employ mine bosses who would have general supervisory responsibility for mine ventilation, maintenance of entries, drainage, and the delivery of adequate supplies of timbers to the rooms. In addition, the act directed mine bosses to visit all working areas to see that they were properly timbered and to ensure that no one worked in an unsafe area except to make needed repairs. A panel made up of an operator, a miner, and the mine inspector was to certify mine bosses, and the mine inspector was to certify firebosses. Operators and mine officials who failed to perform the duties imposed by the law, and miners who damaged the mine plant or equipment, carried lighted pipes or matches, or disobeyed orders to carry out provisions of the law, would be liable for misdemeanor fines of two hundred to five hundred dollars.

As in Colorado and New Mexico, in Wyoming the mine inspector had no direct enforcement authority. When he observed violations he was to notify the operator concerned and inform him of possible penalties. If after five days the operator had failed to make the necessary repairs, the inspector could initiate criminal proceedings. Within fifteen days of their issuance, operators and miners could seek to reverse the mine inspector's orders by appealing to a district court or to a panel of disinterested persons appointed by the court. While the appeal process went on, the disputed orders of the mine inspector would remain in force. Nonetheless, the mine inspector had no power to halt operations in a dangerous mine. Where conditions of imminent danger existed, the inspector had apply to the courts for an injunction to restrain operation of the offending mine.[27]

Statehood for Wyoming briefly reopened the question of coal-mine inspection and regulation. During the constitutional convention, in 1889, a proposal surfaced to eliminate the position of coal-mine inspector and to make the state geologist ex-officio mine inspector. The convention, however, deferred to the advice of delegate John L. Russell, a coal miner from Almy and the author of the 1886 law, who argued that the job of mine inspector was such that only actual mining experience, not a geologist's formal training, could qualify a person for it. The following year the state legislature reenacted the 1886 law with only minor revisions allowing the mine inspector to revoke mine and firebosses' certificates, inspect mine scales, and appoint miners' committees to inspect mines.[28]

The story of Wyoming's first coal-mining law has an ironic postscript. In 1898 John Russell, who authored the original law and helped to preserve it from tampering by the constitutional convention, died fighting a coal-mine fire.[29]

Utah had no coal-mine inspection or regulation until 1891, when the territory's mines came under the jurisdiction of the federal coal-mining law. Regulation apparently was desperately needed, as U.S. Mine Inspector Robert Forrester reported that, with only one or two exceptions, "the mines have been worked in a very primitive and incompetent manner."[30] The federal statute was in effect in Utah for three years, until it was superseded by a state law.

With statehood, in 1896, Utah enacted its own law, one that in many respects resembled the federal act. The act provided for quarterly inspections of all coal mines and spelled out regulations relating to ventilation and other aspects of mine operations. Those regulations, however, applied only to mines employing more than six men unless the mine inspector found it necessary, for the safety and health of the miners, to require smaller operations to observe them. Operators were required to provide one hundred cubic feet of air per man and three hundred cubic feet per animal per minute, and double those amounts in mines known to generate explosive gas. The law required operators to equip their mines with escape shafts. In addition, operators were to deliver timbers to within three hundred feet of working faces. Violation of any portion of the law by owners or managers could bring a fine of five hundred to five thousand dollars.

As in Colorado, New Mexico, and Wyoming, in Utah the coal-mine inspector had no direct enforcement authority. Utah's law, in fact, mimicked the cumbersome procedures of the 1891 federal law. Under the statute, whenever the inspector found unsafe conditions in a mine, he was to report them to the governor, who then would give notice to the operator specifying the repairs required and the time allowed for their completion. If the operator failed to correct the unsafe conditions in the time permitted, it was unlawful for work to continue in the offending mine and the operator would be liable for fines. When an operator failed to make ordered repairs, however, the mine inspector, with the support of the governor, had to apply to the courts for an injunction to close the mine.[31] Another important weakness in the law was the absence of any provision requiring mine bosses or firebosses to conduct daily inspections for gas or other hazards.

As a companion to the coal-mining law, Utah also enacted a law limiting miners to an eight-hour day and prohibiting employment of children under the age of fourteen in the mines. According to the state mine inspector, both the eight-hour law and the coal-mining law were implemented with little resistance. Inspector Gomer Thomas in 1897 commended the state's coal operators for their "willingness to comply with all suggestions . . . relative to providing every possible appliance looking to the safety of their employes."[32] Despite this apparent willingness of operators to comply with both the spirit and the letter of the law, the 1896 statute proved to be inadequate for preventing coal-mine disasters, and only five years later, Utah's legislators were forced to pass a major revision.

On the morning of 1 May 1900 the Pleasant Valley Coal Company's Winter Quarters mine number four, located about one mile west of Scofield, in Carbon County, exploded. The blast probably was caused by a blown-out shot setting off a cache of black powder which, in turn, ignited gas and dust in the mine. Two hundred men died there that day. It was the worst disaster yet in an American coal mine. The bodies of those men caught in the area where the blast originated were torn apart and burned beyond recognition. Most of the victims, however, died in the after-damp. Recovery workers found that "many of them had drawn their coats around or over their heads and laid down where they died in groups; on their faces there was, in most cases, a peaceful expression."[33] The force of the explosion was so great that when it reached the portal of the mine one man was thrown 820 feet; another fell uninjured 200 feet from the mouth of the mine. In town some people thought at first that the explosion's report was a blast set off by a reveler in honor of Dewey Day.

The magnitude of the disaster taxed the resources of not only the coal-mining communities of Carbon County, but the whole state. Public officials appealed to the entire country for help in organizing relief for the survivors. Utah was unable even to bury Scofield's dead without assistance. Because undertakers in Salt Lake City could provide only 125 coffins, a shipment of 75 had to be brought from Denver.

The Scofield disaster and the outbreak of a strike, in January 1901, against the Pleasant Valley Coal Company apparently put the Utah legislature in a conciliatory mood toward the state's coal miners. During its 1901 session the legislature enacted measures strengthening the ability of the State Board of Arbitration to resolve labor disputes and prohibiting coercion of employees to trade at company stores and to live in company boardinghouses.

The legislature also passed a major revision of the state's coal-mining law. Aimed at preventing another disaster such as the Scofield explosion, the law contained new regulations for coal-mine ventilation, dust control, explosives, and supervision. The new law required that abandoned areas of mines be ventilated and that abandoned crosscuts be sealed off. Large mines were to be divided into districts with no more than seventy-five men working in each area. Each district was to be ventilated by a separate current of air, and automatic doors were required in entries to regulate the flow of air. Operators were to provide and maintain safety lamps for use in gassy rooms. To help control dust in the mines, the act required installation of sprinkling systems up to the face in all working rooms. No explosives were to be stored inside the mines, and for daily use, miners could carry in no more than six and one-half pounds of powder unless permitted more by the state mine inspector.

The 1901 law also imposed new responsibilities on supervisors and miners. Committees composed of an operator, a miner, and the mine inspector would examine and certify mine bosses, and the mine inspector would certify firebosses. Foremen and firebosses were to examine all rooms and entries daily for gas. To ensure continuous adequate ventilation, the law required foremen to make weekly measurements of air currents. Possibly in response to the suspicion that non-English-speaking Finns misusing explosives caused the Scofield disaster, the new law required foremen to see to it that all men using explosives were qualified to do so and made it illegal to employ any person incompetent to understand the dangers of explosive gases in coal mines. In addition, the act required that timbers be delivered to within one hundred feet of the faces of rooms and that miners timber the roofs and sides in their rooms as needed before beginning any other work. Miners also were to examine their rooms for hazards both before and after firing shots and immediately report any hazards to the mine boss.

Although the 1901 law contained some new regulations intended to prevent not only explosions but accidents involving roof and coal falls and haulage, and stipulated closer inspection and supervision by mine officials, it did not provide for more effective enforcement. The state mine inspector could notify operators of defects and order repairs, but the law contained no new procedure for closing dangerous mines or mines whose operators ignored the inspector's directives. Moreover, the act reduced the fines for violations. Finally, the new law, like the old, applied only to mines employing more than six men.[34] Utah's legislators and operators, it seems, only partly learned the lesson of Scofield.

Montana's first coal-mining law was enacted in 1891. Like her neighbors' statutes, Montana's law emphasized preventing explosions, and it had serious flaws. The act required operators to provide a minimum of one hundred cubic feet of air per man per minute and six hundred cubic feet for each animal. If needed, the state inspector could order more ventilation. In addition to its ventilation requirements, the act demanded that operators "regularly and thoroughly" sprinkle entries that were "so dry as to become filled with dust." The act also required supervisors of gassy mines to make daily inspections for gas accumulations, lack of adequate ventilation, obstructions in entries, and other hazards. The state inspector was to examine foremen and other mine officials in gassy mines and certify them as to their "competency for managing the underground workings of mines, together with a thorough knowledge of all gases met with in coal mines" and the methods of controlling them.[35]

Provisions for enforcing Montana's coal-mining law were weak and cumbersome. For one thing, there was no requirement for regular inspection of mines. The state mine inspector was to make annual visits only to as many mines as practicable in each mining county and was required to visit any mine when three employees filed a written complaint alleging dangerous conditions. Whenever he discovered hazardous conditions, the inspector was to give the operator a notice stating what hazards existed and requiring "all necessary changes be made without delay." The act gave the inspector no direct authority, however, to force operators to comply with the law or with his orders. When an operator failed to comply with the coal-mining law's ventilation requirements or refused to obey the inspector's orders within a reasonable time, the inspector could only seek an injunction, brought by a county attorney or the state attorney general, to close the offending mine.[36]

Preventing horrible disasters such as the Scofield explosion was the main objective of the various state, territorial, and federal coal-mining statutes. But because governors and legislators feared that stringent regulations might retard economic growth, the early coal-mining laws entered the statute books with fatal weaknesses. Only Utah's law of 1901 and Montana's 1891 act included dust-control measures. Regulations governing the use and storage of explosives and requiring elimination of combustibles from the mines were few and ineffective. And the laws provided no means for practical enforcement of their various regulations. State and territorial mine inspectors had no authority to close hazardous mines or mines whose owners and managers failed or refused to obey the law. Not only did the early laws fail to prevent explosion disasters, they also did not adequately address the other major causes of death and injury in the mines, including roof and coal falls and haulage accidents, which accounted for more deaths than did explosions. These deficiencies in the laws, along with prevailing attitudes about responsibility for job safety, common-law doctrines, and the relations of work in the mines, combined to make western coal mines extremely dangerous places in which to work during the late nineteenth and early twentieth centuries.

Chapter 4

Safety and Regulation, 1884-1912

Colorado State Inspector of Coal Mines John D. Jones in 1908 observed that "the coal miner's calling at the best is hazardous and he should be protected by all the precautionary measures that human skill can provide."[1] Sadly, neither human skill nor state, federal, and territorial coal-mining laws were very effective in protecting the lives of coal miners in Colorado and the other Rocky Mountain states. Compounding the laws' failure was a body of opinion and common-law doctrine that placed most of the responsibility for safety on the shoulders of the miners. The result was an environment of death in the mines.

In Colorado the year 1910 was especially deadly. In three mine explosions, at the Colorado Fuel and Iron Company's Primero and Starkville mines and at Victor-American's Delagua mine, all located in the Trinidad area, 210 miners lost their lives. Headlines told of the horror inside the mines and the grief of widows and orphans. In November, after the third disaster, at Delagua, the state's Progressive Democratic governor, John Franklin Shafroth, appointed a blue-ribbon panel to investigate the mine explosions and recommend measures for preventing such disasters in the future.

On 7 October 1910, one day before the Starkville blast, George Danoff, father of five, died under a fall of rock in the Industrial Mine in Boulder County. On 15 November, a week after the Delagua

TABLE 1: *Coal-Mining Fatalities in the
Rocky Mountain States and U.S., 1884–1912*

Cause	Colorado (1884–1912)		New Mexico (1893–1912)		Utah (1893–1912)	
	Deaths	Per 1,000 Employed	Deaths	Per 1,000 Employed	Deaths	Per 1,000 Employed
Falls of rock and coal	814	3.00	146	3.27	93	2.19
Explosions	588	2.68	72	1.84	208	6.88
Haulage	173	0.68	40	0.89	25	0.56
Machinery	3	0.01	0	0	2	0.09
Electricity	18	0.05	0	0	1	0.01
Total	1,708	6.81	287	6.42	338	10.08

Note: Totals include deaths from other causes as well as the ones listed.

explosion, miner Joe Manini died in a fall of rock while working in the Wootton Mine in Huerfano County. He left four orphans. And three days before the Primero disaster, a Japanese immigrant named Turugori died when part of a roof in the Hastings Mine in Las Animas County collapsed on him.[2] Death struck these miners as suddenly and cruelly as it did the victims of Primero, Starkville, and Delagua. But the deaths of Danoff, Manini, and Turugori aroused no great interest. They were altogether unexceptional.

Because of the arid climate and the frequently very low moisture content of the coals (e.g., 0.5% at Primero), coal mines in Colorado and the rest of the Rocky Mountain region are especially prone to dust explosions. On that account alone, coal-mining laws naturally would focus on preventing explosions. Nonetheless, data collected by the state inspector of coal mines show that Colorado's 1883 coal-mining law failed to forestall major disasters. Moreover, explosion, whether of coal dust, gas, faulty shots, or as was often the case, some combination of factors, was not the most common cause of death in Colorado's coal mines. Instead, death from falling rock and coal and from mishaps involving mine haulage and machinery was far more prevalent. Because of the state's inadequate coal-mining law, and ineffectual enforcement of it by inspectors, operators, and miners, Colorado's coal mines were among the most dangerous in the nation.

During the twenty-nine-year period from 1884 through 1912, 1,708 coal miners died as the result of accidents in Colorado's coal

TABLE 1 *continued*

Wyoming (1886–1912)		Montana (1889–1912)		U.S. (1884–1912)	
Deaths	Per 1,000 Employed	Deaths	Per 1,000 Employed	Deaths	Per 1,000 Employed
212	1.78	102	1.73	20,287	1.49
377	2.32	16	0.29	8,240	0.60
53	0.51	29	0.52	5,169	0.37
2	0.01	2	0.03	576	0.03
0	0	1	0.02	591	0.03
729	6.27	183	3.13	42,898	3.12

mines. The vast majority, 1,402, died in explosions or under falls of rock or coal. Throughout this period Colorado's death rate was much higher than the national rate, averaging 6.81 per thousand employed versus the national rate of 3.12.[3] Colorado's average death rate from explosions for the 1884–1912 period was 2.68 per thousand and that for deaths due to falls of rock and coal was 3.00. Thus, Colorado's death rates from either explosions or falls of rock and coal were comparable to the average national rate of coal-mine deaths from *all* causes.

Colorado's coal mines also were more dangerous than the state's metal mines. During the period from 1896 through 1902, for example, the average fatality rate in the metal mines was 3.08 per thousand, with shaft accidents accounting for the highest rate (1.05), followed by explosions (0.81) and falls of rock (0.70). During the same period the average death rate in the coal mines was 6.14 per thousand, with falls of rock and coal leading at 3.32 per thousand, followed by explosions at 1.91. Haulage accidents killed 0.04 per thousand in metal mines and 0.62 in coal mines.[4]

Comparable (and in the case of Utah, higher) coal-mine fatality rates occurred in three of the other Rocky Mountain states (table 1). Utah and Wyoming differed from the other states in that the explosion fatality rate surpassed that for falls of rock and coal, largely because of two major disasters: the one at Scofield, Utah, in 1900 in which 201 died, and the one at Hanna, Wyoming, in 1903 in which

TABLE 2: *Utah Coal-Mining Fatalities, 1893–1912*

Cause	1893–1912		1893–1895	
	Deaths	Per 1,000 Employed	Deaths	Per 1,000 Employed
Falls of rock and coal	93	2.19	3	1.57
Explosions	208	6.88	1	0.58
Haulage	25	0.56	0	0
Machinery	2	0.09	0	0
Electricity	1	0.01	0	0
Total	338	10.08	4	2.15

Note: Totals include deaths from other causes as well as the ones listed.

169 perished. Only Montana, which luckily had no major disaster before 1913, had a fatality rate comparable to national averages.[5]

Utah also differs from the other states in that three different mining laws applied there at different times before 1913. During the brief period from 1893 through 1895, when the federal coal-mining law applied, Utah had a fairly low fatality rate (2.15 per thousand) with only four deaths. After the state assumed responsibility for regulating the mines, fatality rates soared, averaging 11.47 for the 1896–1912 period. The death rate was even more startling during the life of Utah's first state coal-mining law, averaging 30.41 in the period from 1896 through 1900. After 1901, when a stricter mining law went into effect requiring better ventilation and sprinkling procedures and more frequent inspections by mine officials, Utah's fatality rate fell substantially, to 3.58 per thousand for the 1901–12 period. Clearly, the Scofield disaster must have made everyone involved in coal mining in Utah more alert to the hazard of gas and dust explosion. Unfortunately, no similar improvement occurred in the rate of death due to falls of rock and coal or in recognition of the causes of such accidents (table 2).

By any measure it is evident that the coal mines of the Rocky Mountain West were very dangerous. The high rates of death due to explosions, surpassing national averages, show that state, federal, and territorial coal-mining laws did not achieve their main goal of preventing explosion disasters. In Colorado, by 1913, thirteen major explosions had killed 449 miners; in New Mexico 53 died in seven blasts; in Wyoming 329 were killed in five explosions; and in Utah

TABLE 2 *continued*

	1896–1912			1896–1900			1901–1912	
Deaths	Per 1,000 Employed		Deaths	Per 1,000 Employed		Deaths	Per 1,000 Employed	
90	2.30		8	1.83		82	2.50	
207	7.99		201	26.73		6	0.19	
25	0.66		4	0.69		21	0.65	
2	0.10		1	0.29		1	0.02	
1	0.02		0	0		1	0.02	
334	11.47		217	30.41		117	3.58	

200 miners died at Scofield. In all five states 1,261 coal miners died in explosions of all types. Clearly, laws designed to make working conditions safer by regulating ventilation, dust control, and use of explosives were not working. Furthermore, the fact that 1,367 miners dued under falls of roof and coal shows that regulation was woefully deficient when it came to addressing that problem.

Where they dealt with roof maintenance and timbering at all, the laws imposed specific responsibility on mine bosses only to see that loose coal, slate, and rock overhead in travelways was secured or taken down and that sufficient supplies of timber were available for miners to use in their rooms. Though mine bosses were supposed to see that miners properly timbered their rooms, the reality of the working environment, the miner's general responsibility for his room, and the difficulty of supervising men scattered about the mines put the real, effective responsibility for timbering and other safety-related work squarely on the shoulders of the miner. Thus miners were sometimes forced to chose between safety and income.

During the nineteenth and early twentieth centuries, operators, mine inspectors, coroners, and the courts believed, practically as an article of faith, that miners were responsible for their own safety on the job. Concerned with explaining why miners were killing themselves in such large numbers, industry spokesmen and mine inspectors offered as reasons the inevitability of accidents in a dangerous occupation, the miners' carelessness or deliberate negligence, and the lack of experience and foreign birth of many of them.

The belief that a certain number of accidents was inevitable in a coal mine was common and, given the region's high death rate, understandable. In 1889, for example, Wyoming mine inspector C. G. Epperson wrote that "no law that can be enacted however well-framed and enforced or any system of mine rules rigidly carried out, will secure the coal miner . . . from danger and accident." A decade later another Wyoming mine inspector, Noah Young, expressed a fatalistic attitude about falls of rock and coal, calling them "a class of accidents practically unavoidable" in coal mining. By 1900 Young was reconciled to rock falls as "something utterly unavoidable."[6]

Miners, too, approached their work with a degree of fatalism. One old-timer from Walsenburg, Colorado, talked of accidents and death in the mines as something that "makes you feel bad, but what [are] you going to do, that [is] one of those things that we got to put up with." Contributing to the miners' fatalism was the belief that their employers did not care about their safety. That conviction is illustrated by a story miners often told about the relative worth of men and mules. "If a mule was accidentally killed, boy you got hell . . . if a man got hurt they'd say 'Oh well, they'll hire another Mexican.'"[7]

Coal operators and mine officials, of course, did not see themselves as callous or indifferent to the safety of the miners. They argued, instead, that the carelessness or deliberate negligence of the men in refusing to protect themselves, even when ordered to by supervisors, caused most coal-mine deaths. John Birkinbine, an engineering consultant for the Colorado Fuel and Iron Company, said, in a 1903 edition of the company's *Camp and Plant,* that although faulty machinery or management failures caused some accidents "too many . . . are directly traceable to the miners taking unnecessary risks" to save time by not propping roofs adequately, using too much powder in shots, firing shots at improper times, or using a naked lamp because "it gives better light and is handier than a safety lamp." The Victor-American Fuel Company's chief engineer, F. W. Whiteside, asserted that operators furnished plenty of timbers for their miners and that inspectors watched timbering and did "their utmost to get the men to provide for their own safety." When an accident occurred, Whiteside claimed, "it is usually possible to trace the fault to the carelessness of the injured man or his partner."[8]

State and territorial mine inspectors shared the belief that miners, through their carelessness and negligence, caused their own deaths.

Said Colorado's John McNeil in 1886, "I am inclined to think that disobedience, incompetence and negligence fully explain the cause of as many accidents, if not more, than are due to the hazardous character" of coal mining itself. Eighteen years later, noting that two-thirds of all accidents in 1903 and 1904 were caused by falls of rock and coal, Colorado inspector John Jones reported that "in all such cases" timbers and props were available and that "often instructions had been given . . . to the miner, just prior to the accident, to timber his place, and compliance promised, but postponed."[9] Jones did not explain why the men postponed timbering, and he blamed rising accident rates on the growing number of inexperienced, foreign-born men working in the mines.

Mine inspectors in other Rocky Mountain states held similar views. Wyoming's Noah Young believed it to be human nature for "a large majority of the men following a hazardous occupation gradually . . . to become careless through negligence." Utah's Gomer Thomas complained that "there does not appear to be any method or argument that can be advanced which will induce the miner and the workman to take proper precautions to secure their safety." New Mexico's John Fleming agreed that "the main problem which confronts the mine inspector is to get the miners impressed with the necessity of looking out for themselves and use ordinary precaution in their own behalf." Jo E. Sheridan in 1902 said that most of New Mexico's mine accidents were due to the gross negligence of the miner, a laxness "bred from constant familiarity with dangers incident to his profession." Sheridan objected to "the gross absurdity" of imposing on mine owners the responsibility of trying to protect the miner "while the miner interposes his negligence as an obstacle to the process of protection."[10]

These concerns were by no means limited to the Rocky Mountain region. A *Mining Magazine* editorial in 1906 argued that "it is a well-known fact that miners are inclined to be careless about their safety and frequently are willing to take chances which should not be taken under any circumstances." A West Virginia mine inspector was more blunt. Saying not only that a large percentage of mine accidents were caused by the carelessness of those killed or injured, James W. Paul claimed that "a personal investigation into a number of fatal accidents would almost lead to the belief that they were deliberate suicides."[11] Supposedly, then, through carelessness or deliberate negligence, coal miners were killing themselves, and one another, with apparent reckless abandon.

Mine inspectors and others concerned with high death rates in the coal mines were aware of the underlying cause of this carelessness and negligence: the pressure to produce coal, which too often forced miners to choose between loading coal or doing deadwork such as timbering roofs. A mining engineer employed by the Wootton Land and Fuel Company said that timbering was "very hard . . . to take care of in a mine" because miners "frequently will neglect their places in their eagerness to load more coal." "You almost have to insist on them taking care of themselves," he said. Colorado coal mine inspector Tom Allen, whose career in coal mining spanned much of the twentieth century, considered it natural that "a man being paid so much per car or so much per ton would give more attention to producing coal than to his own personal safety." New Mexico's John Fleming thought that "the overanxious miner trying to get out as much coal per day as possible without regard for his own safety" caused the majority of roof- and coal-fall accidents. Fleming believed that the temptation for the miner to defer timbering in favor of loading coal was "too great for his judgement." A Greek immigrant who worked in Utah recalled the temptation, saying, "We timbered the roofs too quick to get at the digging. Many of our patriots [sic] were killed that way."[12]

Miners avoided timbering and other deadwork even when specifically ordered to do it. Colorado mine inspector John Jones found that miners regularly promised to timber their rooms and then, failing to do so, too often paid for their negligence with their lives. A mine superintendent in New Mexico complained that "time and time again" he had warned his men about working under unpropped top coal but that, "while some would obey his instructions, others would not." All he, as superintendent, could do was to furnish the men with props; "if they would not use them he did not consider the Company responsible for their action." Jo Sheridan in 1900 found similar conditions in the Raton Coal and Coke Company's Blossburg Number 5 mine. Sheridan reported that timbers were readily available for the men, but they "were reckless and would only reluctantly obey the orders [to set props] as they wished to employ all their time taking out coal for which they are paid by the ton." A decade later Wyoming mine inspector Joseph Bird found this situation to be common in his inspection district. Bird reported that in his investigation of roof- and coal-fall accidents he often found timbers lying in the entry ready for use. In many cases, he said, the foreman had ordered them set up, but "the men went ahead and tried to load another car before putting in the timber with the result their lives paid the penalty for the delay."[13]

Timbering was not the only safety procedure miners neglected in favor of more and faster production. For example, miners paid on the run-of-mine basis often shot off the solid, that is, without undermining the coal. Because shooting off the solid required large quantities of blasting powder, it resulted in a greater explosion risk and also led to more falls, as the more powerful shots weakened roofs and sides.

Even if mine inspectors and industry officials recognized the connection among pay systems, deadwork, and safety, few acknowledged, as did F. L. Hoffman, an actuarial statistician writing in the *Engineering and Mining Journal* in 1902, that the problem of mine safety "is not solved by shifting the responsibility upon men who must make their living by producing as much coal as possible in a given length of time."[14] Most simply assumed that deadwork and the risk of accident and death were part of the miner's job and that the responsibility for safety, and death, lay in his hands. A miner's failure to clean roofs and sides, timber his room, prop his coal, or check for gas, whether due to simple carelessness or because of a more willful neglect inspired by his greedy desire to load coal instead of doing deadwork, was no one's fault but his own.

Operators and mine inspectors held miners accountable for their own safety and deaths even when they recognized that the rapid expansion of the coal-mining industry attracted large numbers of inexperienced men into the mines. As early as the mid-1890s Colorado's coal-mine inspector, David Reed, concluded that "a large percent of the accidents in coal mines are the result of inexperienced miners." By the early years of the twentieth century the number of novice miners in Colorado had grown dramatically. Inspector John Jones in 1904 reported that operators had hired thousands of inexperienced men to replace striking miners and that, as a consequence, accidents had increased, especially those due to falls of roof and coal. In 1910 the Colorado Bureau of Labor Statistics found that half of the miners in the state were men "without any previous experience in coal mining." In recommending certification of all miners by a board of examiners and the pairing of inexperienced with experienced men, the bureau declared that it was unfair to all miners "to allow inexperienced workers in dangerous occupations to endanger their own and fellow employes' lives."[15]

Coal miners saw the experience issue in a different light. In a letter to Governor John Franklin Shafroth, John Boyd, a miner from El Paso County, Colorado, claimed that the Pikes View Coal Company fired him after he pointed out safety problems to the mine boss. Boyd said that the mine boss told him he gave "too much attention to little things to work for this company"; implying blacklisting, Boyd also claimed that he was "victimized at the other mines for doing what all miners should do." In Boyd's view the operators' claims that inexperienced miners caused many accidents was true only insofar as the operators "will not keep a miner that is experienced" or who, as in Boyd's case, complained about safety conditions. The *Boulder County Miner* echoed this view, asserting that Colorado had lost both material wealth and moral standing because of coal operators "who have driven from the state thousands of competent miners," replacing them with a lower-paid and "incompetent class of labor." The result, the *Miner* concluded, "has been an appalling death rate among those engaged in the industry."[16]

Coal operators were, in fact, tapping a vast reservoir of inexperienced and inexpensive labor. By the turn of the century "inexperienced" was practically synonymous with "foreign" in the coal mines of the Rocky Mountain West. Although many immigrants came on their own, labor agents lured thousands to the West with promises of good pay and steady work. Frequently, the recruits discovered on their arrival that they had been hired as strikebreakers. In 1910, for example, Bulgarians and Greeks were imported into the northern field of Colorado to replace striking Italian, Slavic, and American miners. One man recalled that the windows of the trains carrying these immigrant strikebreakers were whitewashed or chalked, presumably so that no one could see in or out. Mine guards and bosses unloaded the new men "right at the mines" and quickly set them to work.[17]

As foreign-born workers streamed into the mines, the coal industry was quick to link accidents with ethnicity. F. L. Hoffman, in a 1902 edition of the *Engineering and Mining Journal*, said that, aside from poor inspection, the main cause of rising accident and death rates in the nation's coal mines was "the introduction of inexperienced, non-English speaking common labor, represented by emigrants from southern Europe."[18]

In the West coal-mine inspectors shared this opinion. As early as 1888 Colorado's John McNeil blamed "Italian and other inexperienced miners" for increases in fatal and nonfatal accidents, and in 1906 Inspector John Jones was just as certain in his assessment of the consequences of accident-prone foreigners "taking up coal mining as a livelihood without previous training." Supporting the contention that negligent foreign workers were a major cause of accidents, Inspector James Dalrymple in 1911 said that "coal mining would be rendered vastly safer if a more intelligent class of men could be secured to work in the mines."[19]

Wyoming coal mines, too, employed large numbers of workers "unacquainted with the principles of coal mining, their ignorance often bringing on themselves injury or death, and at the same time endangering the lives of those depending on them for safety." Inspector George Blacker believed that these miners "should on no account be permitted to labor in a coal mine" without constant supervision. Utah's Gomer Thomas found that almost half of the state's coal-mine workers were foreigners "unable to speak our language, and men who have not been trained to exercise care, even for their own protection," and who required "the constant care of those placed over them to protect their health and lives."[20]

If coal-mine inspectors occasionally called for closer supervision of immigrant miners, they did not question the practice of hiring inexperienced, foreign-born men or of sending them into the mines without training. Some critics, however, believed that recruiting the foreign born was a deliberate and brutal policy of the operators. In 1910, in the aftermath of the disaster at Starkville, the *United Mine Workers Journal* declared that "the soulless corporation that . . . employs nothing but inexperienced foreign-speaking miners in order to get cheap coal, is guilty of nothing less than the murder of the victims of those holocausts." In a report on the 1910 strike Colorado Secretary of State James B. Pearce chastised mine owners who, for fear of having "to spend some of their wealth in making it reasonably safe for men to dig coal," preferred the inexperienced, presumably less restive, foreign-born miner. Were those miners to arrive at a full understanding of their rights, he said, coal mines might cease to be "human slaughterhouses."[21]

Labor leaders and some government officials also pointed to poor supervision and violation of the coal-mining laws as factors contributing to high death rates. Edward L. Doyle, a United Mine Workers officer from Colorado, in 1914 told the U.S. Industrial Commission that there had been "a mining law of one kind for years on the books, but no pretense of living up to it" on the part of many operators. Indeed, supposed nonobservance and nonenforcement of ventilation regulations was a grievance in Colorado's strike of 1903–4. Even though state mine inspectors regularly complimented operators for their observance of the mining laws, there is some evidence backing the miners' claims. A committee of the Colorado legislature investigating conditions in the industry in 1901 found poor ventilation in many mines in the state and recommended stricter enforcement of the law by the state mine inspector.[22]

Sometimes investigators blamed accidents on poor supervision, rather than violations of the law. Wyoming's Newell Beeman thought that some roof-fall accidents in 1886 could have been prevented had mine bosses seen to it that miners obeyed their orders. A quarter of a century later another Wyoming inspector, noting one cause for poor supervision, said that some mine bosses overlooked safety requirements because "the tendency of the present day is to rush things to get out the greatest amount of coal at the least possible expense." Supervisors, as well as miners, felt pressure to get the coal out, and sometimes in "trying to attain this end, the safety of the employees is lost sight of to a great extent, until some calamity brings it very forcibly to their mind."[23]

One such calamity, the 1908 disaster at Hanna, Wyoming, in which fifty-nine died (the second there in five years), stirred a greater interest in supervision on the part of Colorado's largest operator. In April 1908 E. H. Weitzel, head of the Fuel Department at Colorado Fuel and Iron, told his superintendents that the Hanna disaster "should awaken all who have mines under their care to a renewed sense of their responsibility." A superintendent's job went beyond managing the company's property and supervising production; "he is also the guardian of the lives and safety of the men who work in the mines." Furthermore, Weitzel said, employees had the right to assume that their superintendent had "at all times assured himself of the safety of the working place." Weitzel urged CF&I's superintendents to exercise greater care in appointing firebosses, enforce safety rules strictly, and promptly implement suggestions of the company mine inspector. Five years later, though, Weitzel still had cause to complain about supervision in CF&I's mines. In a letter to company superintendents Weitzel noted that reports on fifteen roof- and coal-fall fatalities indicated that the mine bosses knew the men killed were careless about timbering. The fact that these men died, said Weitzel, was due to "failure on the part of the mine foreman or his assistant to exercise proper discipline."[24]

Such concern on the part of a prominent coal-industry official was rather exceptional. In the late nineteenth and early twentieth centuries, while the coal industry in the West experienced rapid growth, few operators and government officials believed that coal-mine safety, except as it concerned the welfare of mine properties, was anything but a problem for the individual miner. Strengthening this attitude were the findings of coroners and the prevailing common-law doctrines that guided the courts in their rulings in suits against operators by injured miners or their survivors.

Only rarely did coroners' juries find a coal operator or mine official responsible for fatal accidents in the mines. Instead, they almost always found that accidents either were unavoidable or were due to the carelessness of the deceased or his co-workers. The *United Mine Workers Journal* complained that coroners' inquests were "not as rigid as the inquiry the coal company would make if a dead mule was brought out of the mine, and the miner that is dead is found guilty of suicide by the negligent or careless route."[25]

This tendency did not go unnoticed even by state mine inspectors, who, as shown, also tended to blame miners' carelessness for accidents. Colorado's James Dalrymple noted that in Huerfano County, in the period 1904–14, only one verdict fixed blame on mine management. Dalrymple also complained about the coroner of Las Animas County, who in the same period ruled "in case after case where a miner has been killed—'no inquest necessary,'" even though there had been "a frightful increase in accidents and deaths." In Wyoming, Inspector David Thomas reported that of twenty-nine fatal accidents for the years 1891 and 1892 his investigations and coroners' inquests "in every case exonerate the employing companies from any blame whatever." And in Utah at the turn of the century coroners' verdicts on miners' deaths typically concluded that "no blame is attached to anyone," or "no blame is attached to the company or anyone connected therewith."[26]

With records such as these it is little wonder that miners, labor leaders, and even industry journals considered coroners' juries to be corrupt, serving only the interests of coal operators. More important than the possible corruption of coroners and their inquests, though, is their role in affirming the widely held attitude that the coal miner was primarily responsible for safety in the mines and, therefore, the principal agent of death in the mines.

Until the early twentieth century, legal doctrines and court rulings also reflected that attitude. Prior to about 1915, injured miners or their survivors relied mainly on the largesse of companies and the generosity of friends and unions, or on burial societies and ethnic associations, for financial help. Neighbors of injured or killed miners might give a dance or collect contributions to help families, and companies sometimes paid for medical and burial costs, but these were only short-term measures. Because the Rocky Mountain coal-mining states did not enact workers' compensation programs until 1915 or later, the only way for miners (indeed, all workers) and their families to seek long-term compensation for injury or death was to sue for damages. However, relief through the courts was, for a long time, nearly impossible because plaintiffs confronted a body of common-law doctrine that strongly favored employers.

Three basic common-law concepts—assumption of risk, the fellow-servant rule, and contributory negligence—effectively barred most injured workers or their survivors from collecting financial compensation from employers. When a worker accepted a job, he also assumed all of the risks of injury from hazards ordinarily associated with that job, as well as any extraordinary hazards that a person of normal diligence might be expected to discover and avoid or eliminate. Because such hazards were common to the occupation, coal miners assumed the risk of being injured or killed by roof and coal falls, even when they had timbered their rooms properly; of dying in gas and coal-dust explosions; of being mangled by runaway mine trips or other equipment; or other such ordinary hazards.

In addition, the mine worker also assumed the risk of being injured or killed as a result of the carelessness or negligence of a fellow worker. That is, employers were not liable for the careless or negligent actions of their employees on the job. Until about the turn of the century the fellow-servant rule applied even to supervisors such as firebosses and mine bosses. If a driver or a nipper did not properly sprag a car, thereby allowing it to run away and hit a man walking in an entry; if a day man did not properly clean the roof and timber an entry, resulting in a roof fall; or if a fireboss or mine boss did not discover, or overlooked, a pocket of gas or some bad roof, the injured party, not the operator, assumed the risk for any resulting accident.

If an injured or dead worker's actions in any way contributed to an accident, he or his family could not recover damages from the employer. This doctrine of contributory negligence meant, in practice, that an injured worker, or his survivors, had to prove not only negligence on the part of an operator, but also that there had been no negligence whatever on the worker's part in causing the accident. Given the environment of work in the mines and the miners' tendency to avoid deadwork, contributory negligence was not especially difficult for operators to establish, particularly in accidents such as roof falls. An operator merely had to argue that the accident would not have happened had the miner properly cleaned and timbered his roof.

Contributory negligence could also absolve an operator of liability even when there was evidence of negligence on his part. If a miner or a day man knew of dangerous conditions, such as an exceptionally bad roof or the presence of gas caused by inadequate ventilation, and continued to work knowing of the hazard, the miner, not the operator, was liable for any injury sustained, even if the operator or a supervisor ordered him to work under those conditions. By agreeing to work in exceptionally dangerous conditions, the miner assumed the risk of injury or death. Contributory negligence and assumption of risk also applied to accidents in which the injured party was in a place where his work normally did not require him to be.

These legal roadblocks governed personal injury law in the United States until the beginning of the twentieth century, when courts and legislatures gradually began to modify them in favor of workers. Finally, the enactment of workers' compensation programs resolved much of the legal contention over personal injury and death settlements.

Court cases arising in the Rocky Mountain coal-mining industry in the late nineteenth and early twentieth centuries illustrate the obstacles confronting miners and their families in efforts to recover damages, and help to trace the beginnings of the development of a body of law more sympathetic to injured workers and their survivors. Two cases stemming from a single accident, a roof fall in the Colorado Coal and Iron Company's Berwind Mine, in July 1892, together show the application of the doctrines of assumption of risk, fellow-servant negligence, and contributory negligence. In the accident in question two men, Carpita and Lamb, were killed by a roof fall in an entry. The mine boss had assigned Lamb to clean up a previous fall in the entry and set new props. Carpita was in the entry visiting with Lamb while the latter worked. The Colorado Court of Appeals ruled that Carpita "voluntarily, and without occasion, assumed the risk which caused his death" because "he had no business at the point where the accident happened." That is, Carpita was out of his room, "lingering" at a place known to be dangerous and where his own job did not require his presence. Carpita thus assumed the risk of injury and contributed to his own death by leaving his normal workplace and stopping to talk with a co-worker in a place he knew, or should have known, was dangerous. In Lamb's case the court ruled that the deceased "was employed to assist in the work of making the roof safe for the miners" and that "he took upon himself the risk which might accrue from the circumstances." The court also found that the actions of the mine boss in ordering Lamb to work in an unsafe place could not be held against the company because, as an official whom the law required operators to employ, the mine boss was a fellow servant, not an agent of the company.[27]

The Carpita and Lamb cases were typical of state and federal court rulings during that period. Miners were liable for their own injuries where they knowingly continued to work under dangerous roofs, even though their employers failed to supply them with timbers and even though leaving the area might mean loss of income. A miner who knew, or had the opportunity to know, that a fellow servant was incompetent could not recover damages for an injury caused by that worker even though employers had a positive duty to use "reasonable diligence" in hiring workers. Even when an operator was negligent in not providing a safe workplace, a miner assumed the risks of his employment.[28]

In sum, personal injury law in the nineteenth and early twentieth centuries held miners liable for their own injuries and deaths even if their employers had not obeyed state mining laws, had hired incompetent fellow servants, or placed workers in the charge of incompetent supervisors. Superintendents and mine bosses could order miners into extremely dangerous areas, and if they went, the miners, not the company, assumed the risk of injury or death. Their alternative was to risk loss of income or discharge by refusing to go into, or by leaving, dangerous places. By accepting a job and going into a mine, a coal miner or day man assumed the risk of injury, and any activity that was not clearly part of his work assignment, such as stopping in an entry to chat with a fellow worker, was evidence of contributory negligence.

Gradually, as the Progressive movement, with its concern for ameliorating industrialization's impact on the individual and society, swept over the nation, courts and legislatures lifted some of the legal burden of risk from the individual miner. During the first fifteen years of the twentieth century, court rulings in coal-mining injury cases weakened the doctrines of assumption of risk, fellow-servant negligence, and contributory negligence. In 1911, for example, a Colorado court held the National Fuel Company liable for injuries sustained by a miner when a defective stop block allowed a trip to run away. The court ruled that the injured man neither knew of the defect nor was negligent in not informing himself of it. The court also held that a miner obeying a supervisor's order was not negligent and did not assume risk of injury unless a hazard was "so manifest and imminent that a person of reasonable prudence would refuse obedience," even under threat of discharge.[29] The court thus limited the assumed risk of extraordinary dangers.

In several cases courts, including the United States Supreme Court, held employers liable for injuries caused by fellow servants. The Supreme Court in 1900 ruled that, "where an occupation is attended with danger to life or limb," it was incumbent on employers to "employ competent persons and to take all reasonable and needed precautions to secure safety to the employees." If they failed in that obligation, employers could be held liable "to the extent of any injury inflicted by reason of such neglect."[30]

In the same case the Supreme Court held that the 1891 federal coal-mining law imposed on operators in the territories positive duties to provide safe appliances and adequate ventilation and that the negligence of a fellow servant did not mitigate that duty. Almost a decade later a Colorado court ruled that miners had the right to assume that operators would fulfill legal obligations such as the responsibility to make entries and passageways safe. Thus, a miner killed in a passageway, even though he was away from his normal workplace, had the right to assume that the passageway was properly timbered and safe. Montana's Supreme Court in 1912 made a similar ruling.[31]

The Colorado Court of Appeals in 1914 ruled that miners did not assume the risk of injury when they knew that their employer had not made an area safe when they were required to be in that area. In this case the operator did not provide refuge holes in a haulageway where miners had to walk while cars were running. Finally, in cases from Colorado and New Mexico, courts required employers to prove contributory negligence in cases where injury was caused by a fellow servant or by the employer's own negligence, or where a hazard was not plainly obvious.[32]

Courts were not alone in modifying personal injury law, for state and territorial legislatures also acted, though not always benevolently, to reshape the statutes that guided the courts. In Colorado in 1893 the legislature partially voided the fellow-servant doctrine by making supervisors agents of their employers, not fellow servants, and by making fellow servants "equally liable . . . with the employer" for injury damages. In 1901 the Colorado legislature passed an act making employers liable for injuries caused by the "carelessness, omission of duty or negligence" of the employer or of any "agent, servant or employe" of the employer where the injured party had exercised "due care"; meaning that, except where contributory negligence could be proved, employers were liable for their own negligence or carelessness and that of fellow servants, including supervisors. The state supreme court in 1906 upheld Colorado's fellow-servant law. Montana in 1903 also made employers liable for supervisors' negligence.[33]

The Colorado legislature in 1911 repealed all previous laws on the subject of fellow-servant negligence and replaced them with a statute that, although still holding employers liable for injuries caused by fellow servants, limited damages to five thousand dollars and imposed a two-year time limit from the date of injury or the date of subsequent death for filing suits. Finally, in 1914, Colorado's voters approved a measure that abolished assumption of risk as a defense in suits involving employees injured or killed on account of their employer's negligence or because of defective machinery, tools, or plant facilities that the employer could have corrected through ordinary diligence. The statute also declared that the fact that an injured worker had knowledge of a hazard could not bar recovery of damages.[34]

On 13 May 1908 the U.S. Congress passed a "Joint Resolution Disapproving certain laws enacted by the legislative assembly of the Territory of New Mexico." That resolution nullified a statute passed by the New Mexico territorial legislature in 1903 to limit "the increased cost and annoyance and manifest injury and oppression of the business interests" of the territory caused by personal injury suits.[35] Passed over Governor Miguel A. Otero's veto, the law set up a formidable series of procedural barriers designed to protect businesses from personal injury suits. The act required, among other things, that injured persons or their survivors notify the person or corporation involved of their intention to sue within ninety days of the occurrence of the injury and actually to bring suit within one year; it forbade bringing suit outside of New Mexico; it granted to the business involved the right to file an action requiring the plaintiff to appear and state under oath the nature of his complaint, his evidence, and witnesses; and it provided, if the plaintiff failed to appear, for trial of the matter in his absence.

In modern American civil procedure both parties to a lawsuit may take depositions to obtain information about claims and defenses so that each side can prepare for trial with full information about the case. The parties arrange for taking depositions at their mutual convenience. New Mexico's 1903 law allowed for no such niceties. The plaintiff, who already bore the burden of proving his own case, received the added burden and cost of appearing in a one-sided hearing to disclose information about his case without, at the same time, having the right to examine the defendant's case. If he did not appear, the court could try his case without him or his counsel, and he almost certainly would lose. So even though the law did not forbid personal injury suits, it did, in the opinion of the House Committee on the Territories, set up "so many obstacles around the maintenance of an action for personal injuries as to be in many cases a virtual denial of justice and right."[36] New Mexico's 1903 personal injury statute not only shows an insensitivity to the interests of injured workers, but demonstrates that the legislature of 1903 was just as friendly to corporations as the legislature that passed the 1882 law exempting most of New Mexico's coal mines from regulation. Fortunately, the 1903 law stayed in the statute books only five years before Congress nullified it.

Utah and Wyoming legislatures each passed only one measure changing personal injury laws, but unlike New Mexico's, these showed some sympathy for the injured. Utah in 1896 enacted a law defining fellow servants. That act provided that all persons working for an employer in a supervisory capacity were agents of the employer, not fellow servants. Thus, employers could be held liable for injury or death caused by the negligence of a supervisor. In Wyoming the legislature in 1913 passed a law that, though it directly concerned only railroad employees, had clear implications for personal injury law in general. Under this statute contributory negligence diminished, but did not bar, recovery of damages. Moreover, it declared that workers assumed no risk of injury caused by fellow servants.[37]

By about 1915 case law and statutes had shifted some of the burden of responsibility from the individual miner to the operator, especially by making the latter liable for the actions and negligence of supervisors and fellow servants. Nonetheless, the attitude that the miner assumed most of the risk of injury or death on the job remained basic legal doctrine. In Colorado, for example, courts continued to rule that miners assumed the risk of injury or death in their normal workplaces.[38] Only the operator's failure to perform some specific duty, such as providing adequate ventilation, mitigated the miner's risk.

Common-law doctrines governing personal injury cases were only part of a complex web of legal, industrial, and social attitudes that assigned to miners the major share of responsibility for safety and death on the job. Changes in coal-mining laws during the nineteenth and early twentieth centuries did little to alter that web. In fact, recommendations for changes and actual amendments played to the original tendencies of the laws. State coal-mine inspectors regularly called for amendments to require improved ventilation and dust control, including use of the split system of ventilation, and sprinkling and other dust-control measures; better regulations for the storage and use of explosives; employment of shot firers; use of safety lamps in gassy mines; installation of escape shafts; certification of mine officials; more severe punishment of miners for willful or negligent disobedience of the mining laws; more frequent inspections and the inspection of all mines; larger coal-mine inspection forces; and more authority to close dangerous mines. However, state and territorial legislatures and the U.S. Congress were content mainly to tinker with ventilation requirements. Only in Colorado and Montana did legislatures mandate something as innovative as sprinkling. And only Wyoming gave mine inspectors authority to close mines when operators refused to correct violations.[39]

Western coal-mine inspectors regularly complimented major coal operators not only for observing the laws but for implementing safety programs not required by law. Montana's C. S. Shoemaker in 1893 reported that mine managers spared "neither time nor money to make mines safe and to furnish plenty of good air" and that they were "anxious to provide necessary safeguards for [the] protection and security of employes." Colorado's David Griffiths in 1898 praised operators for complying with the coal-mining law "and in many instances, adopting measures for the safety and welfare of our miners, which are not specified by law." Ten years later John Jones was gratified by "the great desire manifested on [the] part of the mine owners and officials to comply with the demands for safety measures to protect life and health" in the mines. In light of Colorado's inadequate coal-mining law, Jones noted, operators had voluntarily put into effect improvements "for the commendable purpose of increasing the safety and welfare of the mine workers."[40] Though such declarations were practically a standard feature of mine inspectors' reports, there was some basis for the praise.

Major operators, especially the Colorado Fuel and Iron Company and the Victor-American Fuel Company, saw themselves as leaders in promoting mine safety in their own enterprises and for the industry. At the turn of the century a CF&I official discussing the effect of state coal-mining laws said that regulations pertaining to ventilation, escape, appliances, and inspection had "been of no disadvantage to the coal mining industry" because they applied to "just such things as were used prior to the passing of the laws." In fact, he said, "the companies generally go even beyond what the law requires in that respect." Indeed, by about 1913 CF&I's mine-safety programs and policies included efforts to hire more competent firebosses, more frequent inspections by mine and firebosses, employment of shot firers and safety inspectors, more supervision of miners, sprinkling, safeguarding machinery, fireproofing underground construction, and first-aid and rescue training. E. H. Weitzel, head of CF&I's Fuel Department, was proud of these efforts, and he told the U.S. Industrial Commission that the company "has never denied me one dollar that I have asked for for an improvement that tended to create better conditions and safe conditions for the miner."[41]

One especially important project of the Colorado Fuel and Iron Company was equipping a railroad car with rescue equipment and personnel. The company put a rescue car, the first in the nation, into service in 1910, shortly after the disaster at its Primero mine. The newly established U.S. Bureau of Mines quickly recognized the potential value of mobile rescue units and soon equipped its own cars.[42]

The Victor-American Fuel Company also followed CF&I's lead and put a rescue car into service in November 1910. By that time Victor-American also employed safety inspectors, had installed sprinkling systems, and used shot firers to detonate explosives after shifts in the company's mines in Colorado and New Mexico. Victor-American's John C. Osgood was proud that "in advance of any law" his company, and other operators, had spent large sums of money "in introducing improvements not required by law and in making experiments for improvements to promote the safety of our miners."[43]

Many of the safety programs of CF&I and Victor-American, such as equipping rescue cars, employing safety inspectors and extra supervisors, and installing elaborate sprinkling systems, were beyond the financial means of smaller operators. Small companies in Colorado did, however, follow industry leaders at least in the employment of shot firers. In 1908 the state mine inspector reported that the use of shot firers and the firing of shots after shifts were practically standard in the southern, mountain, and western slope fields.[44]

Colorado's operators, however, took second place to Utah in the employment of shot firers. By about 1890 the Utah Fuel Company, in order to reduce the risk of gas and dust explosions, had instituted electric shot firing, as well as sprinkling, in its Castle Gate mine.

According to historian Helen Papanikolas, the coal mines of Carbon County were the first in the nation to fire shots after shifts.[45]

Shot firers were widely employed in New Mexico's mines by about 1910, when the governor and the territorial mine inspector praised operators "for this improvement as well as for many other precautionary measures for the safety of the persons employed in and about the mines." These procedures included daily inspections by firebosses and rules requiring miners to clean and timber roofs and to stop work if timber was not available.[46]

Wyoming's major operator, the Union Pacific Coal Company, was slow to follow other leading western coal companies in instituting safety programs. Reports of the Wyoming coal-mine inspector and a company history show only that, by 1912, the Union Pacific Coal Company had instituted first-aid training and contests and had established a company board of inquiry, composed of mine bosses and superintendents, to investigate accidents. The company did not deploy a rescue car until 1914. By 1916, though, Union Pacific mines had safety inspectors, safety committees of miners and mine officials, and a company safety department. These early efforts of the Union Pacific Coal Company to promote greater mine safety were minimal compared to the programs of other major operators in the West, and as a retired company executive conceded, they "did not show appreciable results."[47]

Company safety policies depended, to a great extent, on the ability and the willingness of superintendents and mine bosses to carry them out. Just as a miner at the face of his room sometimes had to choose between timbering or loading coal, superintendents and mines bosses sometimes had to calculate whether the company's, and their own, greater interest lay in implementing safety policies or in encouraging the men to get coal out as quickly as possible. A 1912 circular letter to Victor-American superintendents from vice-president and general manager W. J. Murray illustrates the problem. Murray instructed his superintendents to do everything possible to increase production but, at the same time, warned them to "watch the safety of your men, and under no circumstances allow your anxiety to get out coal make you forget to watch the safety of the men in your employ."[48] Such instructions required superintendents and other mine officials to calculate how much production the front office was willing to give up in exchange for safety. It was the miners, however, who really paid the price for the choice. A push for safety might mean more deadwork and, therefore, less pay; a push for production might mean less attention to timbering, inspection, or gas and dust abatement and, therefore, more accidents.

The dilemma of production versus safety gained wider recognition in later years. However, the fact that mine superintendents and mine bosses had to choose between safety and production, with miners bearing the consequences, underscores the general tendency of laws, courts, inspectors, and industry to place on the shoulders of the individual mine worker the real burden of safety.

The first laws governing coal mining in the Rocky Mountain region were intended to prevent explosion disasters in the mines. Their failure to achieve this goal is reflected in explosion fatality rates that far exceeded national averages. Just as important, the early laws did not meaningfully address the causes of the deaths of as many, or more, miners as those killed in explosions. Because they did not alter the basic relations of work in the mines, especially the tradition of defining the miner as a contractor and paying him according to the amount of coal he produced, the laws did nothing to eliminate the choice miners had to make between safety and production.

Compounding the failure of laws to protect miners was the attitude of mine inspectors, operators, coroners, and the courts that, whether they died in major disasters or one by one in roof falls, haulage accidents, or other minor incidents, miners ultimately bore primary responsibility for their own deaths. Supposedly, because of their own carelessness, negligence, inexperience, or their inherent inferiority as foreigners, miners recklessly killed themselves and one another despite the existence of laws, inspectors, and company safety policies.

In the latter years of the nineteenth century and the first dozen or so years of the twentieth, there was little recognition of the weaknesses of the coal-mining laws, other than their failure to stop explosions; little recognition of or sympathy for the Hobson's choice that confronted miners; and no acceptance of responsibility by operators and government for allowing untrained, illiterate men to go into the mines and work without close supervision. There was, in short, no serious questioning of the environment of death in the mines.

Chapter 5

Legislation in the Progressive Era

In 1908 the rising tide of the Progressive movement carried John Franklin Shafroth into the office of governor of Colorado. A fixture in Colorado politics by then, Shafroth began his career as a Republican. The silver movement led him to join Henry Teller and others in walking out of the 1896 Republican convention. Six years later Shafroth joined the Democratic party. As a member of Congress from 1894 to 1904, he earned a reputation as a supporter of Progressive causes. Only his advocacy of regional economic interests such as mining in U.S. forest reserves dulled his Progressive reputation. Shafroth in 1904 acquired the nickname "Honest John" when he resigned from Congress after learning of possible vote fraud in his election. By 1908 he was the clear leader among Colorado Progressives and handily defeated a Republican opposition demoralized by corruption and internal strife. Shafroth's four years as governor marked the high point of the Progressive movement in Colorado.

Never a monolithic movement, Progressivism meant different things to different advocates, but at root it was a product of America's struggle to come to terms with itself as an industrial society. Whether they sought economic, political, or moral reforms, Progressives responded to America's industrial transformation. Some aimed to ameliorate the human and physical blight evident in the urban industrial environment. Settlement house projects, tenement laws, improved health and sanitation programs, prohibition and antiprostitution campaigns tried to improve conditions in the industrial city. Lawmakers used antitrust legislation to try to limit the power of corporations in America's economic and political life. And they passed laws to regulate the conditions in which industrial workers toiled. However, reform did not often come without opposition.

During his first two-year term, Governor Shafroth battled a coalition of conservative Democrats, controlled by Denver mayor Robert Speer's machine, and Republicans, many of them tied to powerful corporate interests in Colorado. In control of the state senate, this conservative coalition was determined to keep its grip on state politics and block the reforms advocated by the governor and his supporters. Shafroth's most significant first-term success was forcing the legislature to submit an initiative and referendum amendment to the voters in the 1910 election.

Both the amendment and the governor won resounding victories at the polls in 1910. After his reelection Shafroth won an impressive list of Progressive reforms, including direct primaries, the Australian ballot, civil-service reform, recall of local officials, and home rule for cities. Shafroth also numbered industrial reforms, including a railroad commission, regulation of child and woman labor, and, eventually, a new coal-mining law, among his achievements.

By the time Shafroth became governor, many in the coal-mining industry had come to recognize that accidents not only were costly in terms of property and life, but were symptomatic of an inefficient industry that was not fulfilling its productive potential. Colorado coal-mine inspector John Jones in 1908 observed that the state's operators were "rapidly realizing that a mine conducted on the safest and most sanitary basis is also the most economical to operate." A year later an article in the *Engineering and Mining Journal* summarized this attitude. Accidents, it said, were indicative of lapses in or the absence of discipline and efficiency in a mine. An inefficient mine, naturally, was less productive and, therefore, less profitable than an efficient one. By implementing safety practices, including better supervision and discipline of miners, account books would show that "to economize in blood is to economize in costs." The safest mine, the article concluded, was also the cheapest.[1]

Operators hoped that by promoting efficiency and safety they could forestall a larger government regulatory role, especially in the face of growing Progressive interest in improving conditions for coal miners. Anxious to avoid competitive disadvantages threatened by more stringent, nonuniform state regulation, operators, especially those in the East, began to consider a federal mine department or bureau as a workable alternative. Interest among operators and Progressives in a federal agency gained impetus as a result of a series of mine disasters in the years from 1907 to 1909. Especially fearsome were explosions at Monongah, West Virginia; Jacobs Creek and Marianna, Pennsylvania; and Cherry, Illinois, which together killed more than one thousand miners.

Largely as a result of these disasters, Congress in 1910 established the U.S. Bureau of Mines as an agency of the Department of the Interior. The new bureau had no regulatory authority. Instead, its primary mission was to conduct research into mine-safety problems, especially explosions. In the Bureau of Mines, then, the coal industry, without accepting more stringent regulation, achieved an agency devoted to making the mines safer.[2]

In Colorado, however, the disasters of 1910 at Primero, Delagua, and Starkville forced Governor Shafroth and the legislature to consider strengthening the state's coal-mining law. Three times that year headlines told of explosions blowing men to bits, of fading hopes of finding survivors, of widows and orphans standing vigil, of rituals of grief as bodies were brought out and identified. After each disaster labor leaders and editorialists demanded investigations and reform of the mining law. Following the Primero disaster of 31 January 1910 the *Rocky Mountain News*, whose editors were not generally known for their reform sympathies, demanded a complete investigation by state authorities or some specially appointed panel. Alluding to the coal operators' dominance of local government in the southern counties, the *News* said that, because the public demanded the facts, the investigation could not be left in the hands of Las Animas County authorities, who, the paper claimed, had no "very close acquaintance with facts." The *Denver Post*'s George Creel, a strong supporter of Progressive reform, maintained that the Primero disaster proved that the state's coal-mining law did not adequately take account of the obvious dangers of coal mining. Creel also noted that the underfunded and understaffed state inspector's office could not properly do its job. "The men who died in the Primero mine will have died in vain if public opinion does not insist upon the adoption of adequate mining laws, supported by adequate appropriations," he declared.[3]

Organized labor also demanded action. United Mine Workers of America spokesman John R. Lawson asserted that because of the three disasters "a change has come over the people of this state, and they are finally demanding that the reckless slaughter of our people shall cease." In Trinidad a committee of Austrian-born miners, members of the Western Federation of Miners, demanded the ouster of state mine inspector John Jones, his replacement by an inspector named and paid by the union, and the removal of the Las Animas County coroner. Distrusting local, state, and federal authorities, the miners also demanded an international investigation of conditions in the coal mines of southern Colorado.[4]

The *Denver Post* renewed its call for a more effective coal-mining law after the November 1910 disaster at Delagua. "Colorado wants laws to protect its miners—not reports telling how they came to their death," the *Post* said. Colorado's lawmakers should "forget the corporations, overlook the mine owners . . . and legislate for the protection of the husband, the father, the provider—and in so doing help the men with the pick and shovel."[5]

Colorado's mine laws and mine inspector were not the only subjects of criticism. The Colorado Fuel and Iron Company, operator of the Primero and Starkville mines, in which 131 men died in 1910, was the target of especially vigorous attacks. In the *Denver Post* George Creel blamed the Starkville blast on CF&I's failure to build an air-and-escape shaft, which, he claimed, would have cost the company ten thousand dollars, an amount that "while never begrudged when it comes to buying legislators, was denied when human life was the only consideration." The company angrily refuted the assumption that cost was a factor in its decision not to build the shaft. Fuel Department head E. H. Weitzel said that the company's engineers had determined that enlarging existing air courses would provide much more air in the mine.[6]

The Colorado State Bureau of Labor Statistics also accused the Colorado Fuel and Iron Company of failing to use adequate measures to control dust and gas in its mines. Furthermore, the bureau alleged that at Primero, to obtain timber and rails, men had to go into abandoned areas, where the danger of gas was greatest, a practice the bureau termed "infamous." "To compel men who are working in a gaseous mine filled with dust, to work under conditions imposed by the company at the time of the explosion was cold-blooded barbarism."[7]

The United Mine Workers' John R. Lawson also was unreserved in his criticism of CF&I. Lawson, the union's principal organizer in Colorado, claimed that before the Primero and Starkville disasters the company was warned "times without number" that some major disaster was likely because of the way it operated its mines. "But with a callous greed, which has characterized the operations of this crowd," Lawson said, "they preferred to take a chance . . . rather than spend a reasonable amount to make their mines safe." Lawson also maintained, on the strength of statements of miners and rescuers, that the company tried to cover up the dimensions of the Primero disaster. The actual number killed, he alleged, was 114, not the published figure of 72.[8] (The final official death toll was 75.)

The *United Mine Workers Journal* asserted that "when a single corporation in Colorado nets over $3,000,000 in a year and reports two explosions of this kind, it is not hard to find their cause." To save money the company neglected its property, did not clean up blocked air courses, failed to maintain ventilation equipment, allowed gas and dust to accumulate, and employed non-English-speaking workers. "Then comes an explosion that kills everyone in the mine, and, as usual, it is a 'mystery.'"[9]

The union extended its criticism to the entire state and urged job seekers to disregard any inducements offered by Colorado operators. "If we have to judge by the manner in which human life has been sacrificed during the present year in the coal mines of this state," the *United Mine Workers Journal* said, "we will be compelled to conclude that Colorado is a very good state to keep away from."[10]

Unlike previous explosions, the 1910 disasters, coming at the height of Progressive sentiment in Colorado, set in motion a political process that led, after an abortive first effort, to the passage of a new coal-mining law. In October 1910, in the aftermath of the Starkville disaster, both houses of the legislature passed resolutions calling on the governor to order an investigation into the causes of mining disasters and the adequacy of the state coal-mining law. In November, after the Delagua explosion, Shafroth declared his intention to seek a new coal-mining law. "There is nothing . . . of more pressing importance at present than this subject of better protection for the miners," said the governor as he pledged to "use every possible means to have an effective law placed on the statute books."[11] Shafroth, like almost everyone else, was especially concerned with ensuring adequate ventilation of the mines to prevent explosions.

Shafroth followed through by naming a special commission, headed by the president of the Colorado School of Mines, Victor C. Alderson, to study conditions in the mines and to draft a new law. Other members of the commission were Russell D. George, state geologist and professor of geology at the University of Colorado; John B. Ekeley, professor of chemistry at the university; and James Dalrymple, who, in the aftermath of the Delagua disaster, replaced John D. Jones as state inspector of coal mines. Of the commission members, only Dalrymple, as mine inspector, was involved in the coal-mining industry.

In the course of its work the Alderson Commission interviewed operators, miners, and engineers and examined the literature on coal-mine safety. Its investigation included ventilation, gas and dust problems, mining methods, explosives, mine drainage, surface operations, inspection procedures, rescue equipment and procedures, and training of mine officials. Based on these studies, the commission drafted a new coal-mining law, which was introduced in the legislature on 2 February 1911. In presenting the report of his commission's work, Alderson struck a familiar note, declaring that "mining conditions are bad all over the state" and that "gross carelessness" on the part of the operators and their employees was the rule.[12]

In its original form the bill promised a vast improvement over the obsolete 1883 law. Under the proposed law all coal mines in the state were to come under the jurisdiction of the coal-mine inspector. The bill provided for an expanded coal-mine inspection department, including a chief inspector and seven deputies who were to visit each mine at least once every sixty days. A tax on coal production of one cent per ton would finance the department. Though the bill did not improve the cumbersome injunction process, it did authorize inspectors to order miners out of critically dangerous areas. Operators were to employ their own inspectors, who would be responsible for enforcing the law. Except where authorized by the state inspector, the bill allowed the use of only "permissible" explosives tested and approved by the new federal Bureau of Mines. The bill raised minimum ventilation standards and allowed the mine inspector to require sprinkling. To reduce rock and coal falls, the bill required setting of timbers at seven-foot intervals. To make travel in the mines safer, the bill called for construction of separate manways so that miners would not have to dodge or ride on coal cars. Finally, the measure included rules for the use of electricity and coal-cutting machines and a requirement that operators provide rescue and resuscitation equipment. [13]

The Colorado state representatives approved the Alderson Commission's bill, but the measure did not fare so well in the senate, which, responding to pressure from operators, watered down many of its provisions. Some of the senate amendments clearly aimed to cripple the coal-mine inspection department and reduce costs for operators; others were purely punitive, antilabor provisions. The senate version reduced the mine-inspection force from seven to five deputies without, however, changing the sixty-day inspection cycle, which could only have resulted in less thorough or missed inspections. The senate also cut the proposed coal tax from one cent to one-third cent per ton and weakened the ventilation standards by reducing the volume required for animals and by allowing the state inspector to make further reductions where feasible. Miners, in the senate version, were to pay the salaries of shot firers out of their own wages. The senate also allowed operators to weigh coal after screening, meaning that miners might not be paid for whatever coal operators determined was "slack." [14] Pressure from operators apparently also dampened the representatives' enthusiasm for reform since, with little debate, they accepted the senators' changes and passed the bill in final form on 6 May 1911.

The bill, as it emerged from the legislature, was denounced by labor leaders, who said the amendments, which they recognized as the work of the operators, made it worthless. United Mine Workers leader Edward Doyle urged Governor Shafroth to veto the bill because "the clause requiring the Miner to Pay for the 'Shot Firer' will throw the cost of keeping the mine in a safe condition largely upon the shoulders of the workers instead of the operators." Indeed, a report in the *Denver Times* estimated that the shot firers provision would take as much as $168,000 per year from the miners' pockets. [15]

Governor Shafroth agreed. Saying the bill had been so amended "as to destroy many of its good features, omit many of the provisions originally in the bill for the protection of the life of the miners and to impose very great burdens upon the miners," the governor vetoed it.[16] So ended, for the moment, the effort to reform Colorado's coal-mining law.

There is no question that the operators were the guiding force behind the senate's amendments. John C. Osgood, of Victor-American, in 1914 told a congressional committee that he and other operators opposed the bill as submitted by the Alderson Commission and admitted that "we offered numerous amendments to it." One of those suggesting changes was CF&I's E. H. Weitzel, who proposed the amendments requiring miners to pay shot firers' salaries and allowing screening of coal before weighing.[17]

The absence of industry participation in drafting the original Alderson Commission bill was one factor influencing the operators' attitude toward it. Osgood complained that the operators "had no representative whatever in preparing this law," and he noted that of the Alderson Commission's members only James Dalrymple, the state mine inspector, had experience as a "practical miner." Without operator input, Osgood claimed, many of the bill's provisions "were of such a nature that they could not practically be carried out." The operators thus "opposed the passage of that law in the form it came from the committee and . . . offered numerous amendments to it."[18] That mine operators would view with suspicion a reform bill written by a committee of scholars appointed by a reform-minded governor is not surprising. Perhaps, too, they worried that reform might be viewed as a concession to organized labor at a time of growing labor militance. Or, believing that miners caused their own deaths, perhaps Colorado's coal-mine operators simply were not yet ready to assume the responsibility and the costs of a stronger mine-safety program and sought, in the face of demands for reform, a weak measure that kept most of the burden of safety on the shoulders of the miners.

Industry opposition, the senate's amendments, and the governor's veto of the 1911 bill stalled the effort to rewrite Colorado's coal-mining law. For the moment there would be no new effort to revise the 1883 law. There was no reason for Governor Shafroth to make a proposal until he believed that the operators, especially CF&I and Victor-American, were ready to go along.

In fact, the deadlock over coal-mining reform did not last for long.

In November 1912 more than one hundred coal-mine operators, executives, engineers, and superintendents from the Rocky Mountain region gathered at the state capitol in Denver. Meeting at the suggestion of the editor of the industry journal *Coal Age,* the coal men formed the Rocky Mountain Coal Mining Institute to "increase . . . knowledge relating to coal mining, to encourage education in practical and scientific mining, to promote study and research into mining problems, and to advance the mutual interests" of the members.[19] The group elected CF&I's E. H. Weitzel president of the organization and Victor-American's chief engineer, F. W. Whiteside, secretary-treasurer.

On the second day of the meeting the members heard speeches and papers on conditions in the industry, including an address by former Colorado mine inspector David Griffiths, then working as a superintendent for the Colorado Fuel and Iron Company. The "especial duty" of the institute, said Griffiths, was to educate miners, operators, the press, and government about the problems of the industry. In one curious passage Griffiths linked consumer demand, ethnicity, inexperience, and the press as causes of mine accidents. "The consumer demands our product, and in our necessity we must hire everything that comes along, be it Jap or Greek." Noting that "some of these people never saw a coal mine before," Griffiths said that while they learned their jobs "there must necessarily be more accidents and casualties than would be the case if they were experienced miners." Griffiths then declared that "false representation of the facts by press agents is indirectly contributory to our list of fatalities." Apparently, in Griffiths's view, reporters helped cause accidents by reporting them![20]

Griffiths went on to characterize Colorado's coal-mining law as "inadequate to cope with present necessities." It was time, he said, for the state to "awaken to a sense of duty" and enact a "clear, explicit, practical mining law that will not hamper or impede industry," a law that would define the duty of "every man connected with coal mining," one "with a main motive in view of protecting the life and limb of our workmen."[21] Griffiths called, in effect, for a new coal-mining law that would impose few new costs, at least on major operators, and leave most of the burden of safety on individual mine workers.

Governor Shafroth took Griffiths's speech as a signal that operators now were willing to work on a new law. Two months later, as he was about to leave office, Shafroth called on the incoming legislature to try again to enact a new coal-mining law, one he hoped would be similar to that proposed in 1911. Responding to the governor's call, Representative William C. Gilbert, a coal miner from Fremont County, introduced a bill written largely by state inspector James Dalrymple and UMWA leader John Lawson. The house unanimously approved Gilbert's bill and sent it on to the senate. There, as in 1911, the bill ran into trouble.

The senate Committee on Mines and Mining found the bill unacceptable and requested that the senate appoint a special commission to revise it. That commission included James Dalrymple, John Lawson, CF&I's E. H. Weitzel, George Peart of the Rocky Mountain Fuel Company, and Senator John F. Pearson. These men, representing "the different phases of the coal mining situation," would, the senators believed, guarantee fair treatment for all interests.[22] The commission rewrote the bill and submitted it to the senate, which passed it on 27 March 1913. The house, after a conference committee session, agreed to the amended bill, and Governor Elias Ammons, Shafroth's successor, signed the bill into law.

In many respects the new law was a compromise between the Alderson Commission's bill and the vetoed senate version of it. The reorganized coal-mine inspection department, financed by a coal tax of one-third cent per ton, included a chief inspector and five deputies, each responsible for one of five inspection districts. The statute provided for more frequent inspections and did away with the cumbersome enforcement procedures of the 1883 law. Inspectors were to examine each coal mine at least once every ninety days. When an inspector discovered conditions of imminent danger to the lives of miners, he could order the evacuation of the areas concerned or even of the entire mine. The law required owners to remedy the dangers or seek an injunction in the courts to reverse the inspector's orders before resuming operations.

The act raised coal-mine ventilation requirements to the levels recommended in 1911 by the Alderson Commission; namely, one hundred cubic feet per man per minute and five hundred cubic feet per minute for each animal. In addition, operators were to institute dust-control measures, and firebosses were to inspect mines daily for the presence of explosive gas.

The new law also required mines to use a systematic method of timbering with procedures for each mine approved by the chief inspector. When sufficient timber could not be delivered, the law required that work stop and the area be cleared of miners.

To supervise mine operations, owners of mines employing ten men or more underground were to have foremen examined and certified by a board composed of working miners, operators or company officials, and a mining engineer. Assistant foremen, shot firers, and company inspectors also were to be certified. Foremen were to inspect all workplaces daily; see to the proper operation and condition of ventilation systems, airways, travelways, haulageways, drainage, and timbering; give "prompt attention to the removal of all dangers" reported to them; and, generally, see that employees obeyed the mining law.[23]

The new law also regulated the use of explosives, electricity, and electrical appliances; construction of in-mine installations; provision of rescue and resuscitation equipment; opening of secondary shafts; and use of mine cars. It required mine owners to furnish miners with copies of the essential parts of the new law, "in the language of the employee, if practicable," and instructed the state inspector to have the law translated and printed in the languages and quantities needed.[24] Other provisions allowed miners to appoint checkweighmen and forbade superintendents and other officials to use their positions to extort money or favors from miners in exchange for employment, job security, or favorable work assignments. Violations of the act, including willful negligence by miners, were misdemeanors punishable by fines or imprisonment.

Those most directly interested in the law, labor and industry, expressed satisfaction with it. John Lawson, of the United Mine Workers, was most enthusiastic, saying the new law would give Colorado "the best and safest working conditions for miners in the world." Lawson also predicted that it would help to eliminate the problem of large numbers of inexperienced miners working in the state, since "many of the old-time miners" would return to work in Colorado. The less effusive E. H. Weitzel noted simply that he and the Colorado Fuel and Iron Company were "perfectly satisfied" with the new law.[25] Colorado's major operators, in fact, had good reason to be pleased with the outcome.

Just two years earlier Governor Shafroth had vetoed a coal-mining bill because of crippling amendments made at the instance of the operators. Evidently, something had changed in the interim to make operators more amenable to reform. One obvious difference was in the authorship of the two bills. Whereas a committee of scholars, advised by the state inspector, drafted the 1911 bill, agents of the major interests in the industry—large operators, organized labor, and the state—wrote the 1913 measure. In this setting the operators played a greater, more direct role in shaping the law.

John C. Osgood noted this difference, telling a congressional committee that, in this case, "the operators were given the opportunity to take a hand in the preparation of the law" and "did all in our part to bring about its adoption." The Colorado Fuel and Iron Company's board chairman, L. M. Bowers, boasted that the new law was "almost entirely written by our own . . . E. H. Weitzel." Weitzel himself was more modest, saying that during the work of the special senate commission he was "in constant communication with the officers of our company" as well as with Osgood and W. J. Murray of Victor-American, "and the heads of all of the larger companies."[26]

Major operators were satisfied with the new law because, they claimed, it merely codified practices already followed in their mines. The Colorado Fuel and Iron Company's Jesse F. Welborn said the act "incorporated many of the practices that had been in vogue in our company for some years." Weitzel contended that "the mining law of 1913 was practically brought up to our practices before that time— the practices that we had in effect in our mines were crystallized into the law of 1913."[27] For major operators, a coal-mining law that reflected established practices was neither very threatening nor very costly.

Labor militancy also goes far in explaining the operators' willingness to endorse a new coal-mining law in 1913. Labor unrest had been growing over the preceding decade, and tensions reached new levels with the start of the strike in the northern field in 1910. By 1913 union organizers were at work in the southern fields, where trouble finally erupted in the great strike of 1913–14. The new law, enacted fewer than five months before the strike, implied industry endorsement of safety reform and thus may have been, in part, an effort to placate miners and deny union organizers the useful issue of poor conditions in the mines. Governor Ammons shared the operators' concerns and their hope that the new law might quiet labor agitation. In the aftermath of the 1913–14 strike, Ammons told the U.S. Industrial Commission that he had hoped the new law "would be the means of heading off any strike."[28]

Production and competition were other important factors influencing the industrial environment and making the major operators more amenable to reform than before. The Colorado coal industry's long upward trend in production ended in 1906. From that year through 1912 production leveled off and then declined until 1916, when World War I stimulated temporary increases. Years without significant growth made operators more alert than ever for competitive advantages.

The 1913 law gave major operators such an advantage. The equipment and safety procedures the act required worked to improve the competitive position of large operators such as the Colorado Fuel and Iron Company, Victor-American, and Rocky Mountain Fuel by increasing the relative operating costs of smaller companies. The major operators already owned the equipment and followed many of the procedures required by the act. However, many smaller operators did not, and the increased costs associated with ventilation and dust control, supervision, shot firing, and other regulations represented a huge, even prohibitive investment. In the first several years after 1913 the number of small operators in the major coalfields did not decline from year to year, but most were short-lived and, more important, their share of production fell. In Las Animas County, the heart of the southern field, CF&I had increased its share of production by approximately 8 percent by 1914 and held that lead for the rest of the decade. A similar trend occurred in Boulder County, where Rocky Mountain Fuel increased its lead.[29]

Labor militancy and competition were not the only motives for operator backing of the 1913 law. Operators could support it because it left miners primarily responsible for their own safety, and for their own deaths, without fundamentally changing the conditions in which they worked. Certainly, the 1913 act contained important improvements over the 1883 measure. It enlarged the coal-mine inspection department and gave inspectors greater authority, especially to protect miners from imminent danger. The higher ventilation, equipment, and plant standards and the coal tax imposed greater responsibilities and costs on operators. And more rigid supervision, systematic timbering, and regulations governing explosives, electricity, machinery, and haulage sought to force miners to take greater care of themselves in their workplaces.

In spite of these improvements, however, the law did little or nothing to alter the basic relations of work that were the underlying causes of death in the mines. It did not forbid the hiring of illiterate or incompetent workers or require operators to train them adequately before sending them into the mines. It did not alter the miners' reliance on drivers and machine men. It did not eliminate the incentive to avoid deadwork built into the system of paying according to production. It did not remove the pressure on mine officials to get the coal out as fast as possible. And it did not undo the web of opinion that held miners responsible, because of their supposed carelessness, greed, or inexperience, for their own injuries and deaths.

Similar weaknesses characterized New Mexico's new coal-mining law, passed in June 1912, the result not of disasters in the mines but of the triumph of statehood. The new statute established the office of state inspector of mines with responsibility for enforcing regulations governing mine operations and safety. However, even though the new law included many more specific regulations, it required only that the state inspector visit mines "as often as in his opinion may be necessary," instead of annually, as provided for in the federal law.[30]

The law imposed on operators and mine officials some responsibilities not contained in the federal statute. The act increased ventilation standards and required operators of gassy mines to hire firebosses to make daily inspections for gas. The law also required operators of mines employing more than twenty men to employ shot firers to inspect all shots and fire them after shifts. In mines without separate manways, entries were to be wide enough to permit men to move about without risk of being hit by mine cars. As an alternative to widening entries, shelter holes could be installed at one-hundred-foot intervals. Other safety regulations limited quantities of explosives allowed inside and required operators to provide safety lamps and oxygen masks for use in rescue work. Finally, operators were to deliver timbers to miners "as near as practicable" to the place where they would use them.[31]

The new statute also imposed more duties on coal miners. Miners could not enter their rooms before the fireboss made his daily inspection, and once at work, they were to take down all dangerous rock and coal and make their rooms safe by proper timbering. If a miner discovered his workplace to be dangerous, the act forbade him to stay there except to remove the hazard. It also prohibited operators from requiring miners to work in dangerous areas. Miners also were not to use haulageways when separate manways were available, and they were not to ride on trips unless they notified the haulage operator or rope rider. Finally, the law banned shooting off the solid.

To enforce the law, the act authorized the state mine inspector to notify operators of any improper construction or inadequate machinery and appliances, specify measures to correct defects and dangers, and set the time allowed for making corrections. Operators could challenge the inspector's orders by appealing to a state district court. Violations of the act were misdemeanors carrying fines or prison sentences.

The New Mexico law of 1912 was at least a marginal improvement over the federal act. Though it substituted the mine inspector's discretion for regular inspections, thus risking less frequent government inspection, it promised more supervision through the required daily inspections by firebosses. Other provisions concerning supervision, ventilation, explosives, travelways, and timbering imposed more specific duties on both operators and miners. However, as was the case under the federal statute, the New Mexico mine inspector had no authority to close dangerous mines or remove workers from dangerous places. The act's emphasis on ventilation, inspection for gas, and shot firing indicates that New Mexico's legislators, like their colleagues in Colorado in 1913, were mainly interested in trying to prevent major explosion disasters. Only those provisions regarding supply of timber, roof maintenance, and haulage addressed (inadequately) the causes of most deaths and injuries in New Mexico's coal mines. More important, New Mexico's new law, like Colorado's, did not alter the fundamental relations of work and the attitudes that made miners primarily responsible for safety and death in the mines.

Since 1891, Montana's inspector of mines had been responsible for inspecting both hard-rock and coal mines. Finally, the state legislature in 1907 answered the mine inspector's recommendations and created a separate office of coal-mine inspector. The legislature also tried to improve enforcement of the coal-mining law by requiring the inspector to visit each coal mine at least once every three months.[32]

Montana's legislature in 1911 enacted a general revision of the state's coal-mining code. With an emphasis on preventing explosions, the new code raised the ventilation standard for gassy mines to one hundred fifty cubic feet per man per minute and included new regulations governing the use of explosives, safety lamps, electricity, and mining machines. Although the act did not require shot firers, it did require that mine bosses inspect all shots and that miners wait until the end of their shift to fire them.

The act addressed the problem of falling roof and coal by giving miners the general responsibility for securing roofs in their working places and specifically requiring them to inspect roofs and coal after firing their shots. The act also required operators to deliver timber and other supplies to room entries.

The 1911 code also made some improvements in supervision. Mine bosses and firebosses were to be examined and certified by a board composed of the coal-mine inspector, a working miner, and a mine operator or official. Firebosses were required to visit all working places before each shift, inform miners of any hazards found, and supervise the removal of any gas pockets. Mine bosses were required to visit all working areas at least every other day to see to it that rooms were properly timbered and that adequate supplies of timber were available for miners. Mine bosses also were responsible for seeing to it that novice miners did not work alone.

Though the 1911 revision included some improvements to Montana's coal-mining code, it failed to change the cumbersome enforcement procedure requiring the inspector to secure injunctions to force recalcitrant operators and officials to comply with the law. [33]

The new laws of Colorado, New Mexico, and Montana were the only major changes in coal-mining laws in the Rocky Mountain region during the Progressive era. Utah and Wyoming made no significant changes in their coal-mining laws before World War I.

The U.S. Bureau of Mines and the new state coal-mining laws were enacted in very different contexts. The Bureau of Mines and the Colorado statute primarily were consequences of coal-mining disasters, which aroused public and political concern. Other disasters in other times did not arouse such interest and lead to reform, but the explosions that rocked mines in West Virginia, Pennsylvania, and Illinois from 1907 to 1909, and those in Colorado in 1910, occurred just as the Progressive mood swept over America. Disasters such as Monongah and Delagua touched a sensitive nerve in a nation struggling to come to grips with itself as an industrial society. The problem for legislators was to translate that humane sensitivity into workable legislation—workable in the sense of trying to advance mine safety without seriously harming the operators' interests.

Without minimizing the desire of legislators and industry to improve work and safety conditions in the mines, we may conclude that reform, in the cases of the Bureau of Mines and the Colorado law, more precisely reflected the interests of the operators than those of the coal miners. Because the enactments were immediately inspired by coal-mine explosions and because preventing disasters reflected not only humane but property interests as well, the principal mission of the Bureau of Mines and of the new laws in the West was to prevent future disasters. In Colorado, moreover, major operators got a law that, in focusing on the explosion problem, promised to rationalize the competitive environment by increasing capital costs and forcing smaller operators out of the field. Coming at a time when labor agitation was building toward the strike of 1913–14, the new law also enabled operators to deny union claims that they did not care about the lives of their workers.

In New Mexico the act of 1912 was a product of the transition to statehood as legislators tackled the job of converting territorial and federal laws into state statutes. No major disasters preceded it, nor is there evidence of a strong Progressive movement focusing on working conditions in coal mining or other industries. In fact, New Mexico Progressives were mainly interested in political reforms aimed at breaking the power of the Santa Fe Ring and other entrenched interests in the state's politics and government.[34] Thus New Mexico's legislature, dominated by those interests, did not use the occasion of statehood to make a major revision of the coal-mining law. Instead, they passed a law that contained marginal changes and imposed few serious new burdens on major operators.

In Montana, as in Colorado, a potent Progressive movement developed in the early twentieth century. Unlike Colorado, however, in Montana Progressives did not require the impetus of a great coal-mining disaster to get them to act. Instead, widespread hostility against the power of corporations, especially the copper industry and the railroads, which dominated coal mining, created an atmosphere congenial to reform.

A group of miners, a young driver or nipper, and a mule pose in an entry. The hand tools and open-flame lamps are typical of the early twentieth century. Courtesy Colorado Historical Society, F-43365.

Pick miners, such as these men at work at the face of their room in Starkville, Colorado, in 1905, often worked in cramped conditions. Courtesy Colorado Historical Society, F-44288.

Considered to be deadwork, timbering was one of the miner's most important jobs. By the 1950s, when this photo was taken, hard hats and electric lamps had replaced caps and open-flame lamps, but the job of timbering had changed little. Courtesy CF&I Steel Corporation.

Loading coal, Dawson, New Mexico, 1921. Loading by hand was hard work and something of an art. A well "chunked-up" car could carry two to three tons of coal. Courtesy Museum of New Mexico, neg. no. 5224.

Before mechanized haulage replaced them, mules pulled the loaded coal cars from the mines. These intelligent and hardworking animals spent most of their working lives underground and knew their way around the mine as well as, or better than, most miners. Though most western coal mines had mechanized haulage by the 1950s, when this photo was taken, some used mules as late as the 1970s. Courtesy CF&I Steel Corporation.

Drivers, such as this man employed by the Wootton Land and Fuel Co. around 1910, usually relied on voice commands to guide their animals but sometimes resorted to whips or sprags to persuade a balky mule. Courtesy Colorado Historical Society, F-42847.

The Rocky Mountain West has witnessed numerous coal-mining disasters in which scores, even hundreds, perished. Here rescue workers remove a body from the Pleasant Valley Coal Company's No. 4 mine at Winter Quarters, near Scofield, Utah, where 200 men died in an explosion in May 1900. Courtesy Utah State Historical Society.

Three caskets in front of one home await victims of the Winter Quarters disaster. Courtesy Utah State Historical Society.

An explosion of gas and dust in 1910 killed 79 miners in the Victor-American Fuel Company's Delagua, Colorado, mine. Extensive surface damage shows the power of the blast. Two other disasters that year, at Primero and Starkville, killed an additional 131 miners and created pressure for reform of the state's coal-mining law. Courtesy Colorado Historical Society, F-43009.

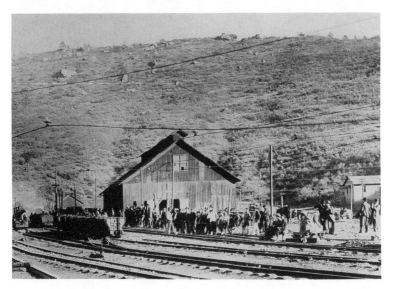

A large crowd gathered at the Phelps-Dodge Company's Stag Canon No. 1 mine after the February 1923 explosion there, which killed 120 men. Photograph by International Newsreel Photo. Courtesy Museum of New Mexico, neg. no. 138143.

A fireboss using a match to relight his safety lamp touched off an explosion in the Kemmerer Coal Company's Frontier No. 1 mine in western Wyoming. The August 1923 disaster claimed 99 lives. Here family members search for their loved ones among the dead. Courtesy American Heritage Center, University of Wyoming.

Relatives and the curious always rushed to the scenes of coal-mining disasters. Here a large crowd is gathered at the Utah Fuel Company's Castle Gate No. 2 mine, where 174 miners died in a March 1924 explosion. Courtesy Utah State Historical Society.

Only a fortunate few ever walked away from the deadly blast, flame, and after-damp of a major coal-mine explosion. Here rescue workers assist a survivor of the 1943 explosion in the Smith Mine, near Red Lodge, Montana, which killed 74 miners. Courtesy Flash's Studio, Red Lodge, Montana.

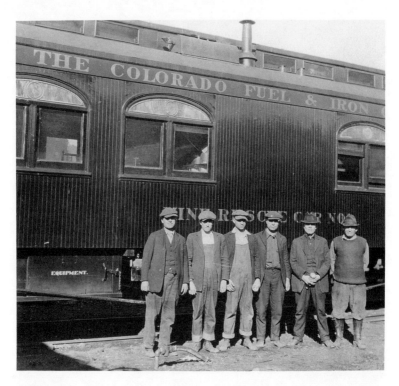

By the early twentieth century, major operators and government agencies were developing safety and rescue programs. The Colorado Fuel and Iron Company in 1910 placed in service a mine rescue car, the first of its kind in the United States. Other operators and the newly established U.S. Bureau of Mines soon followed CF&I's example. Courtesy CF&I Steel Corporation.

Interior of the Colorado Fuel and Iron Company's rescue car, with breathing apparatus and flame safety lamps (*upper right*). Courtesy CF&I Steel Corporation.

A mine rescue team at the Colorado Fuel and Iron Company's Primero Mine practices rescue techniques. An explosion at Primero in 1910 took 75 lives. Courtesy CF&I Steel Corporation.

John D. Rockefeller, Jr. (*front, center*), toured Colorado in 1915 to promote his industrial representation plan, which included worker-management safety committees. CF&I photo, Coal Project Archive, Western Historical Collections, University of Colorado, Boulder.

By the 1930s many coal companies were sponsoring first-aid training programs. Here CF&I employees practice bandaging techniques at a company first-aid contest (probably 1920s). CF&I photo, Coal Project Archive, Western Historical Collections, University of Colorado, Boulder.

Rock dusting in the Colorado Fuel and Iron Company's Allen Mine, 1954. Spraying pulverized limestone, or other soft rock, suppressed explosive coal dust. Sprinkling with water was another technique for controlling dust. Courtesy CF&I Steel Corporation.

Dust barriers in the Colorado Fuel and Iron Company's Robinson Mine. The force of an explosion would blow the heavy rock dust into the air, helping to suppress flames. Courtesy CF&I Steel Corporation.

By the early twentieth century, mechanization had begun to change the nature of work in the coal mines and eventually helped to bring about safer conditions. Miners pose here with a punching machine used for undercutting (probably c. 1910–20). They continued to use dangerous open-flame lamps long after technology changed other aspects of their work.

Cutting machines replaced the skilled miner and his pick and performed the task of undercutting the coal faster. The bulky machines were most suitable for mines with thick, level seams. Courtesy Colorado Historical Society, F-44911.

Electrically powered locomotives, such as this Jeffrey trolley motor, had replaced mules in most western coal mines by the 1930s. Courtesy Colorado Historical Society, F-32454.

Loading machines, such as this Jeffrey L-600, loaded the broken coal directly into cars or onto conveyor belts. Courtesy American Heritage Center, University of Wyoming.

Continuous mining machines completed the mechanization of the coal miner's work. Machines such as this Joy Continuous Miner sheared the coal from the face and loaded it into cars or onto conveyors. Courtesy American Heritage Center, University of Wyoming.

Chapter 6

Death and Rebellion, 1913-1933

"Well, this is my last load of coal," Michael Streeman said to a fellow miner in the Daniels Mine, near Colorado Springs, on the afternoon of 4 May 1913. "I am going to California Monday night with my wife and two children." Seconds later, seven tons of shale crushed Streeman to death. His companion, only twenty feet away, was not injured.[1]

Michael Streeman died exactly one month after Colorado's coal-mining act of 1913 became law. His was one of the first of more than thirteen hundred deaths in the first two decades after 1913. Miners in Colorado continued to die in large numbers in falls of rock and coal, haulage accidents, explosions, and, increasingly, in accidents involving mining machines and electricity. Similar trends occurred in the other Rocky Mountain coal-mining states.

Although continued high casualty rates owed much to defects in the mining laws and to persistent attitudes on safety responsibility that put the greatest burden on miners, the general industrial environment also was an important factor. The year 1913 began two troubled decades in the coal-mining industry: years marked by labor upheaval, industrial paternalism, a new legal environment, and changes in work brought about by economic conditions.

In 1925 the U.S. Coal Commission found irregular production to be the fundamental problem in coal. As competing fuels—petroleum

and natural gas—cut into the demand for coal, the industry experienced cycles of boom and bust. For coal consumers, that meant
fluctuating supplies and prices; for operators and labor, it meant
grappling with the underlying causes of unsteady production: overcapacity and poor labor relations.[2]

Operators' efforts to control costs fell heavily on workers, who
suffered erratic employment and declining wages. Operators fiercely
resisted their employees' attempts to win better wages and job security through unionization and collective bargaining. That resistance, in turn, led to major episodes of labor unrest throughout the
industry.

The coal-producing states of the Rocky Mountain West were not
immune to the industrial and labor conditions described by the Coal
Commission. Throughout the region, production climbed steadily
until the first years of the twentieth century and then declined. After
a brief resurgence during and immediately after World War I, production fell steadily throughout the twenties, especially as oil and
natural gas took over a larger share of the fuel market. The onset of
the Great Depression accelerated coal's decline. In Colorado production fell from 12.6 million tons in 1918 to 5.5 million tons in 1933.
Similar trends occurred in New Mexico, Utah, Wyoming, and Montana, with production reaching highs during or immediately after the
war and declining throughout the twenties and early thirties.

Accompanying the decline in total output was an increase in the
percentage of machine-produced coal, as operators, hoping to make
their product more competitive, sought to replace human labor with
more productive, and less troublesome, mechanical devices. In Colorado, machine-mined coal accounted for 24 percent of total production in 1913. In 1918, the peak year, machines produced 39 percent of
the coal. By 1933 61 percent was machine mined. In Montana,
machine mining in 1933 accounted for about 60 percent of production. Mechanization in Utah and Wyoming was even more pronounced, with machine-mined coal accounting for more than 80
percent of total production in each state in 1933. Only in New
Mexico, where many mines were unsuitable for machines, did pick
mining continue to dominate, producing almost 78 percent of the
state's coal in 1933.

As the industry declined, so too did the condition of the coal miners. Not only did they experience wage instability, but total employment and days worked declined through most of the period. Employment in Colorado, for example, reached 14,374 in 1918, then fell to 8,179 in 1933. Miners in the state worked an average of 192 days in 1913; in 1920 they worked 256 days. Annual workdays rose and fell erratically through most of the twenties but declined steadily after 1927. In 1933 miners averaged only 139.5 days.[3]

Declining wages, fewer jobs, and fewer workdays increased the economic pressure on miners to produce as much coal as possible whenever they had work. Even the growing numbers of machine operators felt this pressure since most of them also were paid tonnage rates. Thus, economic decline in the industry gave miners more incentive to neglect and avoid safety-related work, such as timbering their rooms, in favor of digging and loading coal.

Falling income was, of course, only one of many grievances miners nursed in the second and third decades of the twentieth century. They also resented harassment by mine officials and camp guards, felt cheated by high prices at company stores, and complained of poor housing and sanitary conditions in the camps. Mine workers were far from passive in the face of changing industrial conditions that threatened their livelihoods and their lives. They resisted, and their main weapons were union organization and the strike.

In September 1913, just six months after the passage of Colorado's new coal-mining law, miners in the state's southern field went out on strike, beginning the most dramatic labor upheaval in the state's history. Before it was over, the Ludlow Massacre and ten days of open warfare between strikers and mine guards made the Colorado strike a national issue. Exhaustion, and intervention by the United States Army, brought the strike to its unsuccessful end in December 1914.

Though the main aims of the striking miners were wage increases and recognition of the United Mine Workers of America, safety concerns also figured in their demands. Delegates to the strike convention in September 1913 heard complaints about poor ventilation, inadequate or nonexistent manways, lack of sufficient supplies of timber at working faces, and uncompensated deadwork. Reflecting these complaints, the convention adopted strike demands including pay schedules for deadwork and strict enforcement of the state's mining laws.[4] At the time, miners apparently believed that Colorado's new coal-mining law actually promised safer conditions but was not yet adequately enforced.

During the strike, union broadsides accused coal operators of deliberately sacrificing the lives of coal miners for profits. Colorado's coal companies, the union charged, had long been known for their "wanton disregard and criminal negligence of life." When the operators refused to submit the strike to arbitration, the union answered that "there is something to arbitrate" when mine owners, because of their criminal negligence, disobedience of the law, improper management, and inadequate ventilation, killed almost three times as many men as the average for coal mining in the United States.[5]

Coal operators rejected the union's claims about unsafe conditions in the mines. In a letter to Colorado newspaper editors, Frank E. Gove, attorney for the Victor-American Fuel Company, claimed that "conditions in this state are recognized as far better than in most of the states of the union." Furthermore, he declared, the coal operator was "neither a brute nor a fool" and would not "knowingly subject his property to destruction nor his men to unnecessary danger." Selfish interests alone, he said, dictated a contrary policy. In addition, Gove said, Colorado now had "the most advanced and stringent law of any State . . . regulating the conduct of coal mines." It would be well, he argued, to "await the effect of the enforcement of this law before giving too much heed to careless criticism of existing operating methods affecting the welfare of the miners and employers alike."[6] Six months, and incidents such as the death of Michael Streeman, apparently did not, in Gove's opinion, provide an adequate test of the new law or its enforcement.

Gove's employer, John C. Osgood, also took note of the new coal-mining law in answering the strikers' demand for strict enforcement. Osgood declared that the coal-mine inspection department was enforcing the law and that Chief Inspector James Dalrymple and his deputies enjoyed "the hearty cooperation of every mine operator in the state."[7]

Osgood was a member, with the Colorado Fuel and Iron Company's J. F. Welborn and Rocky Mountain Fuel's D. W. Brown, of a committee of coal-mine operators and managers who acted as spokesmen for the industry during the strike. In a series of pamphlets distributed throughout the country, the committee tried to refute the strikers' grievances and demands, including those concerning dead-work, safety conditions, and regulation. Miners, for example, complained that operators did not pay them for much deadwork, such as carrying timbers and rails long distances. The managers' committee asserted, however, that tonnage rates fully compensated miners for deadwork. Moreover, they claimed that the fact that the union had called for no really major changes in working conditions, other than recognition of the union itself, proved that "there was no substantial cause of complaint" on the strikers' part. As to the coal-mining law and its enforcement, the managers declared that the new law was "second to none . . . particularly in the protection it affords to mine workmen," and that "no fair-minded residents of the State" could doubt "the ability of the regularly constituted authorities to secure its enforcement without the aid of the labor organization."[8]

The 1913–14 strike did not achieve its economic and organizational goals and ended as a major setback for the United Mine Workers of America. In the aftermath the union practically withdrew from Colorado and engaged in little new organizing activity for more than a decade.

Nonetheless, the strike did result in two major official investigations into conditions in the coal mines of Colorado. In hearings conducted during the strike by a congressional committee, and afterward by the U.S. Commission on Industrial Relations, miners, labor leaders, and operators gave their views on all aspects of labor relations in the industry, including safety and death in the mines.

The Committee on Mines and Mining of the U.S. House of Representatives held hearings in the spring and summer of 1914 while the strike was still in progress. The hearings focused on the issues of the miners' right to organize, their economic grievances, social and political conditions in the coalfields, and violence in the strike. The question of safety in the mines also came up as miners and their representatives restated their grievances over poor mine ventilation, inadequate supplies of timbers, and deadwork. The UMWA's Edward L. Doyle, a leader of the strike, summed up the miners' attitude, telling the committee that he had seen enough men hurt in the mines to know that, "if a commodity isn't worth enough to protect life and limb in the production of it, society ought to be ashamed to ask that life be given for" it.[9]

Major operators answered the strikers' complaints by pointing out that they had spent much money and effort trying to make their mines as safe as possible. CF & I's Jesse F. Welborn told the committee that his company's efforts included its rescue cars and first-aid training. The company also had assigned more assistant foremen, "very largely to see that the men carried out their instructions." This was necessary, Welborn said, because "unless they are watched they don't do it."[10] Miners, however, believed that the operators' real motive for increasing supervision was to force them to do more deadwork.

Victor-American's John C. Osgood, assuming the role of industry spokesman, had the most to say at the hearings. Osgood told the committee that his company, and others, had spent large sums of money "in introducing improvements not required by law and in making experiments for improvements to promote the safety of our miners." These expenditures were made "regardless of any provisions of the law."[11] Other than hiring some "special inspectors," however, Osgood did not disclose what improvements and experiments his and other companies had made beyond those required by law.

Asked to compare Colorado's coal-mine fatality rates with those of unionized states, Osgood admitted that he had not studied the statistics but declared, nonetheless, that the state's poor record stemmed from the series of explosions in 1910. Asked again about the high rate of death in Colorado's coal mines, Osgood conceded that he did not even know how many had been killed in his own mines.[12]

Nevertheless, Osgood was emphatic in his view that union mines were no safer than open shops. In fact, he pointed out that a commission of mining experts from Germany, England, France, and Belgium had toured Colorado and told him that they found that "we were very up-to-date in our methods of preventing a coal mine disaster." The only major difference between European and western mines was that in Europe there were "heavy fines and prison sentences to miners who violated the law, endangering the lives of other miners." The Europeans believed that "we ought to have the protection of that kind of a law."[13]

The U.S. Commission on Industrial Relations, like the congressional committee, spent most of its time on the main issues of the strike: recognition of the union, wages, and social and political conditions in the coalfields. Once again, however, safety conditions were discussed and, once again, Osgood had something to say. Asked if any of his employees had ever complained of conditions in the mines or of violations of the coal-mining law, Osgood said that "he had never heard any complaint of that kind." He went on to explain that "a vast number" of accidents were due to recklessness. One of the great difficulties that coal operators contended with, he said, was that "a man will take a chance in that inherent spirit there is in human nature to gamble and take chances and run the risk of receiving injury that is entirely unnecessary." Noting that recklessness was especially a problem with older, experienced miners, Osgood, without realizing it, touched on the economic incentive for miners to take chances. Whereas a new and inexperienced miner "will take every precaution," Osgood noted, the old, seasoned man would say to himself, 'I will load this car out and take a chance.'" Osgood compared such foolhardiness with that of a small boy who "runs out in front of an automobile . . . to see how close he can come to it without being run down."[14]

Though Osgood held the commission's attention for many hours, some of the most important testimony in the hearings came from United Mine Workers leaders and from the man ultimately in charge of the Colorado Fuel and Iron Company, John D. Rockefeller, Jr.

Labor leaders were especially critical of the alleged nonobservance of the coal-mining law by operators. John McLennan, of the Colorado State Federation of Labor, told the commission that the "two greatest contributing causes" of death in the mines were the hiring of inexperienced miners and "the neglect of the companies to enforce the mining laws." Edward L. Doyle agreed that "the mining laws were never paid attention to."[15]

One reason for Colorado's high coal-mine fatality rates, said Frank J. Hayes, international vice-president of the union, was that, without an organization, miners were afraid to complain about dangerous working conditions. "Lots of times," Hayes said, a miner would "rather take a chance with his life than take a chance with his job." John R. Lawson, principal organizer and leader of the strike, agreed that the miners' fears of losing their jobs made them reluctant to complain about working conditions. Lawson explained that in non-union camps miners could not even "notify the mining inspector of the conditions that exist there without jeopardizing their positions."[16]

Lawson worried about other barriers to better conditions in the mines. The complexity of modern industrial organizations, he argued, created a distance between workers and employers that led to an attitude of indifference to the safety and welfare of employees. In modern industry men labored for "an employer who is never seen, and whose power . . . is handed down from man to man until there is a chain that no individual can climb." The "energies and futures" of these workers were "capitalized by financiers in distant cities," and their "conditions of labor held of less account than dividends." "Our masters," Lawson said, too often were "men who have never seen us, who care nothing for us, and will not, or can not hear the cry of our despair."[17] Only through unionization could workers counter the power of modern corporations and close the distance between themselves and their unseen employers.

In describing the institutional distance between workers and employers, Lawson had in mind the relationship between the employees of the Colorado Fuel and Iron Company and their ultimate employer, John D. Rockefeller, Jr. Rockefeller told the Industrial Commission that, as a director of the company, he left day-to-day operations in the hands of his executives, in whom he had great confidence. Rockefeller believed that CF&I's managers had been "diligent in their efforts to reduce to the minimum the possibility of accidents." He did not know, however, how accident rates in Colorado's coal-mining industry compared with those in other states.[18]

Rockefeller asserted that most mishaps were due to miners' carelessness. Hard as the officers and superintendents of a mining company might try, he said, "it is often an exceedings [*sic*] difficult thing to enforce regulations on the men themselves" and to "make them careful not to take risks and not to involve other men in risks." Asked if miners sometimes took risks for economic reasons, Rockefeller was evasive and only restated his view that "men are very careless about observing the requirements and regulations which prevent or help to prevent accidents."[19]

The 1913–14 strike and the Ludlow Massacre were a public relations disaster for the Rockefellers. Following the fighting at Ludlow, the family was the target of attacks in the press and from the pulpit. Anti-Rockefeller street demonstrations occurred around the country, too, including a huge gathering outside the Rockefeller offices in New York City.

In a public relations campaign that included a tour of Colorado,

Rockefeller attempted to counter negative publicity about C F & I and himself. During his trip to the state in 1915 the dapper New York financier donned crisp new overalls and toured company mines, dined with miners, attended a camp dance, and visited the monument at Ludlow. Besides demonstrating his common touch, Rockefeller's visit had another purpose: to promote his plan for building good relations between the company and its workers.

Though Rockefeller believed that he and the corporation bore no responsibility for the events of 1913–14, he was genuinely shocked by the strike and its violence. He had a vision of modern industrial capitalism as a cooperative system. The coalfield war flew in the face of that ideal. Now he set out to show that his vision, not Ludlow, would define the future of industrial relations. Rockefeller told the Industrial Commission that because a corporation was composed of stockholders, directors, officers, and workers, "the real interests of all are one, and . . . neither labor nor capital can permanently prosper unless the just rights of both are conserved." He added that it was his belief that a person rendered the greatest service to society when he cooperated in the organization of industry "to afford to the largest number of men the greatest opportunity for self-development" and to enable each person to enjoy "those benefits which his own work adds to the wealth of civilization."[20] Of course, Rockefeller's idealized notion of modern industry as a cooperative system overlooked the reality that the stockholders, directors, and officers wielded the preponderance of power, especially when the workers remained unorganized.

Because industrialism had wiped out the personal relationship between masters and servants of a bygone era, good intentions alone could not protect the interests of working people. Rockefeller recognized that workers needed a voice, a means of bridging the institutional distance between themselves and their employers. However, he could not bring himself to recognize the United Mine Workers, or any other union, as that voice. Instead, he sought some arrangement that would give C F & I's workers a means of having grievances heard and answered in an orderly and fair way but that required no recognition of outside organizations and no fundamental concession of authority by management.

Rockefeller turned for advice to W. MacKenzie King, a prominent Canadian political figure and labor expert. King devised a program that combined features of a formal grievance procedure and a company union. Accepted by the company's coal miners in 1915, this Colorado Industrial Plan, or Rockefeller Plan, called for the election of employees' representatives to meet regularly with company officers to present grievances and proposals for improving working conditions.[21] Although employees' representatives and company officials would discuss grievances and other issues, management alone would make all decisions. Thus, although the plan established a formal grievance procedure for employees, the company retained full authority.

Along with this grievance procedure, the plan also instituted some management-employee committees to advise the company on ways of improving living and working conditions in its camps, mines, and mills. Among these were the Joint Committees on Safety and Accidents, concerned with "any matter pertaining to the inspection of mines, the prevention of accidents, the safeguarding of machinery and dangerous working places, the use of explosives, fire protection, first aid, etc."[22] Under the plan the company's mining operations were divided into a number of districts, each with a local safety committee that inspected every mine three times per year. The committee reported any problems and recommendations to superintendents and to company officials in Denver, who would decide what, if any, action to take.

A Russell Sage Foundation report on the Rockefeller Plan in 1924 found that, though the safety committees were "useful in urging recommendations upon the superintendent," they actually worked at cross-purposes with management's safety goals. Company officials wanted the committees to emphasize safety training and, at one time, hoped that they would supplement the supervisory role of foremen and firebosses by watching employees and reporting instances of carelessness. The committees, however, frustrated the company's hopes by concerning themselves mainly with physical conditions in the mines.[23]

The reluctance of miners, and even committee members, to pursue grievances beyond the mine also proved to be a major obstacle to the committees' work. Fear of retaliation often kept the men from appealing over the heads of their foremen. That fear did not augur well for the development of the kind of "successful leadership among the miners themselves" necessary to make the entire plan "a vital factor in their relations with the management." The fact was that the employees' representatives did not "take the initiative in discovering, investigating and presenting grievances."[24]

Notwithstanding these problems, state officials and the company itself thought the Rockefeller Plan and its safety program a great success. In a 1917 investigation of complaints against CF&I filed by the United Mine Workers, the Colorado Industrial Commission found that the plan was successful in dealing with problems "that constantly arise between an employer and his employees" and that the employees were "generally satisfied with its workings." The commission found that the joint committees and company officials investigated complaints promptly, considered them carefully, and adjusted them "in most instances to the satisfaction of the employee."[25]

The Colorado Fuel and Iron Company, of course, also gave the Rockefeller Plan high marks, especially for its achievements in the area of coal-mine safety. The company in 1919 reported that it had made "gratifying progress" in improving conditions in the mines as a result of the work of the safety committees. Because of the cooperation between workers and management, "safety conditions at Colorado Fuel and Iron Company mining properties constantly are kept up to the highest standards," the company declared. More than a decade later an independent church group's study of conditions in the coalfields of Colorado supported the company's claims by noting the improved conditions in the camps and mines achieved by the representation plan.[26]

In fact, by the mid-1920s CF&I's safety program included more attention to timbering and shot firing, more sprinkling in rooms and entries, electric illumination in entries, attention to safe installation of electric power and trolley lines, and safety guards on machinery. The company also maintained and enlarged its rescue and first-aid training programs and, beginning in 1926, required first-aid training for all employees.[27]

The Colorado Industrial Plan brought about real improvements in the safety and operations of CF&I's mines. But it did not alter the basic relations of work, nor did it give mine workers an effective means of countering the power of management, from the owner down to the foreman in the pit, over their working and social lives. Superintendents and foremen still had the power to hire, fire, and harass miners. Miners still had to rely on other workers—machine

operators, shot firers, and haulage men—to enable them to mine and
load coal. And most miners, whether pick men or machine operators,
still received tonnage rates. Thus, the plan did not modify the system
of work relations that put primary responsibility for safety on the
shoulders of miners, nor did it eliminate the economic incentive to
risk safety for production.

When the National Industrial Recovery Act (NIRA) of 1933 gave
them the chance, CF&I's mine workers voted to abandon the Rockefeller Plan in favor of organization by the United Mine Workers of
America.[28] Recognizing the strength of union support and the economic advantages, under the NIRA, of dealing with the union, CF&I
did not resist its coal miners' decision to drop the Rockefeller Plan.

The 1913–14 strike and the miners' grievances about safety led to
other changes in the industrial environment besides the Rockefeller
Plan. In 1915 the legislature passed the Colorado Industrial Peace
Act, which established the state Industrial Commission. The act gave
the new Industrial Commission limited authority to investigate and
mediate industrial disputes and required a thirty-day notice before
any strike could begin. During that period the commission, whose
three members included a representative of labor and a representative of employers, could investigate claims and mediate a settlement.
The commission had compulsory investigative authority in industries
such as coal mining, where labor disputes might threaten the public
interest. However, its awards were legally nonbinding unless both
parties agreed in advance to accept them. Lacking authority to arbitrate industrial disputes, the Industrial Commission proved unable
in its early years to prevent strikes and violence in coal mining and
other industries. Nonetheless, limited as its powers were, Colorado's
still was the first state industrial commission in the U.S. to have such
investigative authority.[29]

Organized labor, including the United Mine Workers, opposed
the Industrial Peace Act and, in succeeding sessions of the legislature, worked for its repeal. Labor based its opposition on the claim
that the act effectively prohibited strikes and weakened the independence of unions and their leaders. Labor also believed that the
Industrial Commission was biased in favor of business interests.[30]

In addition to investigating industrial disputes, the commission
administered Colorado's new workers' compensation program. The
program required employers of more than four persons (except ranch,

domestic, and interstate commerce workers) to participate either by contributing to the state's own compensation fund or by providing insurance through private providers, self-insurance, or mutual insurance groups. Because the state compensation fund initially charged them high premiums, most operators elected to participate in mutual insurance groups. Some, including CF&I, became self-insured. Inspector Tom Allen reported that small operators, in particular, resisted participating in the state fund because of the initial fee of one hundred fifty dollars. Operators' preference for self- or mutual insurance was so strong that as late as 1945 the state compensation fund covered only one hundred miners.[31]

Whether their employers were self-insured, joined mutual groups, or participated in the state fund, coal miners were pleased with the workers' compensation program because it assured them at least some benefits for injury or death on the job, without the expense and uncertainty of lawsuits. Miners and their families no longer had to rely on courts or the generosity of companies, unions, neighbors, or social organizations. And with the passage of workers' compensation, some miners believed they detected a new attitude toward their safety on the part of operators and mine officials. One man recalled that, before workers' compensation, a superintendent would ask at the end of the day, "Any mules killed? Any men killed?" After workers' compensation the question would be, "Any men killed? Any mules killed?"[32]

Operators, particularly the major companies, did in fact support workers' compensation. John C. Osgood told the U.S. Commission on Industrial Relations that he supported the principle of workers' compensation and that he had served for four years on a commission appointed by the legislature to study the question. Jesse F. Welborn, of CF&I, also favored workers' compensation, though he worried that if only Colorado, of the Rocky Mountain states, established it, operators in the state would suffer competitive disadvantages. His worries were soon calmed by the enactment of workers' compensation in Wyoming and Montana in 1915 and in Utah and New Mexico in 1917. Welborn also believed that operators should not be required to bear all the costs of workers' compensation. In the interests of fairness, he believed, workers "ought to contribute to the fund which is going to compensate their families for their death and injury."[33] Welborn still believed that the miners were the principal cause of mine accidents and, thus, ought to pay at least part of the costs of compensation.

Another concern was the impact of workers' compensation on small operators. One small company's president said that, though the industry should bear the costs of compensating death and injury in the mines, the burden should be distributed "in some way that will not put all the small representatives of the industry out of business." Colorado's mine inspector, James Dalrymple, was also concerned that workers' compensation might put small operators out of business but believed the risk worthwhile. Asked if the people of Colorado "consider the continuance of a business of more importance than human life," Dalrymple replied that, though he was always inclined to take "the little dog's part," he thought that "if it is necessary to protect life to put the little fellow out of business, then he ought to be put out as quick as we can put him out."[34]

Changes in common-law doctrines, as interpreted by the courts, and the enactment of employer-liability laws also made operators more amenable to workers' compensation. By 1915 legislatures and courts had weakened the doctrines of assumption of risk, fellow-servant negligence, and contributory negligence which for so long had shielded employers from paying damages in personal injury suits. In Colorado the workers' compensation law encouraged participation by voiding the common-law defenses for employers not enrolled in the program. In other words, an employer, such as a coal operator with fewer than four employees, not participating in workers' compensation could no longer use the common-law defenses if sued by an injured employee or his survivors.

Workers' compensation contained trade-offs for operators. It raised somewhat the costs of doing business, but it also freed operators from the expense of defending against lawsuits and limited the financial burden of compensating injury and death on the job to the amounts paid in insurance premiums. Furthermore, the program created positive incentives for operators to work to improve safety in the mines. Mines with low or improved accident rates benefited from lower insurance rates. Safer mines also made for other direct and indirect savings in the form of plant and equipment not damaged and production not lost.

Government officials soon noted the positive impact of workers' compensation on conditions in Colorado's coal mines. A congressional committee in 1916 reported that companies belonging to mutual insurance programs adopted uniform rules and worked together to eliminate unsafe practices. Preventing roof falls seems to have received special attention, as the committee reported that there was "undoubtedly very much more timbering being done . . . than was ever done before."[35] The committee did not state whether that increased timbering was being done by miners as deadwork or by company day men.

The defeat of the 1913–14 strike and succeeding efforts to answer some of the coal miners' grievances through the Rockefeller Plan and workers' compensation helped to produce an interlude of relative calm in Colorado's coalfields that lasted more than a decade. Declining demand and scarcer work also made miners less restive. Coal miners in Colorado struck briefly in 1919 and 1921. In both cases the miners walked out over wage disputes. In neither case was there any violence.

Peace in the Colorado coalfields ended in 1927 when the Industrial Workers of the World led the miners out on strike. The United Mine Workers' withdrawal from Colorado after the 1913–14 strike encouraged the IWW, which had enjoyed some success after World War I, to move into the state. The Wobblies' entry, in turn, prompted the UMWA to renew its own efforts, and in 1925 both unions began organizing drives. The United Mine Workers focused its activities in the southern field, while the IWW was most successful in the north. The battle to organize Colorado's coal miners escalated in October 1927, when the IWW called a strike to protest wage cuts. The strike was strongest in the northern field, and efforts to extend it into the south met with only limited success. More important, the strike became not only a struggle for union recognition and better wages and conditions, but a battle between the IWW and the UMWA.

Still fighting to recover from the defeat of 1914, outraged at the Wobblies' sin of dual unionism, and worried that the tinge of radicalism would further set back organization in Colorado, the United Mine Workers quietly advised state officials on tactics to break the strike. Mike Livoda, a leader of the 1913–14 strike and one of the UMWA's main organizers in the West, suggested using National Guard airplanes to buzz outdoor rallies. In a letter to Governor William H. Adams's secretary, Livoda described how one rally, at the Ludlow Monument, was broken up this way. Livoda also suggested rounding up local strike leaders in order to leave the strike in the hands of inexperienced outsiders.[36]

Grievances over safety and working conditions were an important factor in the 1927–28 strike. Miners complained that operators did not observe the state coal-mining law, including regulations governing ventilation and shot firing. One Rocky Mountain Fuel Company miner complained that his foreman never measured the air current at the faces, as required by law. Others said that mine bosses ordered crosscuts to be driven too far apart and permitted miners to fire shots on-shift. One man claimed that because of illegal shot firing in Rocky Mountain's Columbine Mine, "at times it would be so smokey that it would be impossible to see the trip ahead of you." Striking miners testified that, if they complained about working conditions, "they were told to quit if they did not like it."[37]

Some miners also claimed that mine officials seemed to know when the state inspector was due to visit, enabling them to clean up and attend to repairs and maintenance left undone between inspections. One man said that, when officials expected a visit from the mine inspector, "they sent props in to us," or the foreman would tell them, "I want you to timber your place good." Another man said that "sometimes we would work three or four days to get timbers in . . . before the Mine Inspector come around."[38]

To correct these conditions, the striking miners demanded that operators and mine officials agree to comply with all state mining laws. In addition, they demanded that operators and mine officials agree not to harass or discriminate against employees who complained about working conditions and insisted on enforcement of the laws. The strikers also insisted that foremen not place inexperienced men with experienced miners without the latter's consent. Other demands included a schedule of pay for deadwork; shot firing in accordance with state law; delivery of rails, ties, and timbers to the face; and timbering by company men.[39]

Despite the operators' assertions that they diligently observed the mining laws, the Colorado Industrial Commission's investigation of the strike and its causes sustained many of the miners' claims. The commission found evidence of intimidation of miners by foremen and superintendents; excessive deadwork; delays in delivery of props, ties, and rails; inadequate ventilation; and poor enforcement of the mining law by operators and officials.[40]

In the midst of the strike Josephine Roche took control of the Rocky Mountain Fuel Company, the major operator in the northern fields and, hence, a major target of the strike. Roche sympathized with the miners and was shocked by the outbreak of violence on her company's property, the Columbine Massacre of 21 November 1927, in which state policemen killed six strikers.

To bring the strike to an end, Roche decided to deal with the strikers, though not with the IWW. First, the company got its miners back to work by granting a wage increase and by issuing carefully worded statements indicating its willingness to answer the miners' grievances through some organized means. Then, in May 1928, the company announced that it would negotiate with any union approved by its employees and affiliated with the American Federation of Labor, which could only be the United Mine Workers of America. By September the UMWA had organized the Rocky Mountain Fuel Company's miners and signed a contract with the company. In addition to setting basic wage rates, the contract contained provisions affecting safety and working conditions in the mines. It provided for an eight-hour day, set specific rates for deadwork, established pit committees and grievance procedures, promised delivery of timbers near working faces, and included an explicit commitment by the company and its officials to observe state mining laws. [41]

By the time the Rocky Mountain Fuel Company and the United Mine Workers signed their contract the strike had fallen apart. Dissension among strike leaders, state intervention and harassment, and the operators' ability to hire replacements and keep the mines operating demoralized even the most diehard strikers. The Rocky Mountain Fuel contract and the defeat of the IWW thus did not lead to a stampede of operators to sign with the UMWA. Other companies steadfastly refused to deal with the union until the depression and the New Deal left them no choice.

Colorado was not the only western coal-mining state to experience labor strife in the years from 1913 through 1933. Miners in New Mexico, Utah, and Wyoming joined in local and national strikes to protest falling wages, poor living conditions, and danger in the mines. In New Mexico and Utah the contest between radical unions and the United Mine Workers was acted out, resulting in victories for the UMWA.

Persistent high death rates between 1913 and 1933 demonstrate

TABLE 3: *Coal-Mining Fatalities in the*
Rocky Mountain States and U.S., 1913–1933

Cause	Colorado		New Mexico		Utah	
	Deaths	Per 1,000 Employed	Deaths	Per 1,000 Employed	Deaths	Per 1,000 Employed
Falls of rock and coal	626	2.43	206	2.49	228	2.82
Explosions	276	0.99	430	5.03	223	2.56
Haulage	207	0.81	62	0.81	110	1.33
Machinery	9	0.03	2	0.04	7	0.08
Electricity	56	0.22	9	0.14	18	0.21
Total	1,307	5.02	734	8.81	627	7.51

Note: Totals include deaths from other causes as well as the ones listed.

that there was a real basis to miners' complaints about working conditions. In Colorado 1,307 coal-mine workers were killed in those years. Of these, 626 died in falls of rock and coal, 276 in explosions, 207 in haulage accidents, and 65 were killed by electricity and mining machines. Colorado's death rate continued to surpass national averages. The state's average annual death rate was 5.02 per thousand employed, compared to a national rate of 2.96 per thousand. For deaths from falls of rock and coal the state's rate was 2.43 per thousand, whereas the national rate was 1.46. Colorado's explosion death rate was 0.99 per thousand, far higher than the U.S. rate of 0.49. Haulage accidents killed 0.81 per thousand in Colorado and 0.50 per thousand nationally (table 3).[42]

Dangerous as Colorado was, New Mexico proved to be even worse with the highest rate of coal-mining fatalities (8.81 per thousand employed) in the Rocky Mountain region. Utah, with a death rate of 7.51 per thousand, also was more dangerous than Colorado. Montana and Wyoming, with fatality rates of 3.30 and 4.72 per thousand, were the safest of the Rocky Mountain states. Except in New Mexico, where two disasters took 383 lives, falls of rock and coal continued to be the major cause of death (see table 3).

Clearly, coal-mining laws, workers' compensation, and industrial paternalism did not prevent death in the mines. Miners continued to die in large numbers under falls of rock and coal. At the same time, the rising rates of death due to accidents involving haulage, as well

TABLE 3 *continued*

| | Wyoming | | Montana | | U.S. |
Deaths	Per 1,000 Employed	Deaths	Per 1,000 Employed	Deaths	Per 1,000 Employed
354	2.49	125	1.88	22,320	1.46
172	1.03	10	0.14	7,664	0.49
101	0.70	50	0.75	7,700	0.50
8	0.06	5	0.06	*	*
16	0.10	11	0.19	1,653	0.11
701	4.72	218	3.30	45,425	2.96

*Complete data not available.

as machinery and electricity, indicated the growing importance of mechanization of coal mining and the hazards attendant on it. And laws, regulations, and safety committees did little to reduce the rate of death due to explosions. Although Colorado, Utah, and Montana showed some improvement in that area, the region as a whole far exceeded the national rate.

Especially notable was the failure to prevent major disasters. In the years from 1913 through 1933, 1,043 miners died in eighteen major explosions in the Rocky Mountain states. These included some of the worst disasters ever, such as the explosion at the Phelps-Dodge Company's Stag Canon mine at Dawson, New Mexico, in October 1913, which killed 263. A decade later another 120 men died at Dawson. In 1917 a blast at Victor-American's Hastings mine in southern Colorado killed 121. In 1923 99 were killed at Kemmerer, Wyoming. And in 1924 171 died at Castle Gate, Utah, and 39 at Sublet, Wyoming.

The period from 1913 to 1933 witnessed tragedy and triumph in the western coal miners' struggle to organize. The period also saw a major experiment in industrial paternalism and the enactment of workers' compensation. Tragically, none of these events produced dramatic reductions in fatality rates, despite the fact that they resulted in greater awareness of the safety problem and some tangible improvements in coal-mine safety policies and practices. Continued high rates of death in the Rocky Mountain region, including the large number of deaths in major disasters, owed much to industrial and technological changes affecting the conditions in which the miners worked. Weaknesses in state laws and the persistence of those attitudes and relations of work which held mine workers primarily responsible for their safety and deaths also contributed to the enduring environment of death in the mines.

Chapter 7

Industry and Regulation, 1913-1933

Labor strife, industrial paternalism, workers' compensation, and economic decline were only some of the factors influencing work and safety in the western coal industry in the years between 1913 and 1933. Mechanization, persistent attitudes about the causes of and responsibility for accidents, problems in enforcement of the coal-mining laws, and weaknesses in the laws were just as important in shaping the environment of death in the mines.

Mechanization probably was the most important factor, besides economic conditions, affecting coal mining. Machines changed the way miners worked and how they died. Utah's mine inspector noted that it was "painfully apparent that the introduction of modern improvements, although intended for efficiency and safety," brought new dangers. Electric power lines and equipment were an especially lethal new hazard. Miners and mine officials often were not trained in the proper installation and use of electricity, nor did they appreciate its potential for causing injury and death. Alex Bisulco, a retired miner from southern Colorado, recalled his encounter with a five-hundred-volt trolley line. "It was naked in a lot of places, no shields or nothing. . . . And one time I touched it, it knocked me about fifteen feet and knocked me down." A companion was not so fortunate. "He was all wet from sweat and his lamp touched that trolley line, killed him quick, like that."[1] Improperly wired and grounded undercutting machines were another source of lethal shocks.

Mechanization also increased the risk of death and injury from roof and coal falls and explosions. Machine noise made "sounding" (testing the roof by striking it with a pick) more difficult and increased the risk that miners might not detect bad areas. In addition, machine vibration could weaken roofs thought to be safe. This concerned operators because of the hazard not only to men, but to equipment. A Union Pacific Coal Company superintendent worried that "even with the best mining skill and material there is the ever-present danger of sudden falls of overburden or sides of excavations, with the accompanying hazard of having expensive machinery buried and ruined."[2] The U.P. official said nothing of the hazard of burying and ruining miners.

Mining machines also generated great amounts of dust and, because they rapidly exposed new coal, increased the potential for gas in the rooms. And their electric power lines provided a source of ignition for explosions of gas and dust. In the 1920s and 1930s investigations of coal-mine explosions increasingly found that electric arcs from trolley lines, mining machines, and other electric equipment were probable sources of ignition.

Despite these hazards, some authorities saw mechanization as the key to safer mining. As early as 1916 the U.S. Bureau of Mines described mechanized mines as "more business-like," generally better equipped and managed, and, therefore, safer than pick mines. The U.S. Coal Commission, too, found mechanized mines to be potentially safer due to "concentration of the work area and closer supervision." Indeed, concentration of work areas and better supervision topped one Wyoming coal-mine inspector's list of reasons for his state's improved coal-mine safety record in the decade from 1924 through 1933.[3]

Mechanization, however, was far from universal in the West before 1933. Mining machinery and motorized or electric trolley haulage was expensive and beyond the reach of many small operators. Even some large operations did not mechanize. In 1924, for example, pick miners still produced more than three-fourths of the coal from Colorado Fuel and Iron Company mines. This was due to the gassy condition of many of the mines which made it too dangerous to use electricity. Poor roof conditions also kept machines out of some CF&I mines.[4]

Whether or not they worked in mechanized mines, most miners still received tonnage rates. Thus, the basic incentive to avoid deadwork remained essentially unchanged. In fact, declining production and consequent reductions in work forces and workdays put even more pressure on miners to make the most of every shift. In 1914, for example, Wyoming's mine inspector, George Blacker, linked rising fatality rates that year to economic hard times. Miners lucky enough to have jobs were more inclined to "become indifferent or neglect to exercise that degree of caution so essential to their preservation."[5]

Almost two decades later, as the Great Depression tightened its grip, New Mexico's mine inspector, Warren Bracewell, noted the impact of hard times on mines and miners. Because of declining production, many mines stood idle for days at a time. While they were closed, conditions inside changed as roofs weakened and gas accumulated. When work was again available, the miners preferred to load coal rather than attend to hazards in their rooms. To solve this problem, many New Mexico operators permitted their men to go into the mines to do deadwork, without pay, on days when they were not operating.[6]

Deadwork was a serious point of contention between miners and operators throughout the period. Operators consistently maintained that deadwork was fully compensated through tonnage rates and scheduled pay for extra work. Miners, however, believed that tonnage rates by no means compensated them for the many hours spent timbering, brushing, and laying track. In its investigation of the 1927–28 strike the Colorado Industrial Commission heard more complaints about deadwork and lost time caused by delays in delivery of timbers, track, and ties than about any other work conditions. One miner told the commission that he spent the equivalent of one full shift, eight or nine hours, per week laying track.[7]

Only in 1933, when the United Mine Workers of America and the operators of the northern field signed a contract, were steps taken to resolve the dilemma. Operators agreed to keep work areas dry, deliver timbers close to the faces, and lay track in the entries. Furthermore, the contract specified that "a miner or tonnage worker shall not be required to perform unusual deadwork for which no scale is provided or perform work in deficient places that reduce his earnings."[8]

By the 1930s unionization and mechanization had resulted in important, though not necessarily lifesaving, changes in the environment of coal mining. However, those changes did not alter the attitudes of mine inspectors and operators, who persisted in blaming mine workers for their own deaths. Carelessness and the supposed deliberate negligence of miners continued to receive much notice. Wyoming's George Blacker charged that in many cases the "gross carelessness" of a miner killed on the job was so apparent "as to almost justify the conclusion that suicide was the motive." Blacker also insisted that "the accomplishment of a task along the lines of least resistance is responsible for many serious and occasionally fatal accidents." The solution, he thought, was to teach mine workers that "the longest way around is the surest way to safety."[9]

Choosing the "longest way around," or the line of least resistance, was not just a safety choice, but an economic one as well, and mine inspectors continued to insist that miners greedily chose money over their own lives. Utah's J. F. Pettit in 1916 noted that, despite state laws, company rules, and the efforts of inspectors, "there is a tendency on the part of the miner to postpone the setting up of the prop, or to pull the loose rock or coal, until he has finished loading his car, thus exposing himself to avoidable dangers," bringing disaster to himself and "years of anguish to those left unprotected by his own carelessness." Four years later another Utah inspector was more blunt. Too many men thought only of "loading another carload of coal" and put "the dollar to be earned ahead of their own safety or the safety of their fellow workers." These men were "money mad," and their only desire was "to make as much as possible with as little effort as possible."[10] While recognizing the economic motive for avoiding deadwork, these inspectors were at a loss to explain it except in terms that laid culpability at the feet of miners. The basic fact remained that miners would continue to risk death and injury in favor of production as long as their income depended on how much coal they sent out of their rooms.

A related problem was the miners' opposition to discipline and change. Not only did they delay or avoid deadwork, even when ordered by their foremen, but they also resisted suggestions and orders of state mine inspectors. For example, New Mexico's mine inspector in 1918 found two men shooting off the solid in violation of the state's mining law. When he advised them that the law required them to undermine their coal before shooting, the men told the mine inspector "about what they could do in the Colorado mines . . . gathered up their tools and walked out and called for their time." The following year, when both employment and production declined sharply, the New Mexico inspector attributed higher death rates in the mines to "greater carelessness of the men in general" and to "resentment at strict safety discipline." When he pointed out the dangers of some careless act, the men often replied, "I do not think it is anybody else's business but my own; if I want to take the chance of being hurt, it will not hurt you."[11]

Miners also resisted technological changes in the workplace, some seemingly minor, even when made in the interest of greater safety. The U.S. Coal Commission in 1925 noted that many miners were "suspicious that measures purporting to be in the interests of safety are designed to cut down their earning power or to introduce new conditions that are of advantage to the operator only."[12] Mine workers in Colorado, for example, opposed the introduction of permissible explosives: they were more expensive than black powder and tended to break the coal into smaller pieces, creating more slack (for which the miners were not paid) and increasing the work of loading.

The Colorado Fuel and Iron Company had much difficulty in introducing electric lamps in place of the miners' traditional carbide lamps. Fuel Department manager E. H. Weitzel noted that miners objected to the lamps because "they are cumbersome and can not be worn on the cap, and they give a poor light, and a man's efficiency is reduced" by their use. In 1920, when mine inspector James Dalrymple, finding a high risk of gas explosion in CF&I's Rockvale, Coal Creek, and Fremont mines, ordered miners to use electric lamps, six hundred men struck, briefly, to protest the order, claiming that the mines were not gassy and that the lamps did not give as much light as their flame lamps.[13] Early electric lamps were, in fact, bulky and not very bright. Worse, their battery packs often leaked, causing the wearer to suffer chemical burns. Some operators added insult to injury by requiring miners to pay for recharging batteries.

Foreign-born miners still received much of the blame from inspectors and operators for persistent high death rates in the mines. Mine inspectors continued to complain of the immigrant miners' illiteracy in English and ignorance of the dangers of mining. "Their ignorance," a Wyoming mine inspector said, "brings to themselves injury and death, and at the same time they endanger the lives of others, for it often happens that the ignorance of one, causes the death of many."[14]

Mine inspectors believed that the key to keeping greedy, careless, incompetent miners from killing themselves lay in more and better supervision. James Dalrymple in 1914 told the U.S. Industrial Commission that one of the two major causes of high accident rates was incompetent miners; the other was incompetent or negligent mine officials. He and other Rocky Mountain area coal-mine inspectors held a low opinion of many foremen and superintendents. Dalrymple told the Industrial Commission that, in the case of foremen, "we find some of them who apparently care about nothing else than to sit and see that the coal is coming out all right; very little attention is given to the men working under them." He was even more caustic in his views on superintendents. Conceding that, by 1916, many mines had made "a general great improvement" in supervision, he said that wherever this was not the case the superintendent was "one of those employees who either does not understand his business, or is so lazy or indifferent that he has no interest in anything except pay day, and that only occurs semi-monthly."[15]

Utah's J. F. Pettit agreed and extended his criticism to company inspectors, firebosses, and safety officers, who, he said, were responsible for many accidents that they might have prevented had they made "honest inspections and truthful reports . . . of the findings of those inspections." New Mexico's W. W. Risdon accused foremen of "not doing all that is possible for them to do toward preventing accidents in the mines." In fact, he said, "lack of supervision and indifference to unsafe methods of working on the part of the mine foremen" were responsible for most of the fatal accidents reported in 1929. Merely instructing miners to make needed repairs was not enough, he insisted; foremen had to see to it that the men carried out their orders.[16]

Mine officials' incompetence and negligence were not the only causes of poor supervision, however. Even though state laws required certification of officials and held them responsible for enforcing coal-mine safety regulations, the scope of their jobs often made it difficult or impossible for them to see to it that miners carried out their orders. In many mines, James Dalrymple noted, "the territory to be covered and the number of employees cared for by the mine foremen and firebosses are entirely too great for them to attend to properly." According to figures collected by the Colorado coal-mine inspection department in 1918, there were only 260 foremen to supervise 10,938 underground employees in 249 mines.[17]

The ambiguous position of the foreman and the fireboss complicated the logistics of mine supervision. Responsible for enforcing the law, they were, first, employees of the mine operator. An official who too zealously enforced safety standards at the expense of production might very well find himself unemployed. Sensitive to this problem, Colorado's James Dalrymple urged on operators and superintendents the view that mine officials "should at all times have the support of their superiors in their efforts to enhance the law." Because this was not always the case, foremen and firebosses found themselves "in the position of either allowing the law to be violated or they resign their positions."[18] Dalrymple recommended certifying superintendents, as well as foremen and firebosses, and holding them equally responsible for enforcing the law.

Coal miners and labor leaders also worried about the ambiguous position of mine officials. Former employees of Phelps-Dodge's Stag Canon mine at Dawson, New Mexico, blamed the 1913 disaster there on economy measures instituted by the superintendent, who, they claimed, cut back inspections by firebosses, reduced sprinkling, and failed to act on reports of gas in the mine. Acknowledging that owners did not deliberately court fatalities in their mines, the *United Mine Workers Journal* insisted that "the hired managers, hard driven by the knowledge that their jobs depend on their ability to produce coal cheaply, take chances in order that they may save expenses." The fact that "individual miners cannot insist on the enforcement of the laws, or even the well-known commonest safeguards," further encouraged foremen and firebosses to take chances. The journal held operators and stockholders ultimately responsible for this situation. They, after all, were mainly interested in costs and profits. "Naturally, then, the man who can show the best results in the way of securing large returns on money invested is the man who holds the job of manager."[19]

In its investigation of the 1927–28 strike the Colorado Industrial Commission learned that even small operators relied mainly on reports from mine officials for information on conditions inside the mines rather than going in and seeing for themselves. If this was true of small operators, it was even more a fact of life in large companies. CF&I's E. H. Weitzel was aware that he depended on mine officials for information, and he recognized their power to frustrate company policies. Weitzel observed that company policies might be "the most liberal and of the highest possible character," yet the employees might believe the operator to be "the meanest and most unfair," simply because of a foreman's failure to carry out his instructions, "often through his unwillingness to subscribe to the policy of his superiors." Many higher company officials would be very surprised, Weitzel said, if they could "stand behind a prop . . . and overhear the foreman giving his orders and carrying [out] the policy which they have laid down."[20]

By the mid-1920s industry and government authorities had recognized the potential of mechanization to solve many of the problems of supervision. The U.S. Coal Commission concluded that mechanization, especially mechanical loading equipment, would mean better supervision because of smaller work forces and concentration of operations. In fully mechanized mines foremen could assign deadwork to day men who would have no economic incentive to avoid it. Presumably, too, machine operators would receive daily wages instead of tonnage rates. Furthermore, all workers would be under constant, direct supervision.[21]

Because of the expense, such advanced mechanization was beyond the reach of many western operators. Narrow rooms and entries, or particularly bad roof conditions requiring extensive timbering, made mechanization inappropriate for numerous mines. Thus, many operators translated their concern about the carelessness, negligence, and declining competence of mine workers and officials into other efforts to improve conditions and supervision in the mines. For example, the Rocky Mountain Coal Mining Institute in 1924 adopted a safety code recommending rules for supervision, training, electric power and equipment, ventilation, dust control, use of explosives, timbering, and haulage. The code advocated mechanization wherever possible because of its "tendency to decrease both major and minor accidents."[22] Though the code reflected and anticipated policies implemented by many of the region's mine owners, its recommendations often were too expensive for small operators.

A. C. Watts, chief engineer for the Utah Fuel Company, in 1920 discussed the virtues of the employers in his state, who, he said, were "wide-awake business men, all of a kindly nature." Utah's enlightened operators did everything that was "businessly possible" for their employees, including paying "splendid wages" and studying "the sociological side of their men." The mine workers, he said, were "well cared for" and "well satisfied." By the mid-1920s safety procedures and rules followed in Utah coal mines included the use of electric lights in travelways, electric safety lamps for the men, electric shot firing, and sprinkling. The Utah Fuel Company also offered bonuses for officials who maintained good safety records in their mines.[23]

The existence of safety rules did not guarantee their observance by miners and officials. Shortly before the 1924 Castle Gate disaster, in which 171 miners died in what was supposed to be one of the best-kept and safest mines in Utah, a U.S. Bureau of Mines safety expert reported that some mines did not follow sprinkling procedures and shot-firing regulations. Utah's coal dusts were too explosive to permit taking any chances. Unless the mines were kept up-to-date and carefully maintained, he said prophetically, the Utah coal-mining world would "hear to its dismay, that the very excellent record of the past twenty-three years as to explosions has been shattered."[24]

Following the Castle Gate disaster, Utah operators made numerous changes in their safety programs. One of the most important was the introduction of rock dusting, that is, spraying a dust of pulverized stone (such as limestone and shale) as a method of keeping coal dust down. In 1930 the state Industrial Commission reported that Utah's operators had "progressed wonderfully" in keeping their mines rock dusted. Some larger mines used rock dust not only in entries and to within thirty feet of working faces, but also in abandoned areas where unsuppressed coal dust could add to the fury of an explosion.[25]

In New Mexico, by 1925, the state mine inspector reported that operators generally had adopted the use of permissible explosives, rock dusting, dust barriers (devices containing rock dust and mounted so that the force of an explosion would cause the dust to be expelled before it, thus extinguishing any flames), sprinkling, and closed safety lamps. In addition to such basic policies, some major operators instituted some novel approaches to improving safety conditions in their mines. In 1914, for example, the Stag Canon Fuel Company, which operated Phelps-Dodge's mines at Dawson, began monthly meetings of mine officials to discuss mine-safety methods. After the 1923 disaster at Dawson (120 killed), Phelps-Dodge began experiments with steam humidification, expanded sprinkling operations, and instituted first-aid training for its employees. By 1925 the company had established a safety organization with committees in each of its camps to inspect the mines and recommend and implement safety measures. One such measure required all miners at Dawson to wear a "hard boiled cap" and to use goggles while working at the face. In 1934, as a result of its programs, Phelps-Dodge claimed a general decline in accidents.[26]

Early efforts of the Union Pacific Coal Company to promote safety programs in its mines in Wyoming "did not show appreciable results." However, by 1916 the company had equipped and stationed a rescue car at Rock Springs and set up safety committees at each of its mines. The Union Pacific employed safety inspectors in some mines to see that the miners carried out safety orders, especially in pillar work. "The mere fact of a mine foreman issuing instructions to employes to safeguard themselves," said the company's safety director, "does not always insure those instructions being carried out." Though these inspectors worked under the supervision of mine foremen, the state mine inspector reported that they were allowed "plenty of latitude" to use their judgment "when safety is concerned."[27]

Beginning in 1923 the Union Pacific Coal Company added an incentive program to encourage mine officials to look after safety. The company offered prizes, including watches, pictures, household goods, and even trips to Alaska, for the safest mine. However, it was only when the company began offering an automobile as the grand prize that the incentive program produced significant results. By 1931 the company's safety program included, in addition to contests, a code of standards for its mines, monthly inspections, and regular safety meetings for officials and mine workers. The company also used rock dusting and sprinkling to control coal dust, adopted systematic timbering methods, and required employees to wear hard hats and use electric safety lamps.[28]

In Colorado, mine inspector James Dalrymple had ample praise for operators' efforts to improve conditions in and out of the mines.

In 1919, for example, he noted that there had been "a great outlay of money" to improve tipples, powder magazines, railroad tracks, power plants, and mining machinery. In many camps operators improved housing, water, and sanitation and built churches and schools. "In fact," said Dalrymple, "the coal industry of Colorado is progressive, keeping apace with the most advanced improvements in coal mining." Four years later, in 1923, Dalrymple was enthusiastic about "all the up-to-date machinery" that had been installed during the year and "the work done to improve the underground conditions and safeguard life," as well as "to make living conditions better for the families in the various camps."[29]

Dalrymple also complimented Colorado's coal operators, especially the large companies, for "showing a commendable spirit in complying with the many provisions" of the state's new coal-mining law. Only "a few of the small companies" were not obeying some parts of the law because they were "of the opinion that these provisions" did not apply to them. In most cases, though, Dalrymple praised "the cheerful and prompt acceptance by the operators" of his deputies' suggestions "tending toward safer and more sanitary conditions in the mines." The cooperation of the operators, he said, had produced "a feeling of mutual confidence between them and the Department" which was proving to be "invaluable in our work."[30]

Dalrymple's generous praise of Colorado's operators could not disguise serious problems in coal-mine inspection and regulation. Inadequate funding, disputes over the applicability and enforcement of portions of the law, and certain amendments practically hobbled the inspector and his deputies for much of the two decades after 1913. The coal-mine inspection department's problems began almost immediately after the enactment of the 1913 law. Because of the 1913–14 strike, the coal-mine inspection fund (the revenues of which were to come from a tax on coal production) did not receive enough money to finance the department. The legislature compounded the problem by refusing to appropriate money to finance the department until the fund became solvent. In his report for 1913 Dalrymple stated that he had been unable to put many provisions of the new mining law into force, including the hiring of two additional deputy inspectors, printing vital sections of the law in foreign languages, and examining and certifying foremen, assistant foremen, and firebosses. So short were funds, in fact, that the department had to lay off two deputies for two weeks. In 1914, still working with only three deputies rather than the authorized five, Dalrymple told the U.S. Industrial Commission that "the territory is entirely too big. We cannot do justice to ourselves or to anyone connected with the industry." Asked by a congressional committee why he did not go to the legislature for money to cover his department's expenses, Dalrymple explained that he "would rather ask the devil for transportation to heaven."[31]

The coal-mine inspection department's budget problems became worse during the 1920s as production and, therefore, coal-tax revenues declined. The department in 1923 published advertisements from coal operators and industry suppliers in its annual report in order to defray printing costs. That practice continued through 1927. An increase in the coal tax in 1925 brought some relief but did not end the department's funding troubles. Indeed, in 1928, when the department's automobiles wore out, Dalrymple asked his deputies to consider buying cars of their own to use on the job. This was necessary, he said, because he had had "considerable trouble in getting the Governor to approve our requisitions for new automobiles."[32]

The onset of the depression compounded the department's already serious budget problems. By the end of 1930 the department faced a deficit, and Chief Inspector Dalrymple worried that deputies would have to be laid off and that the ninety-day inspection cycle could not be met. A study by the Federal Council of Churches of Christ in America confirmed his fears. The coal-mine inspection department was "seriously handicapped by the low salaries and inadequate expense allowances for deputy inspectors," which made it "difficult to secure and hold the ablest men for this important work."[33]

In 1932 Dalrymple laid off one deputy and warned Governor William H. Adams that the coal-mine inspection fund soon would be depleted, necessitating further reductions in force. That, he predicted, would lead to worsening conditions in the mines and higher accident rates. In fact, during 1932, staff reductions forced Dalrymple to cut back mine inspections to two per year, even though he considered semiannual visits "absolutely insufficient."[34]

By 1933 declining production had cut the income of Colorado's coal-mine inspection department to half of what it was in 1929 and 60 percent of the 1913 level. During the period from 1913 through 1933, however, the department's workload had increased greatly.

Responsible for inspecting 178 mines in 1913, Dalrymple and his shrinking force of deputies had to look after 269 in 1929 and 421 in 1933. Small mines employing one to five men especially were a problem, since, over the two decades, their number had risen from 23 to 285 and fatality rates in them were far above the state average.

Regulation and inspection of small mines proved to be Dalrymple's greatest problem. As early as 1914 he observed that, though the large coal companies cooperated in carrying out the law, "the greatest trouble we have is with the small fellows." Operated intermittently to supply local, seasonal demands, so-called wagon mines were difficult to monitor because they usually were located in isolated areas with no railroad connections and opened and closed frequently with new names and operators. Dalrymple in 1923 estimated that more than half the mines in the state were wagon mines, "generally handled by men who are unfamiliar with coal mining."[35] By the early 1930s many wagon mines were worked by unemployed men trying to scratch out a living.

Even more vexing was some small operators' resistance to enforcement of basic provisions of the coal-mining law. In 1921 and 1925 the Colorado legislature amended the law to require all mines to install ventilation fans and to employ certified formen.[36] Because of the inspection department's funding problems, aggressive enforcement of these amendments did not occur until late in 1925. When enforcement began, small operators and owners of coal lands reacted with lawsuits and a lobbying campaign to exempt small mines from the ventilation and supervision requirements.

Small operators claimed that enforcement of these regulations forced many of them to shut down. Those who stayed in business had to raise prices. One operator complained to Governor Clarence Morley that "Mr. Dalrymple with his paper jacks, certified men, and his friends, some of the large operators, will have confiscated the property of most of the little fellows" if they were not stopped. Morley, a Ku Klux Klan member who advocated elimination of most state agencies, sympathized with the small operators and answered that "the whole difficulty" arose from Dalrymple's determination "to now rigidly enforce laws which had remained practically without enforcement for about ten years."[37] Apparently, Morley believed that laws inadequately enforced previously ought to be left dormant— especially if enforcement hurt business.

Chief Inspector Dalrymple responded by arguing that owner-operators of small mines had only to install ventilation fans and take the foreman's exam to be in compliance with the law. He pointed out that his department had given numerous examinations throughout the state since 1913 but that "many of the little fellows failed to take" them. Therefore, they, not the law or the coal-mine inspector, were to blame if he shut them down. Dalrymple added that in some cases he had even bent the law by allowing wagon mines to stay open until the next exam.[38]

The chief inspector also claimed that landowners, not the law, were responsible for the higher prices of coal mined by small operators. Landowners, he said, charged royalties of fifty cents to one dollar per ton, making such coal very expensive. That fact, he argued, put to the lie charges that consumers in the remote rural areas served by these mines suffered from the amendments and his enforcement of them.[39]

During 1926 several small operators sued to restrain the inspector from closing them down; others continued to operate in defiance of the law. Early in 1926, small operators won a round when, astonishingly, a judge in Colorado Springs ruled that the ventilation and foreman provisions, as applied to small operators, were an unwarranted use of police power and violated the Fourteenth Amendment by depriving small operators of their property without due process. "The law should not make the same provisions for a one-man mine or one employing only a few men as it does for mines employing a large number of men," Judge Arthur Cornforth declared. Dalrymple vowed to appeal the ruling to the state supreme court. In the meantime, however, he ordered his deputies "not to inspect or interfere with . . . mines employing less than eleven men."[40]

Dalrymple and the coal-mining law won a partial victory when the supreme court heard his appeal of the Colorado Springs ruling. The court declared that it had "no hesitation in saying that requirements of the statute are reasonable and necessary, and a proper exercise of the legislative function." The court noted, however, that it was ruling not on "the validity of the statute as applied to a small mine operated and worked by the owner alone," but only on the facts of the case at hand, which showed that the owner and one employee worked the mine in question. Thus, although it applied to most wagon mines, the ruling potentially exempted mines worked only by owner-operators.[41]

While the battle went on in the courts, Dalrymple gathered data showing that small mines were much more dangerous than larger operations. For the period from 1913 through 1925, mines employing one to five men had an average annual fatality rate of 8.50 per thousand employed, and those employing up to ten men had a rate of 6.74 per thousand. Mines employing eleven men or more had a fatality rate of 5.90 per thousand, almost identical to the average for all mines, 5.93. Despite this evidence, the Colorado legislature in 1927 passed amendments exempting small mines from supervision and ventilation regulations. Mines employing five or fewer persons no longer were required to have certified foremen and could use either natural or artificial methods of ventilation.[42]

Chief Inspector Dalrymple quickly spotted an oversight in the amendments which enabled him to continue requiring small operators to employ certified officials. Although they no longer had to hire certified foremen, Dalrymple noted that the law still required that "all mines where more than one man is employed underground must be examined every morning . . . by a certified Fire Boss." Colorado Attorney General William L. Boatright supported Dalrymple's view that the law required firebosses in all mines, regardless of size.[43]

Dalrymple soon was under fire for requiring certified firebosses in small mines. State senators David Elliot, of Colorado Springs, and Grant Sanders, of Durango, who represented many small operators, led the attack in the statehouse. Sanders complained that he did not know where the state inspector found his authority for requiring certified firebosses, but it looked to him like "a piece of spiteful nagging." Senator Elliot told Governor William H. Adams that Dalrymple and his deputies simply were "up to their old tricks . . . of harassing and annoying the little mines of the State." Having lost on the question of certified foremen, Dalrymple was maliciously demanding that small operators employ a fireboss, "at a fancy price," to take the place of the foreman. Clearly, Elliot argued, Dalrymple was flouting the intent of the legislature, which "wanted to assist these little mines in every way possible and permit them to run in an economical manner, so that they could remain open and furnish coal to their respective communities." Apparently oblivious to the evidence of the higher rates of death and injury in small mines, Senator Elliot asserted that "there have been very few accidents in these little mines" and that Dalrymple would perform a greater public service "if he would attend more carefully to these big mines that are really more dangerous."[44]

Dalrymple disagreed and continued to argue that small mines were more, not less, dangerous than larger operations. Nevertheless, the legislature in 1929 acted to free small mines of the need to employ any certified officials. Mines employing up to five persons no longer had to employ certified foremen, assistant foremen, or fire-bosses. "This amendment," said Dalrymple, "destroys the most vital requirements of the Coal Mining Laws and consequently deprives the miners of the valuable protection guaranteed them under the present law." He pointed out that small mines had a fatality rate 40 percent higher than larger mines. In fact, the death rate in small mines was "so high that no insurance carriers would insure them, thus compelling the State" in 1927 "to pass an insurance law so that their employees might be insured" under workers' compensation. "Now that the state cannot enforce its findings relative to safety in the five-men mines," Dalrymple asked, "would it not have been more consistent to have exempted them from state inspection" altogether? He answered his own question by saying that "the life of a miner working in a five-man mine is as valuable to the country, and entitled to the same protection, as the miner working in a larger mine."[45] Dalrymple thus vowed to continue inspecting small mines and closing them whenever he and his deputies discovered dangerous conditions.

Slight improvement in the laws exempting small mines from ventilation and supervision regulations came in 1931 when the legislature changed them to apply to mines employing three or fewer persons. The same amendment, however, reduced the inspection cycle for all mines from four to two visits each year. In 1937 yet another amendment changed the inspection regimen to three visits per year in mines employing more than three persons.[46]

The amendments exempting small mines from ventilation and supervision regulations were the most important changes in Colorado's coal-mining law passed between 1913 and 1933. There were, however, other changes, mostly aimed at reducing explosion hazards. These included amendments authorizing the coal-mine inspector to require the use of safety lamps in gassy mines, mandating the use of permissible explosives in most mines, and requiring examination of rooms for gas before machine cutting or shot firing. Other amendments made certificates issued to foremen and other mine officials by the states of Wyoming, Utah, and Montana valid in Colorado.[47] This change reduced the burden of examining mine officials and made it easier for those officials to move around in this transient profession.

Wyoming in 1925 reciprocated with a law accepting officials' certificates issued by Colorado, Utah, and Montana. Other changes in Wyoming's coal-mining law included regulations governing electric power and trolley lines, rock dusting, dust barriers, sprinkling, haulage, and lamps. Wyoming also improved its shot-firing regulations and by 1930 required shot firers in all mines.[48]

Like their colleagues in Colorado, Wyoming's legislators eased the burden of inspection on small operators. A 1925 act required only annual, instead of quarterly, inspections of mines employing fewer than ten persons. A 1933 revision required annual inspection of mines employing fewer than five. Wyoming legislators also devised a financial definition of a coal-mine disaster. The state in 1925 enacted a payroll tax on coal operators to fund a special Coal Mine Catastrophe Fund. This act defined a disaster not in terms of number of deaths and injuries, but as an accident that caused payment of more than twenty-five thousand dollars in benefits.[49]

Of the Rocky Mountain states, Utah and New Mexico made the most extensive changes in their coal-mining laws. As early as 1916 Utah's mine inspector, John F. Pettit, recommended appointment of a commission to revise the law and bring it into line with technological developments. Four years later the mine-inspection department, now an agency of the Utah Industrial Commission, issued new coal-mining regulations to supplement the existing state law. The new rules, "discussed and revised by a committee of coal operators," were based on company procedures already in force in some mines and actually "more stringent" than the existing law (a claim that recalls major Colorado operators' assertions that their state's 1913 law reflected practices already employed in their mines).[50]

Disaster occasioned another round of rule making in Utah in 1924. On 8 March the Utah Fuel Company's Number Two mine, at Castle Gate, exploded. One hundred and seventy-one miners and one would-be rescuer died in the blast, which "sounded like the tremble of thunder reverberating across the hills." So powerful was the explosion that "telephone and electric light poles, timber and pipes near the manway were blown across the valley, almost a mile in width."[51] A foreman's open-flame light apparently touched off the explosion.

In the wake of the Castle Gate disaster the Utah Industrial Commission issued new regulations requiring the use of electric lamps in mines employing more than five persons; the use of permissible explosives; electric shot firing after shifts in mines employing more than three persons; rock dusting in entries, slopes, and air courses; installation of dust barriers; sprinkling of coal cutters; and sprinkling at and around working faces.[52]

Although most operators supported the new regulations, not all welcomed them. Some believed that more regulation would not necessarily improve safety in the mines and would harm the industry. William Monay, vice-president of the Kinney Coal Company of Scofield, in 1925 told a meeting of the Rocky Mountain Coal Mining Institute that "the lives and property of the coal industry will find their surest guaranty of protection," not in government regulation, but "in the humanity, and in the self-interest of those operating and working in the mines." "Inelastic, inflexible blanket statutes and rules," he said, would only "stifle and hamper the initiative and progress of our industry." Instead of rules and regulations, Monay advocated more cooperation among operators, employees, and state inspectors to make the mines safer.[53]

New Mexico's revised coal-mining law, passed in 1933, cannot be linked to a major disaster, although explosions at Madrid in 1930 and 1932 caused nineteen fatalities. New Mexico coal-mine inspectors had called for major changes in the law since at least 1924, when Inspector W. W. Risdon had asked the legislature to adopt Utah's new regulations. Larger operators in New Mexico already were following the Utah rules, which, Risdon said, were "copied verbatim" from regulations in force at the Phelps-Dodge mines at Dawson. Risdon's successor, Warren Bracewell, in 1925 also recommended a complete revision of the law, though he did not advocate adopting the Utah regulations.[54]

Finally, in 1933, the New Mexico legislature revised the state's coal-mining law. The new statute contained improvements in the areas of inspection and enforcement, explosives and shot firing, timbering, haulage, and rescue. The law required at least annual inspection of all mines and authorized the mine inspector to order the removal of hazards and prevent employees from working in hazardous areas. The new statute raised ventilation standards and required all mines, except those producing pure anthracite, to be rock dusted to within forty feet of working faces and equipped with dust barriers. With limited exceptions, the act allowed only permissible explosives and required shot firers to detonate all shots. Other regulations governed the installation of electric power lines and machinery, forbade miners to ride on coal trips, and required systematic timbering. The act called for miners to be instructed in proper techniques for testing and removing loose roof material and in correct timbering procedures. Operators were to provide first-aid training and supplies and fire-fighting equipment. Larger mines were to train and maintain rescue teams.

The new law sought to improve coal-mine supervision by requiring examination and certification of all officials, including foremen, assistant foremen, firebosses, and shot firers. The law also authorized the inspector to accept certificates issued by other states. The act required foremen or assistant foremen and firebosses to make daily inspections of all working places and see to the prompt removal of any hazards. Mine officials were to supervise inexperienced workers or pair them with experienced employees.[55]

Of the Rocky Mountain states, only Montana made no notable changes in its coal-mining law between 1913 and 1933.

By 1933 little had changed in the basic patterns of opinion and law on coal-mine safety. Operators and mine inspectors still held miners, because of their supposed carelessness, deliberate negligence, foreign birth, and incompetence, to be the main agents of their own injuries and deaths. Despite improvements in such areas as timbering, electricity, haulage, machine use, and even supervision, the coal-mining laws still focused on preventing major explosion disasters, and they were not especially effective at that. In Colorado, amendments to the coal-mining law exempted the most dangerous mines from regulations governing ventilation and supervision.

The most positive development of the period was the increased concern of mine inspectors and most operators with the quality and extent of supervision in the mines. However, until the mines were more completely mechanized, with attendant reductions of work forces and scale of operations, mine officials would continue to face the challenge of supervising large numbers of men working in pairs and scattered throughout the mine. Even mechanization, however, could not change the ambiguous position of mine officials as enforcers of law and servants of their employers. And of course, mechanization brought with it new hazards.

None of the major developments in the years between 1913 and 1933 altered the basic relations of work in the mines. Even after the coal operators of the West came to terms with the union, coal miners still worked for tonnage rates and still depended on other workers for services that enabled them to blast and load their coal. With poor economic conditions they were even more constrained to produce as much coal as possible, as fast as possible. The ultimate consequence was the same in 1933 as it was before 1913. Work relations, industrial conditions, patterns of law and enforcement, and attitudes on safety combined to create an environment of death in the mines.

The depression and war years would see changes in work relations as mechanization spread and new regulatory concerns arose. Of particular importance would be the expanding role of the federal government in coal-mine safety and regulation.

Chapter 8

Safety and Regulation
in Depression and War

The 1928 contract between Josephine Roche's Rocky Mountain Fuel Company and the United Mine Workers of America inspired a moment of optimism within the ranks of organized labor. Labor leaders and miners hoped that after this breakthrough the remaining unorganized companies in Colorado and the West soon would come to terms with the union. Instead, for the next five years labor waged a struggle against wage cuts and work reductions caused by the deepening depression.

Labor had as one of its strongest assets the argument that organization offered the industry stability in the key area of labor relations. Industrial stability also was a major goal of the new administration of President Franklin D. Roosevelt. The National Industrial Recovery Act (NIRA) of 1933 made union organization an important element in the federal government's economic recovery program. In order to benefit from the NIRA's controls on price and production, operators had to recognize their employees' right to organize and bargain collectively. By the end of 1933 Colorado's coal operators, and most of those in New Mexico, had signed contracts with the United Mine Workers. The National Miners Union originally organized New Mexico's Gallup district but by 1940 had yielded to the United Mine Workers. Utah's coal miners organized by the end of 1934. Miners in Wyoming and Montana organized earlier in the century.

Unionization was only one feature of the industrial environment in the 1930s and 1940s, years of change conditioned by the stresses of depression and war. During these years state mine inspectors began or expanded training programs for miners and supervisors. Federal programs tried to bring economic stability to the industry through controls on production, price, and labor. And for the first time, the federal government became directly involved in coal-mine inspection.

The old cycle of boom and bust continued in the western coal industry during the Great Depression and World War II. In Colorado, production fell to 5.2 million tons in 1934. With the slow economic recovery of the mid-1930s, production rose to 7.2 million tons in 1937, but it fell to below 6 million tons after the recession of 1937–38. Wartime demands pushed production to 8.3 million tons in 1943. In 1945, however, Colorado's coal mines produced 7.6 million tons, little better than the "peak" depression year of 1937. A similar pattern occurred in New Mexico, where production in 1945 (1.4 million tons) exceeded the 1934 level (1.2 million tons) by only 141,391 tons. Wartime production in New Mexico peaked at 1.8 million tons in 1943. Utah, Wyoming, and Montana were able to sustain production levels significantly higher in 1945 than during the depression years. In Utah, production in 1934 was 2.4 million tons, rose to 7.2 million in 1944, and remained at 6.7 million tons in 1945. Wyoming's coal mines produced 4.3 million tons in 1934 and 9.8 million tons in 1945. In Montana, production rose from 2.5 million tons in 1934 and 4.5 million tons in 1945.

Growth, or the lack of it, directly affected the coal miners' fortunes. In four of the five Rocky Mountain coal-mining states, employment declined between 1937 and 1945. Only in Utah were more miners at work in 1945 than in 1937. However, although total employment tended to decline, average annual days worked at the mines increased. In Colorado, for example, the mines operated an average of 143 days in 1934. In 1937 they were open 202 days; in 1945, 207 days. Thus, between 1934 and 1945 the tendency was for fewer men to work more days.

The continued progress of mechanization in the mines largely explains this trend. In Colorado approximately 63 percent of the coal was mined by machines in 1934. Machine production fell to 50 percent in 1937 but rose again to 76 percent in 1945. In Utah and

Wyoming practically all of the coal was machine mined in 1945. Even New Mexico, which had lagged far behind in mechanization, reached 79 percent machine production in 1945. Montana's coal industry contradicted the general trend with the percentage of machine-mined coal from underground mines falling from 52 percent in 1934 to 41 percent in 1945. By 1945, however, almost 58 percent of the state's coal was being taken from surface mines as major operators curtailed underground operations. In general, the growing use of coal-cutting machines and mechanical loaders reduced the need for human labor, especially skilled pick miners.

The shift to mechanization did not, however, immediately reduce the pressure on coal miners to produce as much coal as possible as fast as possible. During the depression years miners were determined to make as much as they could whenever they had work. The war years did not alleviate that pressure. As shown, total employment tended to decline during World War II. Thus, even though the industry enjoyed some growth, miners still faced unemployment. In addition, exhortations from government, employers, and unions to keep the coal coming for national defense added to the pressure on miners to produce.

Throughout the depression and war years the federal government tried to bring a measure of stability to the coal industry through production, price, and wage controls. However, federal concern with conditions in the coal industry did not effectively reach inside the mines. The states retained primary responsibility for regulating safety and working conditions, even after the enactment of the first federal coal-mine inspection law in 1941.

In Colorado, Chief Inspector James Dalrymple continued his fight to restore effective regulation in small coal mines, but he did not live to see the battle through. In October 1934 he was struck and killed by an automobile as he stepped into a street in Florence, Colorado. Dalrymple had served as coal-mine inspector in Colorado for two decades; his successor, Thomas Allen, held the job for three. Like Dalrymple, Allen was an immigrant from Great Britain. In contrast to the dour Scotsman Dalrymple, Tom Allen was an outgoing, sometimes flamboyant son of the Newcastle region of northern England. Trained as a mining engineer, Allen came to the United States in 1907 and worked as a foreman, superintendent, and engineer in Wyoming, Colorado, and New Mexico until 1927, when he joined

Colorado's coal-mine inspection department. Allen did not get along with Dalrymple and left the department in 1930 to form his own mine-engineering firm. Following Dalrymple's death, Allen tested for the position of chief inspector and won the job.

Tom Allen was an early student of the U.S. Bureau of Mines' first-aid and mine-rescue training program and received the bureau's certificate in 1913. During his career as a mine official and engineer, he promoted first-aid and rescue training for coal miners. When he became head of Colorado's coal-mine inspection department, rescue and first-aid training, along with vocational education, became a mainstay of his administration.

Allen also believed that safety, productivity, and good labor relations required a change in the way the industry recruited its workers. The chief inspector in 1935 told a session of the Rocky Mountain Coal Mining Institute that the old ways of recruiting and training miners no longer worked. "You cannot take any farmer anymore, or any foreigner, and put him into your mine," Allen said. Beginning with a period of apprenticeship, "you have to get the kids out of school and take them in and drill them right on through." The industry also had to convince prospective workers that coal mining was "a decent occupation" and not merely "a stepping stone to the position of proprietor of a hot dog stand when you accumulate enough dollars to get away."[1] By 1938 Allen's hopes for a vocational training program for coal miners had borne some fruit. In Lafayette, Colorado, the local school board, in cooperation with the State Board of Vocational Training and the National Youth Administration, opened a coal-mining school.

Still, disaster response—rescue and first aid—remained the main focus of miner training programs in Colorado. The first major rescue and first-aid training program in Colorado began in 1935 as a cooperative effort by the State Board of Vocational Training, the UMWA, and operators. In 1936 the program was expanded to include women, and by the end of the year the U.S. Bureau of Mines had certified a women's team from northern Colorado, the first to be so recognized. Now women would have something to do in a disaster besides waiting at the portal to identify their dead.

Colorado's coal-mine inspection department in 1937 acted to improve its disaster response capability by acquiring and equipping a truck to transport rescue personnel and equipment to disaster scenes.

The Colorado Courtesy Patrol, the National Guard, and the Public Service Company of Colorado agreed to supply additional personnel and equipment for use in coal-mine emergencies. The department assembled a central file of persons trained in first aid and rescue work, and teams of Works Progress Administration workers prepared supplies of bandages and splints. By 1940 some three thousand persons in Colorado had received rescue and first-aid training, and nearly two thousand had taken state or federal accident-prevention courses.

Meanwhile, little state-sponsored training activity occurred in the other Rocky Mountain states. Where rescue and first-aid training programs existed, coal operators and the U.S. Bureau of Mines conducted them.

Budgetary and political problems in the 1930s hampered Chief Inspector Allen's efforts to promote training for coal miners—indeed, to carry out the basic functions of his department. Like his predecessor and his colleagues in other states, Allen faced budget deficiencies that threatened to force cuts in the department's activities and work force. An annual coal-mine license fee, enacted in 1935, provided some additional revenue, but most of the department's budget continued to come from the state coal tax. In March 1934 the Rocky Mountain Mining Institute adopted a resolution in favor of supplementing or replacing the coal-mine inspection fund with a general appropriation. That idea, however, was short-lived. On the same day the institute acted on its resolution, Colorado Attorney General Paul Prosser issued an opinion declaring that "public funds may not be used to supplement the Coal Mine Inspection Fund."[2] The coal-mining law required that all funds for the department come from the coal tax. Allen and his department would have to await either a change in the law to allow supplemental appropriations or increased tax revenues via a return of prosperity in the coal industry, neither of which seemed imminent in the mid-1930s.

An ongoing feud with the Dalrymple family also plagued Tom Allen's administration of the inspection department. The Dalrymples had come to regard the department as a family fiefdom and, to say the least, were distressed when Allen, a family enemy, took over as chief inspector. In the weeks between Allen's interim appointment by Governor Edwin C. Johnson and his final confirmation by the Civil Service Commission, the Dalrymples promoted the candidacy of Deputy Inspector Finley McCallum, a family friend. Allen complained to Governor Johnson that the Dalrymple family "left no stone unturned" to harm him, including soliciting petitions from mine owners, threatening lawsuits, and trying to line up union men against him. In November 1934 the governor answered a letter from an Allen supporter who claimed that many of the new inspector's opponents were mine owners "who are too greedy for earnings with the least expense regardless of the jeopardy to the lives of the workers." Johnson noted that that conclusion "checks exactly with my understanding of the situation."[3]

Once the Civil Service Commission confirmed his appointment, Allen moved quickly to settle the score with the Dalrymples. In December 1934 the new chief inspector proposed to ease the department's budget problems by imposing a new minimum twenty-five-dollar inspection tax on all mines and by laying off deputy inspectors Finley McCallum and George Dalrymple, the latter being one of the former inspector's sons. Governor Johnson thought that the proposed new tax was a good idea but cautioned that the layoffs "might cause such a fight" as to damage prospects for the tax.[4] Despite the governor's concern, Allen proceeded to lay off McCallum and Dalrymple.

The battle was renewed in November 1937 when James Dalrymple, Jr., another son of the late chief inspector, filed formal charges against Allen with the Civil Service Commission. In his complaint Dalrymple accused Allen of "inefficiency, indifference, neglect, and a wilful and unpardonable disregard and violation" of the laws and regulations relating to the coal-mine inspection office. The complaint specifically alleged that Allen was guilty of nepotism in hiring his son as a temporary inspector; that he had failed to appoint a full complement of deputies from the civil-service list; that he had misallocated state funds by creating titles and paying salaries not authorized by law; that he allowed his daughter to use a state-owned vehicle; and that he overassessed operators in collecting the coal tax. Dalrymple also charged Allen with responsibility for the January 1936 explosion at the Monarch Mine, in Boulder County, in which eight miners died. Allen allegedly knew that the mine was gassy but allowed it to continue to operate with inadequate ventilation. Dalrymple concluded his complaint with the assertion that, under Allen's administration, the coal-mine inspection department was "viewed not only with suspicion and distrust, but as an object of ridicule by many fair-minded citizens of this state."[5]

Dalrymple's charges of nepotism and other abuses of office were ironic since he and his brother, George, had served their father as deputy inspectors. In 1929 an anonymous letter to Governor William H. Adams, typed on Colorado Fuel and Iron Company letterhead, complained that for a dozen years one of the Dalrymple sons had placed first in every examination held by the Board of Coal Mine Examiners, the body responsible for examining deputy inspectors and prospective coal-mine officials. In June 1933 Governor Johnson informed Chief Inspector Dalrymple that he had received complaints that James, Jr., "was taking orders for powder from the various coal mines" in Fremont County "and intimating that if the orders were forthcoming it might be easier for the mines to pass inspection." A man who claimed to be friendly with both the Dalrymples and Allen told Johnson's successor, Governor Teller Ammons, that "Jim Dalrymple misses the [inspector's] office influence in selling powder and his business has fallen off."[6]

In addition to personal enmity and business concerns, larger political forces were at work in the Dalrymple-Allen feud. In 1934 the Rocky Mountain Fuel Company's Josephine Roche, a strong supporter of the New Deal, challenged the more conservative incumbent, Edwin C. Johnson, for the Democratic party's gubernatorial nomination. A columnist in the *Pueblo Daily Chieftain* reported that Chief Inspector Dalrymple "and about all the employees under him" supported Roche in the primary. Johnson prevailed and "started in to get the jobs of all who had been against him." Though there is no evidence that the governor tried to remove Dalrymple before his death, Johnson was able to punish the family by denying them continued control of the coal-mine inspection department after Dalrymple died. With Johnson's departure for the U.S. Senate in 1937, the Dalrymples may have seen their chance to settle the score with Allen. The civil-service charges, the *Chieftain* columnist said, were part of the fight. Allen, he concluded, "may be off on some of the things he has done, but the guess of the people who have watched the fight is that he is off more politically than he is through failure to perform his official duties correctly."[7]

The Colorado Civil Service Commission found that Dalrymple's

TABLE 4: *Coal-Mining Fatalities in the*
Rocky Mountain States and U.S., 1934–1940

Cause	Colorado		New Mexico		Utah	
	Deaths	Per 1,000 Employed	Deaths	Per 1,000 Employed	Deaths	Per 1,000 Employed
Falls of rock and coal	102	1.69	30	1.89	30	1.48
Explosions	18	0.29	0	0	0	0
Haulage	23	0.38	11	0.66	18	0.90
Machinery	4	0.07	0	0	3	0.15
Electricity	11	0.18	4	0.24	1	0.04
Total	181	3.00	50	3.12	55	2.73

Note: Totals include deaths from other causes as well as the ones listed.

evidence did not substantiate the charges and dismissed the complaint. This was the last round in the Dalrymple-Allen feud. It was not, however, the last serious attack on Allen and his administration of the coal-mine inspection department.

Allen's battle with the Dalrymples did not adversely affect safety conditions in the mines. In fact, fatality rates in Colorado from 1934 through 1940 showed a slight improvement over those in the previous seven years. Between 1934 and 1940 181 coal-mine workers died in Colorado, at an average annual rate of 3.00 per thousand employed, compared to 249 fatalities and a rate of 3.40 per thousand from 1927 through 1933. Falls of rock and coal continued to be the leading cause of death in the mines. Although the rates of death from rock and coal falls and haulage accidents were better than those of the previous seven years, those for explosions, electricity, and machinery were worse (table 4).

The other Rocky Mountain coal-mining states also reported lower fatality rates from 1934 through 1940 compared to the previous seven years. Nonetheless, the region's coal mines still were more dangerous than the national average.[8]

The most significant trends in coal-mine fatality rates in the years 1934 through 1940 were in explosion and haulage accidents. In all five Rocky Mountain states, as well as nationally, haulage accidents surpassed explosions as the second leading cause of death in the mines. This trend, of course, is indicative both of the declining rate of explosion deaths and of the increasing importance of mechaniza-

TABLE 4 *continued*

Wyoming		Montana		U.S.	
Deaths	Per 1,000 Employed	Deaths	Per 1,000 Employed	Deaths	Per 1,000 Employed
46	1.51	15	1.42	4,671	1.19
12	0.40	0	0	1,005	0.26
23	0.75	9	0.84	1,503	0.38
3	0.09	1	0.09	249	0.06
2	0.06	1	0.09	337	0.08
95	3.13	29	2.71	8,794	2.24

tion in the mines. In Colorado in this period haulage, mining machinery, and electricity accounted for almost 21 percent of all coal-mine deaths. In Utah and Wyoming, the most mechanized states, haulage, machinery, and electricity were involved in 40 percent of coal-mining deaths, and in New Mexico 35 percent of coal-mine fatalities were attributed to those causes. Even in Montana, where machine production declined, haulage, machinery, and electricity accounted for 38 percent of the fatalities. One commentator, noting the decline of explosion fatalities and the overall pattern of death in Utah's coal mines, observed that there were "no mass killings, just picking them off one at a time."[9]

Despite the evidence, opinions remained divided and ambivalent about the impact of mechanization on coal-mine safety. Some emphasized the apparent role of machinery in reducing overall fatality rates, while others argued that mechanization introduced new hazards in the mines. A Bureau of Mines circular in 1940 noted progress in the previous twenty-five to thirty years in reducing accidents involving explosions and explosives. On the other hand, little change had occurred in the rate of accidents caused by falls of roof and coal, and accidents involving haulage and electricity had increased. The introduction of new hazards associated with mechanization negated the progress made in reducing major disasters and even in nondisaster safety areas. Electricity, the circular said, was the most significant new hazard, but problems involving machinery, roof control, and haulage also were important.[10]

A United Mine Workers official, anticipating the Bureau of Mine's findings, told a U.S. Senate committee that declining rates of death due to explosions indicated that that problem had been "fairly well studied" and was "somewhat under control." However, the rates of death associated with haulage and electrical equipment showed "a definitely upward trend, so as practically to destroy the good effect" achieved in preventing explosions. [11]

The *United Mine Workers Journal* also expressed concern about new problems and hazards associated with mechanization. Noise from coal-mining machines prevented adequate roof sounding, and their size sometimes meant inadequate timbering. The *Journal* further noted that electric power lines too often were improperly insulated. On the positive side, the *Journal* admitted that mechanization could bring about better conditions, especially through improved supervision. With mechanical loading, for example, workers would be concentrated in a small area, enabling foremen "to supervise them and the district closely and observe and remedy unsafe practices and conditions relatively promptly." Still, if any of the requirements for the safe and efficient use of machinery were neglected, including good track, safe electrical practices, and systematic timbering, the result likely would be "increased accident occurrence as well as decreased efficiency." [12]

Colorado's Tom Allen believed that mechanization could add to safety by transforming one of the basic relations of work, the tonnage rate. A miner paid a tonnage rate "goes in to dig coal at so much a ton," Allen said, and "the only thing he can see is that so much a ton, therefore he will be prone not to put the timber up and he will take a chance to get another ton of coal." [13] The chief inspector believed that as fewer miners received tonnage rates they would take fewer risks simply because the economic incentive to avoid deadwork was removed.

Mechanization not only affected work relations, but also had an impact on coal-mine safety laws and regulations. John B. Andrews, secretary of the American Association for Labor Legislation and a critic of coal-mine safety laws in the United States, in 1937 argued that mechanization made highly detailed statutes obsolete. Because statutes could not keep up with technological change, Andrews suggested granting state mine inspectors general authority to issue regulations. In the Rocky Mountain states only Utah's Industrial

Commission had such rule-making authority. In the other states the legislatures granted mine inspectors only limited power to make or modify regulations concerning such matters as ventilation and dust control, explosives and shot firing, and use of mine lamps. Nevertheless, Colorado's Tom Allen asserted that he had general rule-making powers and claimed, in 1940, that under the state laws he had "the privilege of making any rules and regulations" he saw fit. "I simply say that is what we are going to do and you better do it."[14] Allen's actions, however, were not as sweeping as his claims. During the 1930s he limited his rule making to regulations concerning shot firing and mechanical loaders. Allen's shot-firing rules proved to be controversial since they allowed limited shooting on shift.

In 1940 a miner from Erie, Colorado, complained that "the coal miners of Colorado would be just as safe on the battle front in France" as working under rules approved by Inspector Allen.[15] By then, the war in Europe was having its effect on the American coal industry as the United States mobilized to aid Britain and France and to prepare for possible direct involvement.

World War II resulted in stepped-up activity in coal mining, in programs to train miners, and in higher rates of death in the mines. Though the war did not cause a major boom in the western coal-mining industry, there were at least modest increases in output. To ensure adequate supplies for national defense and domestic consumption, federal authorities monitored prices and wages in the coal industry. The war years also saw a widening of federal coal-mine inspection activity.

The war gave mine inspectors yet another cause with which to exhort miners and operators to look after mine safety. Preventing accidents became important not only for its own sake, but for winning the war. Tom Allen admonished coal-mine officials that it was "vital that all man-power be conserved 100%," because coal production was critical to the national defense program and because "ACCIDENTS SLOW PRODUCTION."[16] Presumably, patriotic operators and supervisors would make new exertions to provide a safer workplace, and mine workers would advance the war effort by refraining from carelessly killing themselves.

During the war the entry of a new wave of inexperienced workers in the mines became a worry to some coal-mine inspectors. New Mexico's Warren Bracewell in 1942 noted that, with large numbers of employees abandoning the mines in favor of military service or work in defense plants, operators had to employ many novice workers. This trend led operators to mechanize wherever possible and helps to explain the increase in mechanization in New Mexico during the war. Utah's Industrial Commission also was concerned with the problem of inexperienced mine workers but worried, too, about the effect of pressure on operators and employees to keep the coal coming. The commission traced an increase in coal-mine accidents between 1940 and 1942 to the presence in the mines of more "new, inexperienced men, and the pressure being exerted on the producers and from the producers to the employees for more tonnage, necessitating men taking more chances." Though operators did not intend for this pressure to result in more accidents, the commission noted, "it seems to be a natural consequence."[17]

Colorado's Tom Allen did not entirely share his colleagues' concern about the dangers of inexperience. Indeed, he maintained that the experienced miner was the one most likely to be injured or killed on the job. The Colorado coal-mine inspection department in 1944 published figures showing that the average age of men killed in the mines was between forty-eight and fifty years and that they had twenty-five to twenty-six years of experience. Hubris born of a lifetime of working in danger was as much a hazard as inexperience. Mine inspectors and supervisors had to reach the experienced miner, Allen said, "in an effort to stop *over-confidence* in his ability to judge whether or not a piece of coal or rock is safe enough for him to take the chance of working under it."[18]

To Tom Allen, better supervision provided the best solution to the problem of rising wartime fatality rates among coal miners, experienced or inexperienced. "Enforcement of the Coal Mining Laws in *every detail* is the solution," he said. "A Boss who barely enforces the law to avoid trouble, is not doing his job." Supervision of timbering practices was especially important. Foremen had to see to it, personally, that miners obeyed orders to set timbers. "You are doing no favor to anyone in tolerating any laxity in observance of proper timbering in all places in the mines," Allen admonished mine officials.[19]

Training programs continued to be a major feature of Allen's administration of his department during the war. By 1942 he had expanded his training curriculum to include, in addition to first-aid and rescue work, manuals for mine officials dealing with ventilation, timbering, explosives, haulage, machinery, mining methods, and health and sanitation. In addition, instructors from the National Vocational Training Program for Defense Workers conducted courses that Allen called "invaluable in the safe employment of new men for war production."[20]

America's industrial war effort resulted in more than eighty-eight thousand fatalities, more than 25 percent of U.S. combat deaths. A Utah Industrial Commission report claimed that deaths among industrial workers in the first year of the war were "six or seven times as great as the deaths suffered by our armed forces." Coal mining was among those industries that experienced increased fatality rates. Because of the industry's importance to the war effort, coal-mine safety became more than ever a matter of national, as well as local, concern. A series of coal-mine disasters in Kentucky, West Virginia, Ohio, and Pennsylvania in 1939 and 1940, killing almost three hundred miners, sharpened that concern and led to greater federal activity in coal-mine inspection.[21]

Introduced in 1939 and finally passed in 1941, the federal coal-mine inspection law authorized the Bureau of Mines to conduct annual inspections of all coal mines in order to gather information on the health and safety of employees. The act also authorized the bureau to investigate accidents. These inspections would enable the bureau to prepare reports and recommendations for government and industry on ways of improving safety and health conditions in the mines. However, the act established no safety standards and granted no enforcement or rule-making authority. With no authority to enforce its recommendations, the Bureau of Mines, as it had since 1910, continued to rely on voluntary compliance by operators or on action by state officials.

According to its supporters, the new federal inspection law would supplement, not supersede, state coal-mine inspection departments. Secretary of the Interior Harold Ickes pointed out that the act had no regulatory or enforcement provisions and said that its main purpose was "the advancement of health and safety through educational means." The act's principal sponsor, Illinois Representative Kent Keller, said that it was "entirely cooperative with the State laws in all the States that have mines."[22]

In spite of the fact that the act contained no regulatory or enforcement provisions and did not challenge the authority of state coal-mine inspection departments, it provoked almost universal opposition from operators and state inspectors. Opponents of the new law argued that it was unnecessary, that it was costly to operators, that it was only the first step toward a broader and more direct federal regulatory role, and that it was unconstitutional.

Leading the opposition was the National Coal Association (NCA). The NCA urged operators to voice their opposition on the grounds that federal inspection simply was "a new form of business harassment" which would "enable any administration to build up a government police department under the false claim of safety inspectors." The association argued that federal inspection would "lay the foundations for taking out of the hands of the States, and centralizing in the hands of Federal officials in Washington, the control of coal mining operations." It also claimed that federal inspection, and the bill's requirement that operators report all accidents to the Bureau of Mines, would add to the costs of production and harm coal's position in competition with other fuels. This claim exaggerated the impact and costs of federal inspection under the law, and indeed, the NCA offered no serious evidence or arguments to substantiate it. Finally, the NCA asserted that federal coal-mine inspection was unconstitutional. Relying on the U.S. Supreme Court's reasoning in the case of *Schecter Poultry Corporation v. U.S.* (the "sick chicken case" of 1935, in which the Court struck down the National Industrial Recovery Act), the association argued that the production of coal was strictly local in character and, therefore, beyond the authority of the federal government.[23]

Western coal operators also lent their voices in opposition to federal inspection. Echoing the NCA, the Rocky Mountain Coal Mining Institute declared that the act duplicated existing and adequate state inspection, imposed unnecessary burdens on operators, and was an unjustified federal intrusion into local business activity. Other operators' groups followed this line, arguing that federal inspection was unnecessary, unconstitutional, and expensive.[24]

Some operators voiced another concern: the impact of federal inspection on state mine inspection departments. Robert L. Hair, superintendent of fuel mines at the Colorado Fuel and Iron Company, believed federal inspection "would reduce the efficiency of the State mine inspection department and would not result in furthering mine safety." A statement by Northern Colorado Coals, Inc., the self-insurance organization for operators in Colorado, asserted that federal and state inspection would produce "friction between the two corps of inspectors and those in charge of mine operations would, naturally, play one authority against the other."[25]

Not surprisingly, state coal-mine inspectors shared this concern about federal inspectors invading their domain. Tom Allen, representing the state of Colorado and the Mine Inspectors' Institute of America, testified against the act, arguing that it threatened state powers and was a wasteful duplication of effort. Instead of requiring the Bureau of Mines to inspect coal mines, Allen urged, Congress should expand its existing activities, including research, publication, and training programs. In that way, he maintained, the bureau could supplement, not duplicate, the work of state coal-mine inspection departments.[26]

The Utah Industrial Commission also opposed the federal act. The state's inspectors were fully competent, the commission declared, and annual federal inspection would merely duplicate state efforts. Likewise, Wyoming's coal-mine inspector, J. M. Sampson, objected to federal inspection on the grounds that it would be an unnecessary duplication.[27] These arguments ignored the basic purpose of the annual federal inspections, which was systematically to gather information for mine-safety research, not to enforce regulations. And they did not explain how federal inspectors, who would have no enforcement powers, would undermine state inspection departments.

Unlike operators and state mine inspectors, the United Mine Workers of America supported federal coal-mine inspection. The *United Mine Workers Journal* in July 1939 pointed out that, in the three decades since the establishment of the Bureau of Mines, sixty-eight thousand miners had lost their lives in America's coal mines. The time had come for federal legislation to supplement state laws and "to put a stop to this wholesale slaughter of mine employees." Even though it gave the Bureau of Mines no regulatory authority, the proposed federal act would "go a long way toward eliminating hazards and bringing about improved health and safety in the mines."[28]

During Senate hearings a union spokesman acknowledged that state mine inspection departments had, "within the limits of their resources," rendered "effective and heroic services, both in accident

TABLE 5: *Coal-Mining Fatalities in the*
Rocky Mountain States and U.S., 1941–1945

Cause	Colorado		New Mexico		Utah	
	Deaths	Per 1,000 Employed	Deaths	Per 1,000 Employed	Deaths	Per 1,000 Employed
Falls of rock and coal	61	1.68	18	2.13	43	3.25
Explosions	41	1.03	6	0.68	31	2.03
Haulage	32	0.89	6	0.70	21	1.54
Machinery	6	0.17	1	0.10	3	0.24
Electricity	5	0.15	2	0.26	2	0.17
Total	154	4.16	33	3.89	123	6.94

Note: Totals include deaths from other causes as well as the ones listed.

prevention and rescue work." However, conditions and developments in the industry made "supplementary" federal activity necessary in order to protect miners against accident and death. The union also saw federal inspection as a means of reviewing the work of state mine inspection departments and predicted that a federal law would "have the effect of putting state mine inspectors on their toes." Colorado's John Lawson, who led the 1913–14 strike, agreed that a larger federal role would "stimulate the state inspection service."[29]

With the disasters of 1939 and 1940 fresh in mind, Congress rejected the arguments of industry and state government and passed the federal coal-mine inspection act. Opponents of federal inspection ultimately proved correct in at least one of their predictions. The inspection act of 1941 was the first step toward federal regulation of the coal industry. However, that consequence lay more than a quarter of a century in the future. In the short term, opponents also seemed to be correct in their claim that federal inspection would not reduce accidents.

During the debate over the federal coal-mine inspection act the National Coal Association argued that the law contained no "media for accident prevention and safety" and that there was "not a particle of evidence" that federal inspections would save lives.[30] Increased coal-mine fatality rates during the war years, in the West and nationally, seemed to support that contention. Between 1941 and 1945 the average annual total coal-mine fatality rate in the United States was 2.66 per thousand employed, somewhat above the average of

TABLE 5 *continued*

Wyoming		Montana		U.S.	
Deaths	Per 1,000 Employed	Deaths	Per 1,000 Employed	Deaths	Per 1,000 Employed
40	1.71	17	2.25	3,120	1.26
1	0.04	74	9.85	719	0.29
22	0.93	3	0.44	1,317	0.54
7	0.30	1	0.12	213	0.09
3	0.13	0	0	190	0.07
79	3.38	98	13.06	6,554	2.66

2.24 for the period from 1934 through 1940. Falls of rock and coal continued to be the leading cause of death, followed by haulage and explosion fatalities.

Once again western coal mines, with their more unstable roof conditions and drier, more volatile dusts, were more dangerous than the national average. In Colorado, for example, 154 coal miners died between 1941 and 1945 at an average annual rate of 4.16 per thousand employed (table 5). Thirty-four of Colorado's forty-one explosion fatalities occurred in the 27 January 1942 explosion at Victor-American's Wadge Mine, at Mount Harris, in Routt County. Inspector Tom Allen blamed the explosion on negligence and lax enforcement of safety practices by underground officials who permitted an excessive accumulation of coal dust in the mine. Because of the Wadge disaster, Allen later ordered rock dusting in all but "sloppily wet" mines.[31]

Montana, with a fatality rate of 13.06 per thousand employed, was by far the most dangerous of the Rocky Mountain coal-mining states in this period (table 5). Seventy-four of the state's ninety-eight deaths occurred in the 27 February 1943 explosion in the Montana Coal and Iron Company's Smith Mine No. 3, near Red Lodge. It was Montana's worst coal-mine disaster. The explosion probably was ignited by an open-flame lamp; however, miners in the Smith No. 3 were known to smoke underground, and some of the mine's wiring was unsafe. Miner Emil Anderson had time to scratch a message on a chalkboard before he was overcome by the after-damp: "It is five minutes past 11 o'clock Dear Agnes and children. I am sorry we had to go this way. God Bless you. Emil, with lots of kisses." Two other victims left a message assuring their wives and children that "We died an easy death."[32]

After the disaster the head of the Montana State Federation of Labor warned that the Smith Mine was not exceptional. "It was no more than typical of conditions in the state," said James Graham. The state legislature in 1945 responded to the disaster by enacting stricter regulations governing ventilation, including more inspections by mine officials and special rules requiring machine men to check work areas for gas before and during coal-cutting operations. In addition, all but "consistently damp" mines were to be rock dusted. The legislature also passed new rules for the installation of electric power and trolley lines and required that all new electrical equipment be approved by the U.S. Bureau of Mines.[33]

Utah, with 123 fatalities and an average annual fatality rate of 6.94 per thousand employed, also was very dangerous (table 5). Two explosions in Carbon County coal mines, both in 1945, accounted for thirty of Utah's thirty-one explosion deaths. In March the Kenilworth Mine exploded, killing seven; the Sunnyside Number One blew up in May, leaving twenty-three dead. In the wake of these disasters Utah's lawmakers and Industrial Commission again revised the state's coal-mining regulations. As usual, the changes addressed the problem of preventing explosions and dealt only secondarily with more mundane hazards such as rock falls and haulage accidents. The new regulations included a higher ventilation standard, rock dusting, use of permissible explosives, electric battery lamps, and rules for the installation and use of haulage equipment, mining machines, and electric power lines. The orders also included a general requirement that there "be on hand at all times, sufficient materials and supplies to preserve the health and safety of employees."[34]

Thirty-three miners died in New Mexico's coal mines during the war years, at an average rate of 3.89 per thousand employed. Among the Rocky Mountain states, Wyoming, with seventy-nine fatalities and an average rate of 3.38 per thousand, had the safest record during the war.

Despite the surge of the war years, the coal industry by 1945 experienced declining overall fatality rates compared to those of the half-century before 1934. In the area of explosions, especially, regulation and mechanization brought about a significant drop in death rates. In the Rocky Mountain states 157 miners died in major disasters from 1934 through 1945, and 183 in all explosions. The days of the huge disasters in which scores, even hundreds, at a time were blown apart or suffocated to death seemed to be, if not over, at least ending.

Nonetheless, there were other, more disturbing trends. Though the rate was down, falls of rock and coal continued to be the leading cause of death in the mines. Mechanization largely explains that fact. Even though there were fewer miners working for tonnage rates, with the incentive to avoid deadwork in favor of digging and loading coal, the growing use of mining machinery and loading equipment created new hazards. Machine vibration weakened roofs; machine noise prevented proper sounding and drowned out the warning groans and cracks of deteriorating roofs; and the space needed to maneuver machinery in rooms and entries sometimes meant inadequate timbering. Even though mechanization was transforming work in the coal mines and removing the economic incentive for miners to risk their lives for another ton of coal, machines contributed to the persistence of rock and coal falls as the number-one killer in the mines. And mechanization was responsible for growing death rates from other causes. During the 1930s and 1940s, as more mines mechanized, deaths from haulage accidents and electrocution increased.

By 1945, coal-mine inspection departments were just beginning to come to grips with the problems of mechanization in the mines. In Colorado and Utah, government officials responsible for coal-mine inspection had issued some orders concerning the use of machinery, haulage, and electricity in the mines. However, major legislative and regulatory changes still focused on the problem of explosion. As was so often the case, regulatory reform followed major explosion disasters. Tom Allen's most important directive was his 1942 rock-dusting order, following the Wadge disaster. In Utah and Montana the regulatory changes of 1945 followed three deadly explosions. Disaster also led to federal mine inspection. Enacted as the nation geared up for war, the 1941 federal law owed as much or more to the disasters of 1939 and 1940 as it did to concern for stability in the industry in a time of crisis. But because it granted the Bureau of Mines no regulatory authority, the law had no immediate impact on mine safety, a fact demonstrated by rising fatality rates during the war.

The crises of depression and war brought about significant changes in the industrial environment of coal mining. In the West operators, in the face of economic crisis and governmental pressure, recognized their employees' right to organize and bargain collectively, bringing to an end the era of violence in labor relations in the industry. As organized labor won its place at the table, however, its numbers dwindled. Mechanization and falling production reduced the industry's labor needs. And as mechanization cut back the number of men at work in the mines, it also affected how they worked, as skilled miners gave way to machine operators. Mechanization brought with it both new hazards and the potential for bringing about safer conditions through better supervision and, especially, the elimination of the tonnage rate.

The depression and war years also saw important political developments in the area of coal-mine safety and regulation. In Colorado the coal-mine inspection department became an arena of political conflict to a degree unseen in the previous half-century. The Dalrymple-Allen feud began as a battle for control of the department but soon was swept up in depression-era politics. The federal government's entry into the affairs of the coal industry was the most significant political change. Beginning with efforts to bring a measure of stability to coal during the Great Depression, the federal government tried to regulate production, prices, and wages in order to end the pattern of overproduction, cutthroat competition, and labor upheaval which had plagued the industry in the past. As the nation mobilized for war, a stable supply of coal became even more important, and one factor, safety, underscored by the disasters of 1939 and 1940, became a greater national concern. Succeeding decades would witness a gradual broadening of the federal role in coal-mine safety and a corresponding decline in state activity until, finally, the United States government took over most of the responsibility for coal-mining regulation.

Chapter 9

Regulation since World War II: The Federal Takeover

During the debate over the 1941 federal coal-mine inspection law Interior Secretary Harold Ickes argued that the law did not "contemplate establishment of a Federal inspection system superseding or duplicating the work of local safety agencies." Federal inspectors would not be involved in enforcement activities. Instead, the federal role in coal-mine inspection would be to aid state agencies, industry, and labor in improving conditions in the mines. At the same time, however, a congressional committee found the lack of uniformity of regulations and enforcement among the states to be one important reason for supporting the 1941 law.[1] Left unstated was the implication that only federal regulation could bring about such uniformity.

Secretary Ickes and the congressional committee had posed an issue that came to the fore after World War II: whether the states or the federal government would exercise primary regulatory authority. Since the war the federal government has replaced state coal-mine inspection agencies in the forefront of regulation. For a quarter of a century the states and the industry fought a losing battle against the federal takeover. Ironically, by the time the enactment of the Coal Mine Health and Safety Act of 1969 decided the issue, changes in the coal industry itself, especially in the West, had eliminated much of the problem of death in the mines. Indeed, by the 1980s underground coal mining was becoming a thing of the past.

World War II's stimulus to the coal industry ended with the war. Production from western coal mines declined steadily after 1945 until it reached a virtual standstill. Contributing to the industry's troubles was competition from oil and natural gas as sources of fuel for industries and homes. By 1954 production in Colorado had fallen to under 3 million tons, the lowest output since 1889. In New Mexico the industry had all but collapsed by the mid-1950s. In 1954, when production stood at only 255,399 tons, the state coal-mine inspector pronounced coal mining in New Mexico a "dead industry" and expected it to "remain dead for a long, long time."[2] Utah, Wyoming, and Montana experienced more gradual declines, and production did not bottom out until the early 1960s.

Beginning in the 1960s and continuing into the 1980s, the Rocky Mountain coal industry benefited from the region's overall economic growth. New population and new industries, including huge, coal-fired electric generating plants, created a boom in coal mining. By the early 1980s Colorado and New Mexico each were producing approximately 20 million tons per year, Utah more than 12 million tons, and Montana about 30 million tons. Wyoming moved to the top of the region's coal industry, producing more than 100 million tons in 1981.

As the industry recovered, it became apparent that much had changed in the way miners worked. Mechanization took the coal miner out of the depths of the earth and put him in the seat of a gigantic earth-moving machine. And where miners still worked underground, hand methods of cutting and loading coal had essentially disappeared. Since the mid-1970s more than half of Colorado's coal has been produced by strip mining. In Wyoming strip mining surpassed underground production in 1954 and accounted for more than 98 percent of the state's coal production in 1971. The majority of New Mexico's coal was strip mined by 1963. Virtually all of Montana's coal has been strip mined since the industry revived in the early 1970s. Only in Utah, where there is no significant surface mining, is underground mining still predominant. Whether the change from underground to surface mining came early, late, or not at all, by the time the federal government became the primary regulator of the industry, technological change had made coal mining quite different from what it was in 1945.

As the end of World War II approached and the federal government faced the problem of reconversion from a wartime to a peacetime economy, maintaining industrial stability became a major priority. By the spring of 1945 the Roosevelt and Truman administration had become concerned that workers and unions, pressing for wage increases deferred during the war, might use strikes to disrupt industries crucial to postwar economic plans. The government was particularly worried about John L. Lewis and the United Mine Workers of America. A strike in the coal industry would be felt throughout the economy, interfering with basic industries such as steel, transportation, and utilities. As early as January 1945 Secretary Ickes had warned President Roosevelt that Lewis would be "openly truculent and non-cooperative."[3]

Thus, the government expected trouble when negotiations for a national contract began in 1946. The union's demands included wage increases, a retirement fund, and a larger, more direct role for miners in safety enforcement. The union proposed that each mine have a safety committee with authority to inspect the mine and to remove workers from areas where they found conditions of immediate danger. The UMWA also demanded that operators agree to comply with the recommendations of federal mine inspectors. When the operators rejected the union's safety demands, Lewis exclaimed that the miners had "sought surcease from blood-letting" but that the industry had replied with indifference. "When we cried aloud for the safety of our members you answer—Be content—'twas always thus."[4] In mid-May the negotiations broke down and Lewis took his miners out on strike.

The 1946 coal strike brought a vigorous response from the Truman administration which led to a widening of the federal government's regulatory activity. The government's intervention in the strike began on 21 May, when President Truman ordered the Interior Department to take control of the mines. The legal basis for the mine seizure lay in the Smith-Connally War Labor Disputes Act. In 1943, when the United Mine Workers struck for higher wages, President Roosevelt immediately seized the mines and put them under the control of the Interior Department. During the mine seizure John L. Lewis succeeded in negotiating many of his demands. However, public resentment over the wartime strike and fears that other unions might follow the UMWA's example led to calls for legal restraints on the unions. The result was the Smith-Connally Act. Passed over President Roosevelt's veto, the act authorized the president to seize plants vital to the war effort in case labor disputes threatened production.

When President Truman seized the mines in 1946, he ordered Interior Secretary J. A. Krug to negotiate an agreement with the union to return the miners to work. Known as the Krug-Lewis Agreement, the contract between the union and the government included the establishment of safety committees at the mines with authority to withdraw miners from dangerous areas. The government also agreed to issue a comprehensive safety code to regulate coal-mine operations during the seizure.

The Interior Department on 24 July 1946 issued the Federal Mine Safety Code. The code included regulations governing roof, face, and rib (side wall) control; explosives; ventilation and dust control; haulage; electricity; machinery; and supervision. The code required all mines to use a systematic method of timbering, and operators were to deliver props at or near working faces. A ventilation standard of at least 6,000 cubic feet of air per minute was required at the last crosscut of each entry, and more if methane exceeded 1 percent. Miners were to be withdrawn if the methane level reached 1.5 percent. Firebosses were to examine gassy mines (those in which more than 0.25 percent methane was detected at any workings, or where methane had been ignited) within four hours of the beginning of each shift. All mines, except those in which ambient humidity or the presence of incombustibles in the air was adequate to prevent dust explosions, were to be rock dusted to within forty feet of working faces. Haulage regulations included a prohibition of passengers on coal trips, except those with special riding equipment. All electric cables were to have proper capacity and insulation, and electrical equipment was to be frame-grounded and inspected monthly. Coal-mining machinery had to be equipped with safety locks and dust-suppression devices, and hand-held power tools were to have dead-man switches. Finally, all mines were to have foremen, firebosses, and shot firers certified by the states.[5]

The federal safety code elicited a response from the states reminiscent of their opposition to the 1941 mine-inspection law. For example, in a letter to the director of the U.S. Bureau of Mines, Colorado Governor John C. Vivian said that federal inspection was entirely unnecessary because his state had one of the best coal-mine inspection departments in the nation. More important, coal-mine inspection was "unquestionably a state prerogative." Thus, though he had "no particular objection to further examinations" by federal inspectors, Vivian declared that Chief Inspector Tom Allen had to approve their activities.[6]

Governor Vivian did not understand that John L. Lewis had made coal-mine safety a national, and therefore a federal, concern. In agreeing to issue a safety code, the federal government had greatly and, as it turned out, permanently expanded its regulatory role. Originally, the coal-mine safety code was an emergency measure, to be in force only while the government controlled the mines. However, events in 1947 indicated that the federal government was prepared to continue in its new role as regulator of the nation's coal mines.

On 25 March 1947 a coal-mine explosion at Centralia, Illinois, killed 111 miners. Following the disaster, John L. Lewis declared a one-week memorial period during which union miners were to mourn the deaths of their brothers by staying away from work. During this mourning "strike" Lewis vigorously attacked Interior Secretary Krug and demanded his dismissal for his supposed failure to enforce the mining code. Lewis claimed that the victims of the Centralia explosion were "murdered because of the criminal negligence" of the secretary. "This killing must stop," Lewis declared in an appeal to the public conscience. "Coal is heavily saturated with the blood of too many brave men and drenched with the tears of too many widows and orphans."[7]

President Truman rejected Lewis's demand for Krug's removal. Truman even told his cabinet, erroneously, that the union leader "had never displayed any interest on measures looking toward mine safety," a comment suggesting that the president saw the mourning strike as a sham.[8] In fact, Truman and his advisers believed that Lewis was exploiting the Centralia disaster to carry out a strike previously scheduled to begin on 1 April 1947 but cancelled because of a federal court injunction. Under the terms of the Krug-Lewis Agreement, he could not order a strike against the government, but he could legally take the miners out for mourning periods.

Despite the administration's contempt for Lewis, the Interior Secretary acted to demonstrate his willingness and ability to enforce the federal safety code. Secretary Krug ordered 518 mines to remain closed after the mourning period until federal inspectors certified them to be safe. Twenty-three of those mines were in Colorado, Utah, and New Mexico.

In the aftermath of the Centralia disaster and the mourning walkout, Congress began to consider making federal inspections permanent. In August 1947 the House and Senate passed a joint resolution calling on the Bureau of Mines to continue to inspect coal mines and to report to state regulatory agencies any violations of the federal safety code. In its report endorsing the resolution the Senate Committee on Public Lands noted that Congress was placing "squarely upon the States the burden of making the mines safe and keeping them safe for the protection of men underground" and warned that, "if the States do not guard the safety of the miners, the Congress will act further."[9]

In Colorado, Chief Inspector Allen agreed to work with Bureau of Mines inspectors in examining the sixteen mines Secretary Krug had closed during the mourning period. However, Allen's cooperative attitude was inspired less by the threat of a greater federal regulatory role than by his own problems with the United Mine Workers.

Mimicking John L. Lewis's attack on Secretary Krug, UMWA District Fifteen president Frank Hefferly launched a campaign against Inspector Allen during the Centralia mourning period. Hefferly demanded an investigation of the coal-mine inspection department and of coal-mine conditions in Colorado. During hearings conducted by a joint committee of the legislature, he declared that Allen was unfit to hold office; that his "signature is no good, his word is no good, his recommendations are no good, and his performance in office . . . is nil." Hefferly added that "we've had to fight him every minute to get safety measures instituted in the mines." When accidents occurred, Allen always blamed "shift bosses and other workers," instead of prosecuting operators. The union leader also objected to Allen's hiring a woman, Veda Burford, as the department's safety director because state law banned women from the mines and because "miners objected to a woman in the safety job."[10]

Allen responded to Hefferly's charges by noting that his department, which was badly understaffed, was responsible for enforcing a coal-mining law that had become a "legislative patchwork." It was time, he believed, for the legislature to make a major revision in the law to include mandatory rock dusting, electric shot firing, training of rescue teams, and a prohibition of the use of black powder. Allen also defended his safety director, saying that Burford was fully qualified for her job. Speaking for herself, Burford accused Hefferly of trying to excuse his own "unwillingness to cooperate with the department by hiding behind a woman's skirts."[11]

In its report the joint committee found that Hefferly's charges against Allen were unjustified. The report went on to urge more cooperation among state and federal agencies, more frequent inspection of the mines, and joint efforts by operators, miners, and public officials to enforce safety regulations. The committee did support the union's objections to Veda Burford in the job of safety director. Burford nevertheless remained on the job. A disappointed Frank Hefferly called the report a whitewash and noted that the committee chairman, Senator Sam Taylor of Walsenburg, was a mine operator, a suggestion that there was a pro-industry and pro-Allen bias in the committee's investigation and report.[12]

Senator Taylor's own comments reveal no proindustry bias. During the hearings Taylor identified the real problem with coal-mine safety and inspection in Colorado as the "woeful inadequacies" in the state's coal-mining law, which he said was "perhaps the worst in the United States." His opinion was shared by U.S. Bureau of Mines inspector Earl R. Maize, who told the committee that the law was "entirely inadequate." Maize also argued that "operator control over the legislature is responsible for the inadequacy" of the state law. Legislators, he said, should stop paying attention "to the wishes of coal operators" and provide the coal-mine inspection department with enough men to do its job properly.[13]

Having failed in his battle against Allen, Hefferly decided to follow the path suggested by Senator Taylor and prepared to work for a new law in the upcoming 1949 session of the legislature. During 1948 Hefferly drafted a bill based on the federal safety code. It called for creating the position of deputy chief inspector for safety work and authorized an increase in the number of deputy inspectors from six to ten. Chief Inspector Allen endorsed Hefferly's bill, with reservations, as did local representatives of the U.S. Bureau of Mines. Allen said the bill was generally sound, except that some penalties on operators were too harsh. Senators Ben Veltri and Sam Taylor sponsored the bill in the legislature.[14]

Many of the state's coal operators strongly opposed the United Mine Workers' bill. Opponents claimed that, in incorporating the federal safety code, the bill contained numerous provisions irrelevant to conditions in Colorado. The code, and the bill, could not easily be amended to take advantage of technological developments. Instead of passing a new law, the operators maintained, the legislature and the coal-mine inspection department could remedy any defects in the 1913 act through amendments or through administrative rules and regulations. The operators also opposed a proposed increase in the state coal tax to finance the enlargement of the coal-mine inspection department. Rather than add to the industry's tax burden, they believed, the department should be financed from the state's general fund. Much of the criticism of the bill came from Northern Colorado Coals, Inc., the self-insurance organization of operators in the northern field. Interestingly, officials of the state's largest operator, the Colorado Fuel and Iron Company, did not comment on the bill.[15]

As in 1911, a coal-mining law strongly opposed by the state's operators had little chance of being enacted. Though it passed in the state house of representatives, the senate refused to approve it.

Frank Hefferly learned from the defeat in 1949 and took the lead in preparing another bill for the 1951 legislature to consider. This time, however, Tom Allen, representatives of the U.S. Bureau of Mines, and industry officials, including Robert Hair of the Colorado Fuel and Iron Company, participated in writing the bill. With support from labor, state and federal officials, and the coal industry, the 1951 bill easily passed both houses of the legislature, and Governor Dan T. Thornton signed it into law on 21 March 1951.

The *United Mine Workers Journal* called the new law "sensational," and Tom Allen pronounced it "the best coal code west of the Mississippi." In addition to incorporating most of the provisions of the federal coal-mine safety code, the act ended the exemption of small mines from inspection by requiring that all coal mines be inspected at least four times per year. Inspectors were to notify persons in charge of mines when they discovered conditions of imminent danger. If mine officials did not immediately act to remedy those conditions, inspectors could remove workers from the area or close the entire mine. To finance the coal-mine inspection department, the act raised the coal tax to seven mills and, in case of deficits, provided for the appropriation of additional funds. (That provision, however, did not end the department's budget problems because the act did not *require* the legislature to appropriate needed additional funds. In 1952, because of inadequate funding, Allen, who had opposed federal inspection, deputized federal mine inspectors in Colorado to enforce the state law.)[16]

The 1951 law provided some improvement in supervision in most small mines. It required all mines employing more than three persons, including owners, to employ a certified foreman. Where mines were so extensive that a single foreman could not personally carry out all of the duties imposed by the law, operators were to employ certified assistant foremen. Foremen and assistant foremen were to have full charge of all inside workings and employees; were to be responsible for supervising ventilation, haulage, timbering, drainage, machinery, and construction work; and were to see to the prompt removal of all dangers reported to them. In short, they were responsible for enforcing the law. Mine officials who failed to perform their duties properly could lose their certificates and faced criminal liability. In small mines employing fewer than three persons, workers were to be supervised by a certified official with at least the rank of shot firer. Thus, the new law corrected most of the deficiencies in supervision in small mines which had existed since the 1920s and 1930s.

To guide mine officials, the act included detailed regulations governing roof control, ventilation and dust control, and explosives. All mines were to employ a systematic method of roof control approved by the chief inspector, and operators were to deliver adequate supplies of timbers and other roof-control equipment at or near working faces. Miners were to set posts, jacks, or crossbars close to the face, where falls were most likely to occur. In addition to daily examinations of roofs, sides, and faces by foremen, the act required miners to examine their areas and correct all hazards. Supervisors in mechanized mines were to examine work areas and see to the removal of dangers.

Like previous statutes, the 1951 law focused on explosion hazards and ventilation. The law's ventilation and air-quality standards were the same as those in the federal safety code. In addition to the ventilation standards, the act required wetting down dust at its sources and rock dusting to within forty feet of working faces in all but naturally very wet mines. The law prohibited the use of any form of black powder and allowed only permissible explosives fired by certified shot firers. In addition, the act included elaborate rules for surface and underground storage and transport of explosives. In all mines firebosses were to make daily visits to each working place and examine it for gas, as well as inspecting roofs, sides, and faces, and haulageways and travelways.

Although the law emphasized ventilation and explosion problems, it also spelled out regulations governing haulage, machinery, and electricity. Like the ventilation and air-quality standards, most of these rules followed the 1946 federal safety code.

In addition to these regulations, the 1951 law required that mines be equipped with fire-fighting equipment. The statute also reflected Chief Inspector Allen's enthusiasm for first-aid and rescue training. The act recommended, but did not require, that operators train 50 percent of their employees in first-aid methods. It did require that all mine officials have first-aid training. The statute also provided for the organization of rescue teams. Mines with more than one hundred employees were to have at least three five-man teams; mines with twenty-five to one hundred employees, two teams. The coal-mine inspection department would group mines with fewer than twenty-five workers into districts and organize teams of five men for every fifty miners.[17]

The question of why the 1949 bill failed and the 1951 act passed the legislature is an interesting one. They were, after all, very similar in content, both being based on the 1946 federal coal-mine safety code. The answer is reminiscent of the setting for the enactment of Colorado's 1913 law: the participation of the major interests—the state, organized labor, and the largest coal operator—in drafting the statute. In 1949 the UMWA's Frank Hefferly wrote his bill without consulting Tom Allen or the state's operators. When the bill reached the legislature, the small operators opposed it strongly. They, of course, would incur the greatest expenses in implementing the proposed law. Meanwhile, the Colorado Fuel and Iron Company sat out the debate. In 1951 both the coal-mine inspection department and CF&I played major roles in drafting the legislation. The support of the state's dominant coal producer, which already followed many of the act's regulations, outweighed any objection by smaller operators. Thus the 1951 law, like the 1913 act, was the product of an agreement among the state, organized labor, and the major operators, or operator.

Montana in 1949 and Wyoming in 1951 also passed major revisions of their coal-mining laws based on the federal coal-mine safety code. The Wyoming statute differed significantly from Colorado's only in that it mandated mine inspections at least every two months and required foremen in mines employing five workers or more. Montana's law allowed the state coal-mine inspector to permit small mines employing fewer than six men on any shift to operate without a certified foreman.[18]

Utah and New Mexico enacted only a few amendments in this period. A 1949 Utah law required certified foremen in all mines classified as gassy and in mines employing five or more workers. In smaller mines the owner could designate a foreman, who had to pass an oral exam given by the state mine inspector. Another amendment passed in 1949 eliminated the existing ventilation standard of one hundred fifty cubic feet per man per minute in favor of a general requirement that ventilation be sufficient to keep all working areas free of smoke and gases. In New Mexico a 1947 amendment permitted shot firing in mechanized mines at any time, even if workers were still inside, if the operator obtained permission from both the state mine inspector and the local mine committee.[19]

These laws, especially those of Colorado, Wyoming, and Montana, were mainly the products of local concerns and interests. Everyone— miners, labor leaders, government officials, and operators—wanted to improve working conditions and reduce injury and death rates in the mines. Beyond that, the states hoped to block the growth of federal regulatory power and to answer criticism by federal officials about the weakness and nonuniformity of state laws. However, the force of events and the momentum of public and political opinion continued to favor a stronger federal role.

On 12 December 1951 the Orient Number Two mine in West Frankfurt, Illinois, exploded, killing 119 miners. Seven months later, on 16 July 1952, President Truman signed the Federal Coal Mine Safety Act, giving the Bureau of Mines regulatory and enforcement powers intended to prevent such disasters as the Illinois explosion. However, the new law, based on the 1946 safety code, applied only to mines employing more than fourteen workers. As had been the case in Colorado in the 1920s, the contention that regulation would drive many small operators out of business prevailed over the fact that these mines contributed disproportionately to coal-mining fatality rates.

The new federal statute authorized Bureau of Mines inspectors to make annual inspections of those mines subject to the law. Where they discovered conditions of imminent danger, the federal inspectors could order the evacuation and closure of mines. Inspectors also could order correction of less serious hazards, and if operators did not comply within a reasonable time, the inspectors could close those mines. The Bureau of Mines could enforce only those regulations specified in the act and had no rule-making authority. Only Congress could enact new regulations.

Congress, in the 1952 law, went to great lengths to preserve state regulatory authority. The act provided that state laws requiring higher safety standards would supersede the federal act. State and federal agencies were encouraged to make cooperative agreements to share inspection, research, and other safety activities. As part of such agreements, the law required that state inspectors accompany federal agents on their inspections. Furthermore, state inspectors could override federal mine-closure orders if they believed the hazards in question did not present an imminent threat to life.[20]

Limited as it was, operators and state officials strongly opposed the new federal law. As it had in 1941, the National Coal Association led the industry in opposing this enlargement of the federal role in inspection and regulation. As before, the NCA based its opposition on contentions that federal regulation would weaken state agencies and was unconstitutional. Federal regulation, said an NCA spokesman, would "inevitably force the state mining departments out of the field or bring about serious curtailment of their important and vital activities." The NCA argued that federal regulation was unconstitutional because it was an inappropriate use of the commerce power to regulate local business activity and because it threatened to deny operators due process of law. The goals and provisions of the act, it asserted, were too vague and general; it delegated too much authority to the secretary of the interior; and it allowed mine inspectors to close mines without proper judicial proceedings.[21]

Western operators joined in opposing the federal law. The Colorado and New Mexico Coal Operators Association argued that existing state laws, most notably Colorado's, were up-to-date, fully adequate, and gave state inspectors authority to protect workers from imminent hazards. The operators also contended that state and federal inspectors already worked together closely and that centralization of authority in federal hands would be "a needless and serious encroachment" on the right of the states to control their own affairs.[22]

Western coal-mine inspectors also voiced opposition to federal regulation and inspection. At the 1952 meeting of the Rocky Mountain Coal Mining Institute, Wyoming's Lyman Fearn and New Mexico's John Garcia both expressed their dislike of granting enforcement powers to federal inspectors. Fearn maintained that state inspectors could do just as good a job as federal agents and that federal enforcement would be an encroachment on states' rights.[23]

Countering the opposition of industry and state officials was the strong support of the United Mine Workers of America. John L. Lewis, at his sarcastic best, told a House committee that it was easy for the industry to oppose federal regulation because only coal miners were being killed, not coal operators. That, he said, made it easier for the coal operators to say to Congress, "Leave us alone. . . . None of us have been injured at the country club, and we are thinking about this situation. We might do something about it." In a similar vein Lewis characterized operators as saying, in effect, "Leave us alone. We have only been working on this job for 150 years. We have only killed 114,000 men in disasters since 1839. We have only injured a few million."[24]

In a less sarcastic mood Lewis recognized that many coal operators, especially those sincerely interested in safety, were in a competitive bind. Without uniform regulation of the industry, "the benevolent minded coal operator" who worked to maintain high safety standards in his mine was "penalized" by the unfair competition of operators who, because of their "chiseling" on safety, could sell their coal at a lower price.[25] He failed to note, however, that many major operators, such as the Colorado Fuel and Iron Company, already practiced a large number of the measures required by the proposed law. The real problem was with small operators, most of whom would be exempt from federal inspection.

In its editorial columns the *United Mine Workers Journal* discussed political and other considerations for favoring federal over state regulation and inspection. Because state mine inspection agencies were more susceptible to pressure by mine operators, who enjoyed "more direct and immediate influence in state governments than in the Federal Government," these agencies were "unlikely to have the independence of the federal Bureau of Mines." Too many state mining departments, the *Journal* asserted, were "staffed by persons more responsive to the mining industry or to politics than they should be." The *Journal* also cited as a major problem the lack of uniformity among state regulations. If all states worked together and accepted a uniform code, "the miners' hope of a nation-wide protection from unsafe mines could well be achieved through state efforts." However, the *Journal* had no faith in such a solution and concluded that "the tragedies that have sprung from inadequate state mine safety regulations and lax state enforcement can be corrected only by a firm federal code with teeth in it."[26]

The 1952 law was a major step toward the uniformity desired by critics of state coal-mine inspection. But because it applied only to mines employing fourteen workers or more underground, it left many mines solely under the jurisdiction of state laws and agencies. In signing the bill into law, President Truman took note of this and other defects. Probably the most important weakness, besides its exemption of small mines, was the act's exclusive goal of preventing disasters. Congress, in passing the law, was fully aware of this shortcoming. The report of the House Committee on Education and Labor acknowledged that in addressing only disaster prevention the new law would not deal with the causes of the overwhelming majority of coal-mine fatalities. "The bill is not designed to prevent the day-to-day accidents which occur in the mine industry nor for the general health and welfare of the miners," the committee noted. Instead, "the enforcement of rules and regulations in the field of day-to-day accidents . . . is clearly left within the jurisdiction of the several states."[27]

Experience soon showed that small coal mines, as they had in the past, contributed a disproportionate share of fatalities. Over the next fourteen years critics of state inspection worked to extend the federal law to all coal mines. In 1958 and 1959 the U.S. Senate Subcommittee on Labor, chaired by John F. Kennedy, held hearings on bills to repeal the exemption of small mines from federal inspection. In those hearings John L. Lewis explained that small mines employing fewer than fifteen workers accounted for only 7 percent of the coal produced in the United States, but nearly 26 percent of coal-mine fatalities. Bureau of Mines director Marling J. Ankeny told the subcommittee that small mines in the West were especially dangerous.

In Colorado, for example, 20 percent of small mines had serious roof hazards, compared to 15 percent with such hazards nationally. In addition, more than 40 percent of small mines in Colorado, Utah, and New Mexico did not meet federal rock-dusting standards.[28] If, indeed, that was the case in Colorado, those mines were in violation of the state law, which followed the federal standard.

Utah's Senator Frank E. Moss sponsored one of the bills to bring small coal mines under federal regulation. Moss argued that the small operators' claim that federal regulation would force them out of business "is not based on fact," and he declared that the miners employed in small mines "are just as valuable human beings as the miners in the larger mines, and are entitled to the same protection."[29] The Senate passed the bill to bring small mines under federal authority, but the House of Representatives killed the measure.

As president, John Kennedy must have recalled his subcommittee's study of the problem of small mines, but it took two coal-mine explosions, in December 1962 and April 1963, in which fifty-nine died, to move him to action. In April 1963 Kennedy ordered the Interior Department to form a task force on coal-mine safety to study the issue and recommend changes in the law. In its report the task force recommended eliminating the exemption of small mines from federal regulation. The group took particular note of claims that federal regulation would drive many small mines out of business. Such allegations, it concluded, were not well-founded since some 30 percent of mines already under federal jurisdiction employed only fifteen to nineteen workers and more than half employed fewer than fifty. The task force also recommended giving federal inspectors greater authority to close hazardous mines; suggested repeal of "grandfather" clauses in the law permitting older mines to continue to use outdated ventilation methods; advocated more safety education and training for miners; and called for increased research funding, more training, and more uniform inspection procedures for the Bureau of Mines and its inspectors.[30]

The task force began a legislative effort that eventually led to the extension of federal regulation to small mines. The opposition of operators and state officials ultimately could not overcome the evidence that the fatality rate in small mines was almost twice as high as in larger operations. Finally, in 1966, Congress acted on the task force's recommendations and ended the exemption of small

TABLE 6: *Coal-Mining Fatalities in the Rocky Mountain States and U.S., 1953–1969*

	Colorado		New Mexico		Utah	
Cause	Deaths	Per 1,000 Employed	Deaths	Per 1,000 Employed	Deaths	Per 1,000 Employed
Falls of rock and coal	31	0.97	4	0.88	52	1.27
Explosions	12	0.47	0	0	11	0.37
Haulage	10	0.37	0	0	10	0.22
Machinery	4	0.13	1	0.08	4	0.09
Electricity	0	0	0	0	2	0.07
Total	61	2.05	6	1.16	90	2.32

Note: Totals include deaths from other causes as well as the ones listed.

mines. The amended coal-mine safety act also gave federal inspectors stronger enforcement powers and called for cooperation with the states in safety education programs.[31]

Operators hoped that the 1966 amendments would be the last step in the expansion of federal authority in coal-mine safety and regulation. In a 1967 report, for example, the Bituminous Coal Operators Association argued that the federal coal-mining law "does not materially lack sufficiency" and that "considerations for further amendment should be few, if any."[32]

Fatality rates in the United States and the Rocky Mountain region give a clearer picture of the "sufficiency" of federal coal-mine regulation under the 1952 law. Between 1953 and 1969, 5,516 mine workers died in the United States at an average annual rate of 1.66 per thousand employed. Falls of rock and coal continued to be the leading cause of death, followed by haulage, explosion, machinery, and electrical accidents. Of the Rocky Mountain states, only New Mexico and Wyoming compared favorably with the national average, and Colorado, Utah, and Montana were well above it (table 6).

During the period from 1953 through 1965, when the federal law regulated only mines employing fourteen or more workers, the average annual fatality rate nationally was 1.64 per thousand employed, slightly better than the rate for the entire 1953–69 period. Again, falls of rock and coal killed the largest number of miners, followed by haulage, explosions, machinery, and electricity. Among the Rocky Mountain states, only Wyoming and New Mexico were safer than the

TABLE 6 *continued*

	Wyoming		Montana		U.S.
Deaths	Per 1,000 Employed	Deaths	Per 1,000 Employed	Deaths	Per 1,000 Employed
5	0.33	8	1.86	2,683	0.79
0	0	1	0.37	503	0.16
8	0.69	0	0	853	0.25
2	0.22	1	0.57	256	0.08
0	0	0	0	176	0.05
16	1.40	10	2.80	5,516	1.66

national average. And only in Wyoming were falls of rock and coal not the leading cause of death in the mines (table 7).

In the brief period from 1967 through 1969, when the federal coal-mine safety law applied to all mines, the average annual U.S. fatality rate rose to 1.77 per thousand employed, with falls of rock and coal still the leading cause of death. Of the western states, Colorado was by far the most dangerous, killing miners at a rate of 2.93 per thousand, followed by Wyoming with a rate of 2.23. Utah's death rate was about half the national average, and New Mexico and Montana had no fatalities (table 8).[33]

Overall, national and regional coal-mining fatality rates improved during the first decade and a half of federal regulation. However, although there was a marginal improvement in the rate of deaths due to explosions, the law's failure to address the day-to-day leading causes of death in the mines also is apparent. From 1953 through 1969, falls of rock and coal, and haulage, machinery, and electrical accidents, accounted for 68 percent of all coal-mining deaths. Explosions accounted for 9 percent. That the coal-mine fatality rate increased after small coal mines came under federal jurisdiction simply underscores the essential failure of the federal coal-mining law to affect nondisaster hazards.

Yet another major disaster had to occur before Congress acted to improve the law and expand federal authority. On 20 November 1968 the Consolidation Coal Mining Company's Number Nine mine at Farmington, West Virginia, exploded, killing seventy-eight workers.

TABLE 7: *Coal-Mining Fatalities in the
Rocky Mountain States and U.S., 1953–1965*

Cause	Colorado		New Mexico		Utah	
	Deaths	Per 1,000 Employed	Deaths	Per 1,000 Employed	Deaths	Per 1,000 Employed
Falls of rock and coal	21	0.72	4	1.15	45	1.22
Explosions	9	0.46	0	0	11	0.48
Haulage	7	0.31	0	0	9	0.24
Machinery	4	0.17	1	0.11	4	0.13
Electricity	0	0	0	0	2	0.08
Total	45	1.80	6	1.52	82	2.54

Note: Totals include deaths from other causes as well as the ones listed.

The Farmington disaster aroused union, political, and public opinion in favor of stronger federal regulation of coal mining not only to control conditions leading to great disasters, but also to reduce the number of "day-to-day" deaths. Taking advantage of this climate of opinion, miners' groups and public health officials also pressed for regulations to reduce the incidence, and to compensate the victims, of the number-one occupational disease among coal miners: pneumoconiosis, or black lung disease.

In short order the Nixon administration, the United Mine Workers of America, and the Mine Inspectors' Institute of America all submitted bills to Congress. A basic difference among these bills concerned the question of granting the secretary of the interior authority to make regulations, the position favored by the administration, or specifying regulations in the law and allowing changes only by congressional action, the approach favored by the union and the inspectors. The bills also differed on the level of coal dust to be permitted in the mines. The administration and the mine inspectors favored an initial standard of 4.5 milligrams per cubic yard and an eventual level of 3.0 milligrams. The union, however, advocated the lower level, 3.0 milligrams, as the initial standard.

In testimony on the bills Bureau of Mines director John F. O'Leary quickly summarized the weaknesses in the existing federal coal-mine safety law. First, he said, "we have a mechanism which is imperfect for dealing with disaster type occurrences"; that is, existing state and federal laws simply did not prevent disasters. Second, the law gave

TABLE 7 *continued*

Wyoming		Montana		U.S.	
Deaths	Per 1,000 Employed	Deaths	Per 1,000 Employed	Deaths	Per 1,000 Employed
5	0.44	8	2.43	2,290	0.82
0	0	1	0.48	384	0.15
6	0.55	0	0	720	0.26
1	0.12	0	0	196	0.07
0	0	0	0	140	0.05
13	1.32	9	2.92	4,547	1.64

federal inspectors no authority to deal with the "day-to-day accidents that take ninety percent of the lives." And third, the law did not address the problem of black lung disease, "the health hazard which takes perhaps two or three times as many lives as the visible accidents take." O'Leary noted that in the interval between the Farmington disaster and his testimony in March 1969 an additional forty-four coal-mine workers died "from those kinds of conditions and practices that the Bureau has no power to control."[34]

Representative John Erlenborn of Illinois was surprised to hear of those forty-four deaths and observed that, although major disasters "get a great deal of publicity," accidents involving one or two fatalities "just are not brought to our attention." Another representative, Pennsylvania's John Dent, noted that many existing federal regulations, based on hand-mining techniques, were irrelevant to actual working conditions.[35] The reality of work and death in the mines, it seems, finally was seeping into the halls and committee rooms of Congress.

Interior Secretary Walter Hickel, speaking for the Nixon administration's bill, declared that "we must . . . eliminate the accidents that kill miners by the ones, twos, or threes as well as prevent major disasters." Reducing overall accident rates, Hickel noted, was important not only for humanitarian but for economic reasons, for without improvement it would become increasingly difficult to recruit coal miners, a problem that, in turn, could jeopardize future energy supplies.[36]

TABLE 8: *Coal-Mining Fatalities in the Rocky Mountain States and U.S., 1967–1969*

Cause	Colorado		New Mexico		Utah	
	Deaths	Per 1,000 Employed	Deaths	Per 1,000 Employed	Deaths	Per 1,000 Employed
Falls of rock and coal	9	2.20	0	0	3	0.94
Explosions	0	0	0	0	0	0
Haulage	3	0.73	0	0	0	0
Machinery	0	0	0	0	0	0
Electricity	0	0	0	0	0	0
Total	12	2.93	0	0	3	0.94

Note: Totals include deaths from other causes as well as the ones listed.

Western coal operators were among the few interests strongly opposed to a new federal coal-mine law. Just three weeks after the Farmington disaster Rocky Mountain Coal Mining Institute president John A. Reeves told an Interior Department conference on coal-mining safety that his group believed that "the present mining laws as they now exist with the states and the federal government are adequate." In a familiar refrain Reeves said cooperation among managers and workers in observing safety procedures, and research and education, not more legislation, were the solution to the problem of mine safety. "To legislate more punitive mining laws," Reeves said, "will have the effect of discouraging men from entering our industry" at a time when it needed to attract "the very finest people available."[37]

Such opposition could not stem the tide of opinion in favor of stronger federal regulation, and on 30 December 1969 President Nixon signed into law the new Federal Coal Mine Health and Safety Act. This stronger federal law directed the secretary of the interior to establish mandatory health and safety standards to apply to all mines and set interim standards to apply until the secretary could act. The act required all mines to develop roof-control plans; set a minimum ventilation standard of nine thousand cubic feet per minute at the last crosscut and three thousand cubic feet per minute at the face; required the use of permissible explosives; and called for rock dusting to within forty feet of working faces, except in very wet mines. The law also set standards for electrical equipment and power lines

TABLE 8 *continued*

Wyoming		Montana		U.S.	
Deaths	Per 1,000 Employed	Deaths	Per 1,000 Employed	Deaths	Per 1,000 Employed
0	0	0	0	278	0.67
0	0	0	0	106	0.26
2	1.49	0	0	93	0.22
1	0.74	0	0	48	0.11
0	0	0	0	34	0.08
3	2.23	0	0	736	1.77

and lighting, required safety devices on haulage and man-trips, and specified necessary fire-fighting equipment.

The new law also set standards for coal-dust concentrations, requiring by 30 June 1970 a level of no more than 3.0 milligrams per cubic meter of air and no more than 2.0 milligrams by 31 December 1972. The secretary could grant noncompliance exemptions for up to one year where owners could demonstrate progress in reducing dust levels. In addition to setting dust standards, the law required operators to provide approved respirators for all workers whenever they were exposed to dust levels above the standards. The act also provided compensation for miners disabled by black lung disease, or for their surviving widows and dependents. Miners filing for benefits by the end of 1972 were eligible for federally funded compensation. After 1972 state workers' compensation or employers' self-insurance programs would pay benefits.

To enforce the act, Bureau of Mines inspectors were to visit every mine four times per year and could close mines where they found conditions of imminent danger. In addition, they were to notify operators of other potentially dangerous conditions and fix a time limit for their correction. If an operator failed to make the required repairs in the time allowed, inspectors could then close the offending mine. Operators were liable for fines of up to ten thousand dollars for each violation. The act gave operators another incentive to obey the law by requiring them to pay employees their regular wages during any period when their mine was closed for violations.[38]

Passage of the Coal Mine Health and Safety Act did not silence opposition to federal regulation, and small operators and state officials were especially vocal in their criticism. When a group of small operators gathered at Florence, Colorado, in April 1970 to demonstrate their disapproval of the new law, they found they had an ally in state inspector Donald Haske. (Tom Allen, who had held the job since 1934, retired at the end of 1963 and died in March 1964. Haske, who began working in Colorado coal mines in 1926, joined the coal-mine inspection department in 1959. He succeeded Allen as chief inspector in February 1964.) Responding to the operators' complaints, Haske said the new law was "just impractical," especially in its equipment and ventilation requirements. Haske repeated the old industry argument that stiffer regulation would drive the small operators out of business. "The small operator couldn't comply even if he had the financial means," he said, adding that "in some respects we're creating greater problems than we have now."[39] How different Haske's statement is from that of James Dalrymple, who, a half-century earlier, had observed that, if stricter safety standards put the "little fellow" out of business, then the sooner the better.

Haske restated his criticism in his annual report for 1970, saying that "many of our small mines may find it difficult to remain in operation unless constructive revisions" were made in the act. The state inspector also voiced his complaints to the 1971 meeting of the Rocky Mountain Coal Mining Institute, where he declared that if the government fully enforced the 1969 law "there will not be a small coal mine operating in Colorado." Haske related the comment of one Colorado operator who told him that "when you have to hire an attorney and a bookkeeper for a one man operation the only way you want to get is out."[40]

Another friend of the small operators was Colorado's U.S. Senator Gordon Allott, who in April 1970 carried their complaints to the Interior Department. In asking for a review of the impact of the new law on small operators, Allott expressed concern not only that the law might drive many of them out of business, but also that many southern Colorado communities were worried about resulting rising costs and shortages of coal.[41]

The small operators' protests continued into 1971, sometimes escalating to outright resistance against federal inspectors. In June operator Violet Smith, of Hesperus, told of chasing a federal inspector from her property, telling him to "get your goddamned self out of here." Smith also confessed to hauling another inspector out of his car to "give him a few" after he ordered her mine shut. [42]

In August 1971 the Bureau of Mines held hearings in Denver to listen to the small operators' complaints. One owner, Bonita Steele, of Oak Creek, said that "without an act of God" her family's mine would be out of business by the end of 1972. Steele complained that the law had forced her to fill the mine with expensive "gadgets and trinkets" and that ventilation regulations subjected her employees to a constant twenty-mile-per-hour wind that, she claimed, resulted in sub-zero wind-chill factors in the winter. [43]

There was, in fact, some evidence to support claims that the federal law was hurting the small operators. The Bureau of Mines reported that 272 small mines had closed nationwide by April 1970. It was not clear, however, that all of them had shut down because of federal regulation. In 1973 Colorado's deputy commissioner of mines, Norman R. Blake, reported that during the first two and one-half years under the law the state lost thirty-three producing operations. He conceded, however, that there had been no loss in total employment in the mines. Still, Blake summed up the feelings of operators and state officials when he said that the U.S. Bureau of Mines was "acting as the coal mine superintendent" and the inspectors had taken over for foremen and firebosses. "All the operator does is sign the paychecks and pay the bills. The Federal government is running the mine." [44]

The Bureau of Mines caught criticism from all directions. Soon it was under attack from those who believed that it was not enforcing the law strictly enough. In a report on problems in implementing the law during its first year, the General Accounting Office (GAO) found that there were many recurring violations due to lenient, confusing, and inequitable regulations; that inspections were inadequate because of shortages of manpower and equipment; and that many operators had failed to comply with roof-control and ventilation requirements. To correct these problems the GAO recommended increasing the Bureau of Mines' staff, clarifying and making regulations more uniform, using more vigorous authority in closing mines of repeat violators, providing more guidelines for local offices and inspectors regarding regulations, and giving more guidance for operators to help them comply with the law. Scholars and industry critics

TABLE 9: *Coal-Mining Fatalities in the*
Rocky Mountain States and U.S., 1970–1980

Cause	Colorado Deaths	Colorado Per 1,000 Employed	New Mexico Deaths	New Mexico Per 1,000 Employed	Utah Deaths	Utah Per 1,000 Employed
Falls of rock and coal	15	0.66	0	0	18	0.68
Explosions	0	0	0	0	0	0
Haulage	2	0.09	0	0	5	0.20
Machinery	3	0.15	3	0.36	3	0.14
Electricity	2	0.08	0	0	1	0.03
Total	27	1.23	9	0.99	32	1.27

Note: Totals include deaths from other causes as well as the ones listed.

also noted the inspectors' reluctance to use their authority, including closing mines. This was owing, in part, to the absence of strong leadership in Washington and to the supposed tradition of cooperation between the Bureau of Mines and operators. Bureau officials feared that aggressive enforcement would antagonize operators and increase resistance to the law.[45]

These criticisms, coupled with a series of explosions and flooding disasters in coal and other mines, prompted Congress in 1977 to revise the federal mining law. The new legislation took responsibility for mine-safety enforcement from the Interior Department and the Bureau of Mines and entrusted it to the Department of Labor and a new Mine Safety and Health Administration. Congress also extended the 1969 law to cover metal and nonmetal as well as coal mines and strengthened the government's rule-making and enforcement authority. In addition, the secretary of labor was authorized to issue mandatory regulations requiring operators to provide health and safety training for their employees.[46]

Despite implementation and enforcement problems, fatality rates did improve after the enactment of the Coal Mine Health and Safety Act. In the first decade under the law the rate of death in the mines nationally was half of that experienced during the life of the 1952 federal law (tables 8 and 9). In the Rocky Mountain region New Mexico, Wyoming, and Montana compared well with the national average while Utah and Colorado remained considerably higher (table 9). Falls of rock and coal continued to be the leading cause of

TABLE 9 *continued*

Wyoming		Montana		U.S.	
Deaths	Per 1,000 Employed	Deaths	Per 1,000 Employed	Deaths	Per 1,000 Employed
1	0.03	0	0	554	0.27
1	0.02	0	0	106	0.05
0	0	1	0.11	297	0.15
2	0.22	0	0	175	0.09
1	0.09	0	0	81	0.04
10	0.52	1	0.11	1,687	0.83

death, though two states, New Mexico and Montana (which by 1980 had virtually no underground mining) had no deaths from rock and coal falls.[47]

Much of the credit for lower fatality rates must go to the stronger role of the federal government in inspection and regulation. However, it is notable that of the Rocky Mountain states those with the largest percentage of underground mining, Colorado and Utah, also had the highest fatality rates, indicative of the role of technological change, especially the shift from underground to surface mining, in reducing the incidence of death and injury in the coal-mining industry. In short, technological change had as much or more to do with declining death rates as did regulation.

All of the federal coal-mining laws, from the first inspection act passed in 1941 to the amendments of 1977, intended that federal and state agencies cooperate not only in inspection and enforcement but also in mine-safety research and training programs. In fact, the larger federal regulatory role gave the states an incentive to reduce their own regulatory activities. One scholar noted that, by effectively superseding state regulatory functions, federal control left "the principal remaining role of the States . . . the training of mine personnel."[48]

Under "state plan" agreements provided for in the 1969 law, the states and the Bureau of Mines were to work together to bring state and federal laws into conformity, conduct mine inspections, and exchange information and reports. To that end, the Colorado legislature in 1971 directed the coal-mine inspection office, by then a division of the Department of Natural Resources, to accept operators' plans for roof support and ventilation approved by the Bureau of Mines. The legislature also directed the state inspector to work with the bureau in certifying mine officials. More significantly, the legislature also told the inspection division to accept Bureau of Mines inspection reports in lieu of state inspection.[49] Thus, fewer than two years after passage of the Federal Coal Mine Health and Safety Act, the state of Colorado began to withdraw from active coal-mine inspection work.

New Mexico made a bolder start than Colorado in contending with the new federal law, but it, too, eventually handed the job of inspection over to the Bureau of Mines. In February 1972 the state and the bureau concluded an agreement delegating to the New Mexico mine inspector authority to enforce the federal, as well as state, coal-mining laws. Six years later, however, the state cancelled the agreement, and the bureau's Mine Enforcement and Safety Administration took over the job of inspecting New Mexico's mines.[50]

The decline of state inspection activity gives a clear measure of the impact of the expanded federal role on state agencies. In Wyoming the state conducted 260 regular inspections in 1972, down from 391 in 1969. In Colorado in 1969 the state inspectors made 359 inspections. Inspections increased to 390 in 1970. For the rest of the decade the annual number of inspections fluctuated, but the trend was generally downward until, in 1980, the division made only 122 inspections. In 1981 the Colorado legislature mandated a further reduction in state inspection activity by requiring inspections only of those mines employing an average of more than seventy-five full-time employees. Montana in the same year abolished the office of state coal-mine inspector.[51]

In the 1970s, as state inspection activity decreased, coal-mine inspection agencies shifted their attention and resources toward safety education and training programs. In Colorado the legislature in 1971 mandated this shift in emphasis and instructed the coal-mine inspection division to "expand programs for the education and training of operators . . . and of miners in recognition, avoidance, and prevention of accidents." The legislature was especially concerned that mine workers and supervisors be trained in the use of flame safety lamps and other devices for detecting explosive gas. Thus, in training programs, as they had been in inspection, lawmakers in Colorado were particularly concerned with preventing explosion disasters. To its credit, the coal-mine inspection division set about developing programs to train miners in other aspects of mine safety. By the mid-1970s junior and community colleges and high schools were conducting training programs, including courses in electricity, ventilation and dust control, roof control, machinery operation, supervisory skills, and safety and rescue techniques.[52]

As state training programs grew, however, officials in charge of them sounded notes familiar for more than a century. Training, Colorado's coal-mine inspector said, would enable miners to "upgrade themselves and work more safely." Through miner training, the state could combat "the carelessness, negligence, and unsafe acts which are the predominant cause of most needless worker injury, illness and incapacitation." "As we enter the 1980s," the inspector said, "there is an opportunity to have better trained miners who should have knowledge of potential hazards and a 'safety awareness' to safely produce when facing a hostile workplace."[53] In the 1980s, as in the 1880s, officials continued to place the main burden of safety and death in the mines on the shoulders of the miners.

Chapter 10

Conclusion

"Utah Mine Fire Traps 27," the headline reported. The fire, in the Wilberg Mine near the town of Orangeville in Emery County, erupted on 19 December 1984. At first, rescuers hoped that some or all of the trapped miners and company executives might have found safety and fresh air deep inside the mine. As the days passed, however, that slim hope faded. A member of the rescue team described the scene inside the mine as an inferno in which the fire was heard more than seen. "Fire was mostly on the floor. It was on the ribs, up on the top; it was everywhere. . . . It was so smokey all you could see is six inches in front of your mask. All you could do was hear it."[1] Then they found the bodies. Twenty-five of the dead were recovered right away; the other two could not be found in the dense smoke and fire. They were brought out a year later, after the fire had burned itself out.

At the time of the fire, investigation and speculation focused on the mine's conveyor belt. The miners that night were working for a production record. The prize was a steak dinner. Five executives of the Emery Mining Company, which operated the mine for the Utah Light and Power Company, were on hand for the event. The furious pace of work that evening, it was thought, might have overburdened the conveyor. An overheated bearing could have ignited dust and fine particles of coal which the conveyor quickly spread throughout the mine.

Two years later, however, the U.S. Labor Department's Mine Safety and Health Administration (MSHA) concluded that the conveyor and the production drive did not cause the fire. The blaze, the agency reported, began in an overheated air compressor. The compressor was not equipped with required heat-sensing and fire-fighting equipment. MSHA also cited the operator for some other violations, including failure to provide adequate escapeways, inadequate emergency evacuation training (including the use of emergency respirators), and failure to maintain the mine's telephone system. Even though MSHA's report dismissed the production drive of the night of 19 December as a direct cause of the disaster, it still revealed that basic safety procedures were ignored or forgotten in the effort to produce coal. However, a spokesman for the Utah Power and Light Company called the report "severely flawed" and accused the agency of attempting to "deflect any responsibility away from itself."[2]

Shock and anger over the Wilberg disaster spread beyond the boundaries of Utah, across the entire Rocky Mountain region. A *Denver Post* editorial was typical. "Like other Westerners," the *Post* said, "Coloradans will react from our bitter heritage of mining disasters." Recalling the April 1917 Hastings disaster, in which 121 miners died, the editorial found that "the circumstances were similar to last week's Wilberg fire" and concluded that, "when the Hastings disaster can be replicated 68 years later in Utah, we obviously haven't made enough progress." The *Post* suggested that the time had come for a public policy decision to eliminate underground coal mining altogether.[3]

In fact, much had changed in those sixty-eight years. The Wilberg miners worked, and died, in a very different environment than did the Hastings miners. At Hastings the miners still used pick-mining methods. At Wilberg they worked in a highly mechanized operation. In 1917 the union was in defeat; in 1984 it was an accepted part of the industrial environment. The men in the Hastings mine worked hard to dig and load as much coal as they could, but they were not striving for a group achievement and a fancy steak dinner. They merely were toiling to feed and house themselves and their families.

Coal mining is a very dangerous job, but death in the mines owed less to the inherent dangers of the coal miner's work than to the complex human, economic, and technological relations of work. In the pick-mining era, and even after the introduction of undercutting machinery, the miner in his room did most of the work of producing coal. He undercut the seam, drilled and loaded shots, brushed floors and ribs, laid track, and cleaned and timbered the roof. Considered to be a contract worker, the miner received a tonnage rate; the more coal he loaded, the more he earned.

As an "independent" contractor, however, the miner was not free of dependence on others. He could not do his job without the mule driver or haulage operator, the day men who maintained the entries, and, later, the machine operator and the shot firer. That dependence gave other workers, especially drivers and shot firers, an element of control over the coal miner. Exercising more formal authority in the mine were foremen and firebosses who could hire and fire, assign good and bad workplaces, require miners to do deadwork, or close their rooms. Mine officials, especially foremen and superintendents, often had their own agendas, separate from those of miners and even of their employers. Faced with their employer's desire that they run a mine that was both safe and productive, foremen and superintendents too often chose production over safety. In that sense Hastings and Wilberg shared a deadly similarity: the willingness to risk safety in favor of more production.

In the pick-mining era, however, that choice most often fell not to managers and executives, but to the miner at the face. Every hour he spent taking down bad roof, fetching and putting up timbers, brushing floors and ribs, and laying track was time not spent loading coal. The contract system thus contained a built-in economic incentive for miners to avoid doing such deadwork, to choose earnings over safety. Cycles of boom and bust in the industry added to that incentive. In periods of decline, such as the 1920s and 1930s, miners facing fewer workdays or outright unemployment sought to make the most of each day on the job.

Altogether, this complex web of work relations created an environment of death in the mines. Coal-mine fatality rates in the five Rocky Mountain states consistently surpassed national averages. Unfortunately, consideration of why the West's mines were more dangerous yields few conclusive answers.

Coal mining in the Rocky Mountain region differed from the rest of the industry in few significant ways. Nationally, large operators dominated the industry, though small companies also were found. Miners everywhere worked for tonnage rates and had the same problems with foremen, shot firers, drivers, and day men. The introduction of mining machines altered work and safety conditions everywhere. Among western coal-mining states, those least or latest mechanized tended to have the highest death rates. However, the progress of mechanization in the West, beginning as early as the 1880s and becoming widespread in the 1930s, did not differ dramatically from the national trend. No evidence suggests that employers, supervisors, and state officials in the West were any more or less callous of miners' lives. All generally believed that the men themselves were liable for their own safety. Personal injury laws were similar all over the United States. Coal camps in the East and Midwest were, by the early twentieth century, heavily populated by ethnic minorities. The ethnic mosaic in the West differed to the extent that Mexican and Asian miners were more likely to be found there than in other areas. Coal camps everywhere in the country were controlled, if not owned outright, by operators, who dominated economic, social, and political life. Coal-mining laws did not differ greatly from region to region. All tended to focus on preventing explosion disasters. Western laws, at the time of their enactment, often were considered to be very advanced. Even the pattern of death in western coal mines did not differ from the national trend. Though the Rocky Mountain states recorded higher-than-average overall rates, falls of rock and coal, haulage accidents, and other day-to-day hazards caused more deaths than did explosions.

Why, then, did the Rocky Mountain West produce such high fatality rates? One answer is climate. Aridity, combined with the frequently very low moisture content of the coals, was conducive to the generation and suspension of great quantities of dust in the air. The West's arid climate, then, made for a greater explosion hazard. But historically, as we have seen, falls of roof and coal—not explosions—were the leading cause of death in the mines. In many western coalfields the overburden of rock and shale covering coal seams was very unstable. Layers of shale, especially, often were thin and very friable. CF&I's E. H. Weitzel in 1914 told both the U.S. Industrial Commission and a congressional committee that he considered the

Rocky Mountain region to be the most hazardous coal-mining area in the country, especially for falls of rock and coal. All coal seams, Weitzel said, "were formed level." However, the violent upheavals that built the Rockies pitched many seams and left the overlying strata broken. These breaks, exposed and weakened when the coal was mined, were the cause of the region's high rock- and coal-fall death rate. "In the Eastern States, where the coal seams have not been subject to these upheavals," Weitzel said, "they do not have those difficulties." Several years later a U.S. Bureau of Mines official noted that the practice of pulling pillars (unmined coal left standing between rooms and entries) in worked-out areas—more common in the West than in other regions—made unstable roof conditions more dangerous.[4]

In addition to these factors of climate and geology, the progress of organized labor differed in the West. Coal miners in three of the five Rocky Mountain states were not successfully organized until the 1930s. In some eastern and midwestern fields miners worked under union contracts, which included important safety and deadwork rules, many years earlier. Nonetheless, the successful organization of Montana and Wyoming coal miners early in the twentieth century led to no immediate, dramatic improvement in fatality rates in those states.

These differences, especially of climate and geology, help to explain at least in part the Rocky Mountain region's higher coal-mining death rate. However, they are not entirely convincing. The rate of death due to haulage accidents in the West, which would not have been influenced by aridity or geology, also consistently surpassed national averages. It may be that definitive answers to this problem lie outside of the mines and beyond laws and regulations, in more in-depth study of the miners' communities. Or it may be that there are no definitive answers and that this riddle will remain unsolved.

Scholars of western coal mining are not alone in this problem, for the riddle of higher-than-average death rates also applies to the West's hard-rock mines. For example, Mark Wyman has found that mines in Colorado, Montana, and Idaho in the late nineteenth and early twentieth centuries had fatality rates two and three times higher than similar mines in Europe. Montana, in the period from 1894 through 1908, had a rate of 3.53 deaths per thousand employed, and Idaho, from 1903 through 1908, reported a rate of 2.47, compared to rates of 1.14 in the United Kingdom, 1.07 in Germany, 2.02 in France, and 0.75 in Belgium from 1899 through 1906. In Colorado, from 1896 through 1908, hard-rock miners died at an average rate of 2.80 per thousand.[5] In the same period Colorado's coal-mine fatality rate averaged 6.28 per thousand.

In comparing hard-rock and coal-mining death rates, Wyman has repeated the old error of emphasizing explosion disasters. Coal mining received more publicity about accidents, he writes, "largely due to the fact that coal-mine disasters left large numbers of men killed, while metal-mine fatalities usually occurred one or two at a time."[6] In fact, in terms of hazards, patterns of death, work relations, and regulation, coal and metal mining had much in common.

Falling objects—rocks, timbers, tools—were the leading cause of accidents among hard-rock miners, followed by haulage, drilling, and machinery accidents. Falls down shafts and holes also were common. Explosives typically caused about 2 or 3 percent of accidents and usually involved delayed or misfired shots. In addition to these hazards, hard-rock miners encountered danger from noxious gases, generated by dynamite, which sometimes caused them to lose consciousness or, possibly worse, dulled their senses and reactions, making it difficult for them to work safely or keep their balance on fast-moving mine cages. Extreme heat, a problem rarely found in western coal mines, also plagued hard-rock miners. As miners drove shafts deeper into the earth, they often encountered natural hot water, which raised air temperatures to as high as 150 degrees. The heat sapped the miners' strength and, like the blasting gases, sometimes dulled their senses. Tired, unalert, or inattentive men sometimes slipped and fell into scalding water or injured themselves with tools and explosives. Occupational diseases also plagued the hard-rock miners. In silver mines workers risked lead poisoning from inhaling lead-carbonate ore dust. Silicosis, or "miner's con," caused by breathing in fine particles of rock dust, destroyed the metal miner's lungs as surely as coal dust ruined the coal miner's.[7]

Silicosis was largely a disease of technology. High-speed drills generated great volumes of rock dust that inadequate or nonexistent ventilation did not carry away. Indeed, technology affected work and safety conditions in the hard-rock mines as it did in the coal mines. In the gold, silver, and copper mines, the miner's traditional skills gave way to machinery. Especially important was the air-powered drill, introduced in the 1860s and 1870s, which replaced the hammer and hand-held drill of the skilled double-jacking team. As it did in coal mining, mechanization not only speeded production, but also brought with it new hazards. Power drills, high-speed cages, electric haulage, and other devices intended to make work easier, more efficient, and more productive had, at least initially, the effect of increasing work and health hazards. Eventually, though, as miners became accustomed to new technologies, mechanization did reduce accident and death rates.[8]

In hard-rock mining, as in coal mining, owners and managers pressed for maximum production, often at the expense of safety. In *Hard Rock Epic* Mark Wyman recorded a miner's recollection of how pressure for production could compromise safety as demands for more ore came down the line from management to the shift boss. As he traveled from stope to stope (the hard-rock miner's room) yelling "Rock, Rock, Rock!" the shift boss looked on the timberman as "a nuisance who blocks the tracks and stations with his timber, thus decreasing production."[9] How similar this is to the coal miners' frequent complaints about foremen and superintendents who placed a higher priority on production than on lives.

Western states and territories enacted laws for the regulation and inspection of hard-rock mines beginning in the 1870s, though one, Arizona, did not act until 1912. Wyman calls the state inspectors of the late nineteenth and early twentieth centuries "the conscience of the West" on the subject of mining safety.[10] As in coal mining, however, early laws were not very effective, and inspectors found themselves hobbled by weak, cumbersome enforcement procedures and by the industry's resistance to regulation.

Although hard-rock and coal mining had much in common, there were important differences. Even though explosion disasters were not the leading cause of death in the coal mines, they did occur. For all their hazards, hard-rock mines did not produce explosive dusts that could turn the very air into a deadly tongue of flame. More important, however, than any specific work hazard in distinguishing the two kinds of mining was the fundamental factor of wages. Some hard-rock miners worked under the contract system, in which the job went to the lowest bidder. That may have encouraged those miners to cut corners and run unnecessary risks. However, most hard-rock miners worked for day wages. Since their earnings did not depend directly on their daily output, they did not labor under an immediate, personal incentive to avoid safety work, even though owners and managers pressed them to maximize production. More than any other single factor, the tonnage rate distinguished the work and safety environment of the coal miner from that of the hard-rock miner and explains the coal industry's higher death rates.

By the time of Wilberg, pick mining had all but disappeared from the coal mines of the West. Except in Utah, in fact, underground mining had given way to surface extraction. Where miners still worked underground, they usually labored in highly mechanized and closely supervised operations. And they received daily wages, not tonnage rates. As coal mines mechanized, death rates declined dramatically.

From the early days of the Rocky Mountain coal-mining industry, government tried to regulate working conditions in the mines. Until at least the middle of the twentieth century, however, those efforts generally were ineffective. For decades the West's coal-producing states registered fatality rates far above national averages. Occasionally, the states tried to improve their coal-mining laws, but major reform efforts usually followed some great disaster or, worse, a series of disasters. This was the case in Utah, in 1901, when the state passed a new law in the wake of the Scofield disaster. Wyoming's first coal-mining law came in the wake of the 1886 explosion at Almy. In Colorado the 1913 law, partly the result of Progressive ideals, owed much to the uproar over the disasters at Primero, Starkville, and Delagua.

The tendency for major disasters to lead to legislative initiatives also characterized the federal government's involvement in coal-mine inspection and regulation. The *United Mine Workers Journal* once called it an unwritten law of political behavior in the United States "that Congressional action on coal mine safety occurs only after some appalling disaster has taken a fearful toll of miners' lives and shocked the conscience of the nation."[11] The first federal coal-mine inspection law, passed in 1891, was the product of concern over rising coal-mine fatalities in the territories, including New Mexico. A series of disasters in the first decade of the twentieth century led to the creation of the U.S. Bureau of Mines. A research agency, the bureau was established to study the problem of mine safety and recommend solutions to industry and state governments. However, the agency had no authority to inspect mines and enforce regulations. Disasters in 1939 and 1940, coupled with growing concern about the economic and strategic importance of coal as the nation moved toward war, prompted Congress to grant the Bureau of Mines the right to make annual inspections of coal mines in the United States; nonetheless, the agency still had no police powers.

The federal government exercised direct regulatory authority over the nation's coal mines for the first time in 1946, when President Truman seized the mines. During the seizure the Bureau of Mines enforced a coal-mine safety code issued by the Interior Department. That code became the basis for several major changes in state laws, including those of Colorado, Wyoming, and Montana.

Following the Orient Number Two disaster in Illinois, Congress gave the Bureau of Mines permanent inspection and regulatory authority. The Coal Mine Safety Act of 1952 included the provisions of the 1946 code but applied only to mines employing at least fifteen workers underground. Fourteen years later, however, the evidence showing small mines to be more dangerous than larger operations finally led Congress to apply the law to all mines.

Yet another federal law, the Coal Mine Health and Safety Act of 1969, was the product of a major disaster, the November 1968 explosion in the Consolidation Number Nine at Farmington, West Virginia. This law gave the Interior Department the authority to formulate and enforce coal-mine safety regulations. And it included dust standards to try to reduce the incidence of black lung disease.

Time after time state and federal lawmakers passed reform laws, and time after time the result was, at best, only a marginal improvement in death rates. Coal-mining laws, at least until the federal act of 1969, failed mainly because they did not deal with the major, day-to-day causes of death in the mines. Recall the surprise of Illinois congressman John Erlenborn, who, during the hearings on the 1969 law, learned of the high rate of death due to nondisaster causes such as falls of roof and coal. Erlenborn noted that he and his fellow legislators heard only of the great disasters, whereas the day-to-day fatalities "just are not brought to our attention."[12] What was true in 1969 also was true in 1886, 1901, and 1913.

Political expedience largely explains the emphasis on preventing the great explosion catastrophes. Lawmakers, like a stream of water, follow the path of least resistance. In the climate of opinion surrounding reform efforts, usually following some disaster, it was easiest to develop the necessary consensus among operators, labor leaders, and government officials to pass laws raising ventilation and dust-control standards but doing little or nothing effective about roof and coal falls or accidents from haulage, machinery, or electricity. Besides, for many years government and industry officials reckoned that death and injuries from those day-to-day causes were the fault of careless, negligent, greedy miners.

Preventing major disasters also served the interests of the larger corporations. Higher ventilation and dust-control standards not only promised to prevent catastrophic loss of plant and equipment, but also created competitive disadvantages for smaller operators in the form of higher equipment and operating costs. Following the enactment of Colorado's 1913 law, for example, both the Colorado Fuel and Iron Company and the Rocky Mountain Fuel Company increased their shares of production at the expense of smaller competitors.

Small operators always complained about the impact of more stringent regulation on their businesses, and sometimes they were vocal enough to win some legislative concessions. In the 1920s and 1930s they succeeded in getting the Colorado legislature to exempt them from crucial portions of the law, much to the frustration of State Inspector James Dalrymple. In 1952, 1966, 1969, and later they complained (with less success) that the expensive "gadgets and trinkets" required by federal regulation would drive them out of business.

The small operators' problems illustrate a larger public policy dilemma: the desire of legislatures to protect society and promote a social good versus the equally strong impulse not to dampen or restrain enterprise. How, if at all, could Congress and the states protect coal-mine workers without forcing small operators out of business and, consequently, increasing the grip of large corporations on the industry? The long-term tendency, at least in the area of disaster prevention, was to err on the side of safety and on the side of consolidation.

The fact that the coal-mining laws did not shift the major responsibility for mine safety, and death, from the individual miner to industry or government gave major operators another reason to accept safety regulation. Until the federal government assumed the main role in mine regulation and inspection, laws did not adequately address the major day-to-day causes of death. Thus they imposed on the industry few significant duties or costs other than helping to compensate the injured or their survivors after the fact.

Coal-mining laws also did not address the underlying causes of high death rates found in the relations of work in the mines. They did little or nothing to alter the tradition of paying miners tonnage rates; they did not alter the relationship between miners and other workers, such as drivers, machine operators, and shot firers, who could affect their ability to earn; and they did little, beyond nominally forbidding certain forms of harassment, to alter the authority of foremen and superintendents over the miners' lives.

Nor did the laws do much to change the persistent attitudes of industry and government officials, who believed that miners, through their greed, negligence, illiteracy, or ethnic inferiority, deliberately killed themselves and their colleagues. Colorado's John McNeil in 1886 said that "disobedience, incompetence and negligence fully explain the cause of as many accidents, if not more" than were due to any inherent hazards in coal mining. McNeil's comment differs little from the 1978 statement of the Colorado Division of Mines that the key to safer mines lay in combating "the carelessness, negligence, and unsafe acts which are the predominant cause of most needless worker injury, illness and incapacitation." Even when operators and mine inspectors were aware of the connection between work relations and death in the mines, they continued to insist that the miners were responsible, that they ought to know better, and that their grievances about deadwork were "simply a quibble."[13]

Nevertheless, fatality rates have declined in the twentieth century, especially in the decades since World War II. That improvement, however, was not so much the result of coal-mining laws, but the consequence of fundamental changes in the coal-mining industry and in the relations of work. Also at work were changes in the larger political and legal environment.

Influenced by the spirit of Progressivism, the law, if not personal opinions, on responsibility for the costs of coal-mining accidents began to change in the first two decades of the century. The enactment of workers' compensation laws and the dismantling of the common-law doctrines of assumption of risk, fellow-servant negligence, and contributory negligence, which so often barred injured workers or their survivors from financial compensation, led industry and government to accept the expenses of coal-mine accidents as part of the economic and social costs of the business. In practice, workers' compensation protected operators as much as workers by limiting the costs of compensation and insulating them from expensive lawsuits.

A major industrial change affecting work relations occurred when miners won the right to organize and bargain collectively. Unionization brought better and more stable wages, agreements on deadwork, safety standards and grievance procedures, and rules governing the relations between workers and mine officials. These gains, in turn, lessened somewhat the pressure on miners to choose production and earnings over safety.

Mechanization brought about the most important changes in work relations and safety. As machines took over the various functions and skills of mining coal, the tonnage rate disappeared and with it went the single most important incentive for miners to choose production over safety. In a mechanized mine smaller work forces labored in closely supervised teams in concentrated areas, rather than in teams of two or three scattered throughout the mine. The closer supervision afforded by mechanized production meant greater management responsibility for safety, including more concern with training miners. If nothing else, mechanization gave operators larger capital investments to protect. Ultimately, the shift from underground to surface mining in many areas simply eliminated the necessity of sending workers into the hazardous underground environment.

In the 1980s the shock and outrage accompanying a disaster such as that at Wilberg may be greater than was the reaction to a Dawson, or a Castle Gate, or a Starkville earlier in the century. Declining death rates, tougher laws, and faith in the ability of machines to do better the work of error-prone humans convince us that such things ought not to be possible. But they remain possible as long as society needs to extract fuel from the earth and as long as men and women are willing to go deep into the earth to get it.

Notes

Chapter 1

1. J. M. Sampson, "Mine Inspection in Wyoming Mines," Rocky Mountain Coal Mining Institute, *Proceedings, 1942*, 21; Leroy Hafen, ed., *The Far West and the Rockies Historical Series, 1820–1875* (Glendale, Calif.: Arthur H. Clark Co., 1956), 4:91, 5:73, 235; Frederick Athearn, "Black Diamonds: A History of Federal Coal Policy in the Western United States, 1862–1981," *Journal of the West* 31, no. 4 (October 1982): 44; William G. B. Carson, ed., "William Carr Lane Diary," *New Mexico Historical Review* 39, no. 4 (October 1964): 292–93; Donald Joseph McClurg, "Labor Organization in the Coal Mines of Colorado, 1878–1933" (Ph.D. dissertation, University of California, Berkeley, 1959), 3–4.

2. Maynard A. Peck, "Some Economic Aspects of the Coal Industry in Boulder County, Colorado" (Ph.D. dissertation, University of Colorado, Boulder, 1947), 10; R. A. Pierce, "The Lignite Fields of Colorado," *Coal Age*, 3 February 1912, 534.

3. Robert G. Athearn, *Rebel of the Rockies: A History of the Denver and Rio Grande Western Railroad* (New Haven: Yale University Press, 1962), 32.

4. "Statement and Reports of the Belle Monte Iron and Coal Company of Colorado" (New York: Sackett and Mackay, 1866), 8, in Denver Public Library, Western History Department, Mining Collection, Boulder, envelope "be"; Denver *Republican*, quoted in *Engineering and Mining Journal*, 3 December 1881, 377.

5. *Boulder County News*, 20 November 1869, 3.

6. "Second Inaugural Address of His Excellency, Frederick W. Pitkin To

The Two Branches of The Legislature of Colorado, January 11, 1881" (Denver: Tribune Publishing Co., 1881), 7–8, in Library of Congress, Records of the States of the United States, Colorado, 1861–1891, microfilm, Col. D. 2., reel 1a.

7. Colorado Fuel and Iron Company, "The Rise of a Great Industry" (n.d.), copy in Colorado Division of State Archives and Public Records, Governor's Council of National Defense, Box 22378, ff. 26; John Stirling Fischer, *A Builder of the West: The Life of William Jackson Palmer* (Caldwell, Idaho: Caxton Printers, 1939), 24, 34.

8. U.S. Commission on Industrial Relations, *Report on the Relations and Conditions of Capital and Labor Employed in the Mining Industry* (Washington, D.C.: Government Printing Office, 1901), 12:268–69; *Engineering and Mining Journal*, 29 December 1906, quoted in Duane A. Smith, *When Coal Was King: A History of Crested Butte, Colorado, 1880–1952* (Golden, Colorado: School of Mines Press, 1984), 51.

9. Charles Monroe Chase, *The Editor's Run in New Mexico and Colorado* (1882; reprint, Ft. Davis, Texas: Frontier Book Co., 1968), 162–64; LeBaron Bradford Prince, "New Mexico: Resources and Business Opportunities. Chief Justice Prince's Letter to the Tribune" (New York: 1879?).

10. Utah Investigating Committee of Governmental Units, Subcommittee on Coal Resources (1936), *Economic Study of the Development of Utah Coal Resources*, 3.

11. Salt Lake City *Daily Herald*, 22 April 1881, 26 October 1881, quoted in Athearn, *Rebel of the Rockies*, 118.

12. Colorado Bureau of Labor Statistics, *12th Biennial Report* (1909–10), 24–25.

13. Bowers to Charles Heydt, 13 May 1913, in U.S. Commission on Industrial Relations, *Final Report and Testimony*, S. Doc. 415, 64th Cong., 1st sess., 1916, 8:8411–12.

14. Edmund G. Ross, quoted in Howard R. Lamar, *The Far Southwest, 1846–1912: A Territorial History* (New Haven: Yale University Press, 1966), 150–51.

15. Mike Livoda, interview, 1 August 1975, in Eric Margolis, "Western Coal Mining as a Way of Life: An Oral History of the Colorado Coal Miners to 1914," *Journal of the West* 24, no. 3 (July 1985): 72; group interview, Biondi's Sporting Goods, Walsenburg, Colorado, 3 February 1978, ibid., 51.

16. U.S. Commission on Industrial Relations, *Final Report and Testimony* (1916), 7:6786; Colorado Bureau of Labor Statistics, *Biennial Report, 1909–1910*, quoted in U.S. Congress, House Committee on Mines and Mining, *Investigation of Conditions in the Coal Mines of Colorado*, 63d Cong., 2d sess., 1914, 176–77; *United Mine Workers Journal*, 23 July 1914, 1; U.S. Congress, House Committee on Mines and Mining, *Investigation of Conditions in the Coal Mines of Colorado*, 2:1831.

17. *Coal Age*, 27 January 1912, 501; *Engineering and Mining Journal*, 11 May 1907, 917, and 9 January 1909, 84.

18. Helen Z. Papanikolas, "Unionism, Communism, and the Great Depression: The Carbon County Coal Strike of 1933," *Utah Historical Quarterly*, 41, no. 3 (Summer 1973): 266; James B. Allen, "The Company-Owned Mining Town in the West: Exploitation or Benevolent Paternalism," in *Reflections of Western Historians*, ed. John A. Carroll (Tucson: University of Arizona Press, 1976), 179, cited in Margolis, "Western Coal Mining as a Way of Life," 51.

19. Lawrence Lewis, "Uplifting 17,000 Employees," *World's Work* 9, no. 5 (March 1905): 5939; *Denver Republican*, undated clipping [1906?] in Colorado Division of State Archives and Public Records, Department of Natural Resources, Division of Mines, Box 18337, Scrapbooks.

20. Wyoming Inspector of Coal Mines, *Annual Report, 1919*, 6; New Mexico Inspector of Mines, *Annual Report, 1918*, 65.

21. Richard Melzer, *Madrid Revisited: Life and Labor in a New Mexican Mining Camp in the Years of the Great Depression* (Santa Fe: Lightning Tree, 1976), 9–10.

22. *Trinidad Daily Advocate*, 28 August 1886, 4; Wyoming State Inspector of Coal Mines, *Annual Report, 1893*, 16, typescript in Wyoming State Archives, Museums and Historical Department, Mining Records, State Inspector of Coal Mines.

23. Message of Miguel A. Otero, Governor of New Mexico, to the 36th Legislative Assembly, January 16, 1905, in U.S. National Archives, Record Group 48, Micro M 364, reel #9, Department of the Interior, Territorial Papers, New Mexico, Letters Received, April 1851–May 27, 1907, rel. to Misc. Subjects.

24. Ben F. Selekman and Mary Van Kleeck, *Employes' Representation in Coal Mines: A Study of the Industrial Representation Plan of the Colorado Fuel and Iron Company* (New York: Russell Sage Foundation, 1924), 3.

25. Kenneth Boulding Interview, Oral History of Colorado Project, 4 March 1975, quoted in Carl Abbott, Stephen J. Leonard, and David McComb, *Colorado: A History of the Centennial State* (Boulder: Colorado Associated University Press, 1982), 316.

Chapter 2

1. *History of the Arkansas Valley* (Chicago: O. L. Baskin & Co., 1881), 597–98.

2. *Trinidad Daily Advertiser*, 30 January 1883, 2.

3. Eric Margolis, "Western Coal Mining as a Way of Life: An Oral History of the Colorado Coal Miners to 1914," *Journal of the West* 24, no. 3 (July 1985), 14.

4. William McShane, interview by H. Lee Scamehorn, January–July 1968.

5. Thomas Allen, interview by Marjorie Harkness, March 1962, in Colorado Division of State Archives and Public Records, Department of Natural Resources, Division of Mines, Administrative Files, 1883–1972, Box 43919, p. 9.

6. Ibid., 8.

7. Utah Industrial Commission, *Biennial Report, 1924–1926*, Bulletin #4, 16; *Greeley Tribune*, 26 May 1970, 24.

8. William McShane, interview by H. Lee Scamehorn, January–July 1968.

9. U.S. Congress, Senate, *Report of the United States Coal Commission*, S. Doc. 195, 68th Cong., 2d sess., 1925, pt. 3:1321.

10. David Brody, *Workers in Industrial America: Essays on the Twentieth-Century Struggle* (New York and Oxford: Oxford University Press, 1980), 3–4.

11. Thomas Allen, interview by Marjorie Harkness, March 1962.

12. James Dalrymple, "Qualifications of Coal Mine Inspectors as to Practical Ability and Technical Knowledge," Mine Inspectors' Institute of America, *Proceedings, 1924*, 21–22; Colorado Industrial Commission, Hearings, 21 December 1927, typescript in University of Colorado, Boulder, Western History Collection, Josephine Roche Papers, Box 7, "RMF CO.— Colo. Industrial Hearings—Miners' Wages and Working Conditions, Dec. 19 thru 22, 1927," 241.

13. Walt Celeski, interview, 1976, in Ronald Loren McMahon, "Visual Sociology: A Study of the Western Coal Miner" (Ph.D. dissertation, University of Colorado, Boulder, 1978), 108; William N. Page, "The Economics of Coal Mining," *The Mineral Industry*, 3 (1894): 149.

14. Lawrence Amicarella, interview, 1978, in McMahon, "Visual Sociology," 108; U.S. Congress, House, *Annual Report of the Mine Inspector for the Territory of New Mexico* (1901), H. Exec. Docs., 57th Cong., 1st sess., 1901–2, 25:312.

15. Walt Celeski, interview, 1976, University of Colorado, Institute of Behavioral Science, Coal Project.

16. Colorado State Inspector of Coal Mines, *17th Annual Report, 1929*, 8–9.

17. Henry Mathias, interview, 2 July 1975, University of Colorado, Institute of Behavioral Science, Coal Project.

18. Attorney General Theodore Thomas to Governor Benjamin Eaton, 24 May 1886, in Colorado Division of State Archives and Public Records, Governor Benjamin H. Eaton Papers, Box 26689, folder #7, "Correspondence, Appointments, Petitions, 1885; 1886; 1887."

19. Colorado General Assembly, Senate Committee to Investigate Con-

ditions in Relation to Coal Strike, *Report,* in *Senate Journal of the General Assembly of the State of Colorado, 13th Session, 1901,* 566.

20.   U.S. Commission on Industrial Relations, *The Foreign Born in Coal Mines* (Washington, D.C.: Government Printing Office, 1901), 389; H. Lee Scamehorn, "Coal-Mining in the Rocky Mountains: Boom, Bust, and Boom," in *The Twentieth Century American West,* ed. Thomas G. Alexander and John F. Bluth (Provo, Utah: Brigham Young University, Charles Redd Center for Western Studies, 1983), 35–36; "Nationalities Employed in Mines of Colorado During the Year 1912, and Per Centages," typescript in Denver Public Library, Western History Department, Edward Lawrence Doyle Papers, Box #2, Envelope #18; U.S. Commission on Industrial Relations, *Final Report and Testimony,* S. Doc. 415, 64th Cong., 1st sess., 1916, 7240; U.S. Congress, House Committee on Mines and Mining, *Investigation of Conditions in the Coal Mines of Colorado,* 63d Cong., 2d sess., 1914, 2615.

21.   Wyoming Inspector of Coal Mines, *Annual Report, 1915,* 5.

22.   New Mexico Inspector of Mines, *Annual Report, 1919,* 10.

23.   U.S. Commission on Industrial Relations, *Final Report and Testimony,* 6531.

24.   Bill Lloyd, interview, May 1978, University of Colorado, Institute of Behavioral Science, Coal Project; Jack Miller, interview, 1976, in McMahon, "Visual Sociology," 94; Jack Miller, interview in Margolis, "Western Coal Mining as a Way of Life," 18.

25.   U.S. Congress, Senate, *Report of the United States Coal Commission,* S. Doc. 195, 68th Cong., 2d sess., 1925, 1310–11; U.S. Congress, House Committee on Mines and Mining, *Investigation of Conditions in the Coal Mines of Colorado,* 1:1003, 861–62.

26.   Colorado General Assembly, Committee to Investigate Conditions in Relation to Coal Strike, *Report,* 548.

27.   *Pueblo Star-Journal,* 16 November 1913, 7.

28.   U.S. Congress, House Committee on Mines and Mining, *Investigation of Conditions in the Coal Mines of Colorado,* 2373; O. A. Adams to Governor Elias Ammons, 3 November 1913, in Colorado Division of State Archives and Public Records, Governor Elias M. Ammons Papers, Box 26751, "Corr. re Coal Miners Strike, Misc. letters in opposition to Governor's sending militia to coal fields."

29.   *Pueblo Star-Journal,* 16 November 1913, 8, 6.

30.   University of Colorado, Institute of Behavioral Science, Coal Project, "The Life of the Western Coal Miner; Part I, Toil and Rage in a New Land," videotape, 1982; U.S. Congress, Senate, *Report of the United States Coal Commission,* pt. 3:1683; Tom Allen, interview by Marjorie Harkness, 9 March 1962, 1; Victor "Tooley" Calmette, interview by Ellen Arquimbau, 25 March 1975, 7, University of Colorado, Western History Collection, Coal Creek Interviews.

31. *United Mine Workers Journal,* 17 December 1914, 4; U.S. Congress, Senate, *Report of the United States Coal Commission,* pt. 3:1773.

Chapter 3

1. The Roche anecdote is recorded in the *Denver Post,* 16 June 1958, 6; *United Mine Workers Journal,* 15 June 1965, 15; Marjorie Hornbein, "Josephine Roche: Social Worker and Coal Miner," *Colorado Magazine* 53, no. 3 (Summer 1976): 244; and David Fridtjof Halaas, "Josephine Roche, 1886–1976: Social Reformer, Mine Operator," *Colorado Heritage News* (March 1985): 4.

2. U.S. Commission on Industrial Relations, *Report on the Relations and Conditions of Capital and Labor Employed in the Mining Industry* (Washington, D.C.: Government Printing Office, 1901), 12:266.

3. Colorado General Assembly, *Session Laws, 1877,* 130.

4. Colorado General Assembly, *Session Laws, 1881,* 62–63; Carl Abbott, Stephen J. Leonard, and David McComb, *Colorado: A History of the Centennial State,* rev. ed. (Boulder: Colorado Associated University Press, 1982), 127, 344; "Second Biennial Message of His Excellency, Frederick W. Pitkin, to the Two Branches of the Legislature of Colorado, January 4th, 1883" (Denver: Daily Times Steam Printing House and Book Manufactory, 1883), 32, in Library of Congress, Records of the States of the United States, Colorado, 1861–91, microform, Col. D.2, reel 1a.

5. *Trinidad Daily Democrat,* 23 December 1882, 1; Trinidad *Daily News,* 27 January 1883, 1; and *Rocky Mountain News,* 7 February 1883, 3.

6. U.S. Department of the Interior, Bureau of Mines, *Milestones in Mine Safety Legislation,* Information Circular 6904 (1936), 8.

7. "Second Biennial Message of His Excellency, Frederick W. Pitkin," 32.

8. "Inaugural Address of His Excellency, James B. Grant, Governor of Colorado, to the Fourth General Assembly of the State of Colorado, January 9th, 1883," 6, in Library of Congress, Records of the States of the United States, Colorado, 1861–91, microform, Col. D.2, reel 1a. B. F. Rockafellow, "Incidents leading up to town building and deep coal mining at Rockvale, Colorado, by a participant, Captain B. F. Rockafellow, March 6, 1919," typescript, p.6, Colorado Historical Society, B. F. Rockafellow Collection.

9. *Leadville Democrat,* January 1883, reprinted in *Rocky Mountain News,* 8 January 1883, 6; *Rocky Mountain News,* 6 February 1883, 4.

10. *Trinidad Daily Advertiser,* 4 February 1883, 2.

11. Colorado, *Session Laws, 1883,* 102–12; Colorado State Inspector of Coal Mines (hereafter cited as CMI), *17th Annual Report, 1929,* 10. Research on the role of coal dust in explosions was fairly new and still controversial. Inspector John McNeil in 1888 recommended revising the state law to

require wetting down mine dust. CMI, *3rd Biennial Report, 1887–1888*, 8, 26–33.

12. CMI, *2nd Biennial Report, 1885–1886*, 12. The law was revised in 1885 to apply to mines employing ten men or more. Colorado General Assembly, *Session Laws, 1885*, 141.

13. CMI, *13th Biennial Report, 1907–1908*, 18.

14. CMI, *1st Annual Report, 1884*, 4; *2nd Biennial Report, 1885–1886*, 34–76; *8th Biennial Report, 1897–1898*, 3.

15. CMI, *1st Annual Report, 1884*, 3–4; John B. Ekeley, "The New Proposed Coal Mining Law for Colorado," *University of Colorado Journal of Engineering* 7 (1910–11): 27.

16. U.S. Commission on Industrial Relations, *Report on the Relations and Conditions of Capital and Labor Employed in the Mining Industry*, 12:327.

17. New Mexico (Territory), *Session Laws, 1882*, 96–98.

18. Ibid., 98. Governor Miguel A. Otero in 1902 said that "Sec. 11 of the act of our legislature, expressly limits its operation to mines then in operation." Otero to Secretary of the Interior, 20 April 1902, in U.S. National Archives, Record Group 48, Department of the Interior, Territorial Papers of New Mexico, Letters Received Relating to Inspection of Coal Mines, microform M 364, reel 7.

19. C. W. Kennedy to Governor Edmund G. Ross, 4 January 1889, in New Mexico State Records Center and Archives, Governor Edmund G. Ross Papers, Letters Received, microfilm, Roll #101, fr. 788–91.

20. Act of March 3, 1891, ch. 564, secs. 1–19; 26 Stat. L. 1104; Supp. to Rev. Stats., 1:948–50, in Daniel M. Barringer and John Stokes Adams, *The Law of Mines and Mining in the United States* (1897; reprint, St. Paul: Keef-Davidson Co., 1900), 811–14; U.S. Congress, H. Rept. 2588, 51st Cong., 1st sess., 1890, 1, 2.

21. *Congressional Record* 21 (1 September 1890): 9489–90; 22 (28 February 1891): 3537.

22. U.S. National Archives, Record Group 48, Department of the Interior, Territorial Papers of New Mexico, Letters Received Relating to Inspection of Coal Mines, microform M 364, reel 7.

23. Spears to Prince, 31 July 1892, in New Mexico State Records Center and Archives, L. Bradford Prince Papers, letters received, May–December 1892, microfilm 112, fr. 523.

24. Bartlett to Acting Governor Silas Alexander, 16 December 1892, in U.S. National Archives, Record Group 48, Department of the Interior, Territorial Papers of New Mexico, Letters Received Relating to Inspection of Coal Mines, microform M 364, reel 5; Alexander to secretary of the interior, 16 December 1892, ibid.; "The Governor's Message, 28 December 1892,"

xxxiv–xxv, in New Mexico State Records Center and Archives, L. Bradford Prince Papers, Appointments, Resignations, Proclamations, Reports to the Governor, microfilm 121, fr. 418.

25. U.S. Mine Inspector, New Mexico, *Third Annual Report, 1894–1895*, 673; *First Annual Report, 1893*, 2, in National Archives, Record Group 48, Territorial Papers of New Mexico, microform M 364; *Third Annual Report, 1894–1895*, 673.

26. Wyoming (Territory) Inspector of Coal Mines, *Annual Report, 1889*, 18, typescript in Wyoming State Archives, Museums and Historical Department, Mining Records, State Inspector of Coal Mines.

27. Wyoming (Territory), *Session Laws, 1886*, 44–57.

28. Wyoming, *Session Laws, 1890*, 340–51.

29. Walter R. Jones, "Coal Mine Explosions at Almy, Wyoming: Their Influence on Wyoming's First Coal Mining Laws," *Annals of Wyoming* 56, no. 1 (Spring 1984): 63.

30. U.S. Mine Inspector, Utah, *Annual Report, 1893*, 421.

31. See Utah Mine Inspector, *Annual Report, 1896*, 41–46.

32. Ibid., 47; *Annual Report, 1897*, 4.

33. Don Maguire, "Scofield Disaster," *Mines and Minerals* 20, no. 2 (June 1900): 486.

34. Utah, *Laws, 1901*, 83–92.

35. Montana, *Session Laws, 1891*, 282–91.

36. Montana, *Codes Annotated, 1895*, "Political Code," 75–78, sec. 580–90; *Session Laws, 1891*, 286.

Chapter 4

1. Colorado State Inspector of Coal Mines (hereafter cited as CMI), *13th Biennial Report, 1907–1908*, 20.

2. CMI, *14th Biennial Report, 1909–1910*, 130, 133, 136–46, 149–53, 154–60.

3. U.S. death rates are based on data in U.S. Department of the Interior, Bureau of Mines, Bulletin 115, *Coal Mine Fatalities in the U.S., 1870–1914* (1916), and U.S. Department of the Interior, Mine Enforcement and Safety Administration, *Injury Experience in Coal Mining, 1975*, Information Report 1077 (1978).

4. *Engineering and Mining Journal* 77 (14 January 1904): 80.

5. Data on coal-mining fatalities are derived from the reports of state and federal coal-mine inspectors and from U.S. Department of the Interior, U.S. Geological Survey, *Mineral Resources of the United States* (various years).

6. Wyoming Inspector of Coal Mines (hereafter cited as WMI), *Annual Report, 1889*, 9, typescript in Wyoming Archives, Museums and Historical Department, State Inspector of Coal Mines (hereafter cited as Wyoming

Archives); WMI, *Annual Report, 1898,* 2, and *Annual Report, 1900,* 1, typescripts in Wyoming Archives.

7. Pete Gergich, interview, 7 February 1978, University of Colorado, Boulder, Institute of Behavioral Science, Coal Project, "The Life of the Western Coal Miner; Part I, Toil and Rage in a New Land," videotape, 1982.

8. Colorado Fuel and Iron Company, *Camp and Plant* 3, no. 9 (7 March 1903): 199; F. W. Whiteside, "The Trinidad District in Colorado," *Coal Age* 1, no. 20 (24 February 1912): 634.

9. CMI, *2d Biennial Report, 1885–1886,* 28; *11th Biennial Report, 1903–1904,* 6.

10. WMI, District 2, *Annual Report, 1906,* 4, typescript in Wyoming Archives; Utah Mine Inspector (hereafter cited as UMI), *Annual Report, 1905,* 7; U.S. Mine Inspector, New Mexico (hereafter cited as USMI/NM), *Annual Report, 1896,* 699; *Annual Report, 1902,* 402; *Annual Report, 1901,* 719.

11. *Mining Magazine,* March 1906, 223, quoted in Keith Dix, *Work Relations in the Coal Industry: The Hand Loading Era, 1880–1930* (Morgantown: West Virginia University, Institute for Labor Studies, 1977), 74; *Engineering and Mining Journal* 80 (2 December 1905): 1016.

12. Mark O. Danford, in U.S. Congress, House Committee on Mines and Mining, *Investigation of Conditions in the Coal Mines of Colorado,* 63d Cong., 2d sess., 1914, 1:1029; Tom Allen, interview by Marjorie Harkness, 9 March 1962, 1, in Colorado Division of State Archives and Public Records (hereafter cited as Colorado Archives), Department of Natural Resources, Division of Mines, Box 43919, Adm. Files, 1883–1972; USMI/NM, *Annual Report, 1895,* 699; Helen Z. Papanikolas, "Utah's Coal Lands: A Vital Example of How America Became a Great Nation," *Utah Historical Quarterly* 43, no. 2 (Spring 1975): 104.

13. CMI, *11th Biennial Report, 1903–1904,* 6; USMI/NM, monthly report, 3 May 1900, in U.S. National Archives, Record Group 48, Interior Department, Territorial Papers of New Mexico, "Letters Relating to Inspection of Coal Mines," microform M 364, reel 6; USMI/NM, monthly report, 1 November 1900, ibid.; WMI, District 1, *Annual Report, 1910,* 23.

14. *Engineering and Mining Journal* 74 (20 December 1902): 811.

15. CMI, *6th Biennial Report, 1893–1894,* 5; *11th Biennial Report, 1903–1904,* 6; Colorado Bureau of Labor Statistics, *12th Biennial Report, 1909–1910,* 13.

16. John J. Boyd to Shafroth, 26 December 1910, in Colorado Archives, Governor John Franklin Shafroth, Correspondence, Box 26727. *Boulder County Miner,* 6 February 1913, clipping in Denver Public Library, Western History Department, John R. Lawson Scrapbooks, vol. 1.

17. Henry Mathias, interview, 1975, in Ronald Loren McMahon, "Visual

Sociology: A Study of the Western Coal Miner" (Ph. D. dissertation, University of Colorado, Boulder, 1978), 92.

18. *Engineering and Mining Journal* 74 (25 October 1902): 542.

19. CMI, *3d Biennial Report, 1887–1888*, 24; *12th Biennial Report, 1905–1906*, 5; *Engineering and Mining Journal*, 91 (14 January 1911): 135.

20. WMI, District 1, *Annual Report, 1911*, 3; UMI, *Annual Report, 1905*, 5–6.

21. *United Mine Workers Journal*, 10 October 1910, 4; Colorado Bureau of Labor Statistics, *12th Biennial Report, 1909–1910*, 11.

22. Edward L. Doyle, in U.S. Commission on Industrial Relations, *Final Report and Testimony*, S. Doc. 415, 64th Cong., 1st sess., 1916, 7:6954; ibid., 6512; United Mine Workers of America, District 15, "A Manifesto. An open letter to the Governor of the State of Colorado and the Public at Large," in Colorado Archives, Governor James H. Peabody, Adm. Corr. (1903–4), box 26713, "U"; Colorado, General Assembly, Committee to Investigate Conditions in Relation to Coal Strike, *Report*, in *Senate Journal*, 13th General Assembly, 1901, 556–57, 568–69.

23. WMI, *Annual Report, 1886*, news clipping in Wyoming Archives; WMI, District 2, *Annual Report, 1910*, 6.

24. Weitzel to CF&I superintendents, 8 April 1908, in U.S. Commission on Industrial Relations, *Final Report and Testimony*, 7:6738–39; Weitzel to CF&I superintendents, 17 January 1913, ibid., 6748.

25. *United Mine Workers Journal*, 27 January 1910, 12.

26. U.S. Commission on Industrial Relations, *Final Report and Testimony*, 7:6786; see copies of verdicts, ibid., 7265–96; *United Mine Workers Journal*, 23 July 1914, 11; WMI, *Annual Report, 1891 and 1892*, 16; UMI, *6th Annual Report, 1901*, 59–62.

27. *Colorado Coal and Iron Company v. Carpita*, 40 *Pacific Reporter* 248 (1895), p. 250; *Colorado Coal and Iron Company v. Lamb*, 40 *Pacific Reporter* 251 (1895), p. 255.

28. *The Victor Coal Company v. Muir*, 20 *Colorado* 320 (1894); *Acme Coal Mining Company v. McIver*, 5 *Colorado Appeals* 267 (1894); *Burke v. Union Coal and Coke Company*, 157 *Federal Reports* 178 (1907); *Maki v. Union Pacific Coal Company*, 187 *Federal Reports* 389 (1911).

29. *National Fuel Company v. Green*, 50 *Colorado* 307 (1911), p. 308. See also *Victor-American Fuel Company v. Peccarich*, 209 *Federal Reports* 568 (1913).

30. *Deserant v. Cerrillos Coal Railroad Company*, 178 *U.S.* 409 (1900), p. 415; *Parkdale Fuel Company v. Taylor*, 144 *Pacific Reporter* 1138 (1914); *National Fuel Company v. Maccia*, 139 *Pacific Reporter* 22 (1914).

31. *Deserant v. Cerrillos Coal Railroad Company*, 178 *U.S.* 409 (1900); *Northern Coal and Coke Company v. Allera*, 46 *Colorado* 224 (1909); *Kallio v. Northwestern Improvement Co.*, 47 *Montana* 314 (1913).

32. *Parkdale Fuel Company v. Taylor*, 144 *Pacific Reporter* 1138 (1914); *Victor-American Fuel Company v. Peccarich*, 209 *Federal Reports* 568 (1913); *National Fuel Company v. Maccia*, 138 *Pacific Reporter* 22 (1914).

33. Colorado, *Session Laws, 1893*, 129–31; Colorado, *Session Laws, 1901*, 161; *Engineering and Mining Journal* 81 (16 June 1906), 1162; Gordon M. Bakken, *The Development of Law on the Rocky Mountain Frontier: Civil Law and Society, 1850–1912* (Westport, Conn.: Greenwood Press, 1983), 104.

34. Colorado, *Session Laws, 1913*, 115; *Session Laws, 1915*, 197.

35. U.S., *Statutes at Large*, 60th Cong., 1st sess., 1908, vol. 35, pt. 1, public resolution no. 22, 573–75; New Mexico (Territory), *Laws, 1903*, 51.

36. U.S. Congress, House Committee on the Territories, *Report to Accompany House Joint Resolution 94*, 60th Cong., 1st sess., 1908, in National Archives, Record Group 48, Interior Department, Territorial Papers, New Mexico, file 957, microform M 364, reel 13, 0226–32.

37. Utah, *Session Laws, 1896*, 99–100; Wyoming, *Session Laws, 1913*, 200–201.

38. *Baldi v. Cedar Hill Coal and Coke Company*, 173 *Federal Reports* 781 (1909); *Calumet Fuel Company v. Rossi*, 60 *Colorado* 87 (1915).

39. Colorado, *Session Laws, 1889*, 70; Montana, *Session Laws, 1891*, 287; Wyoming, *Session Laws, 1909*, 104–5.

40. Montana Inspector of Mines, *5th Annual Report, 1893*, 10–11. CMI, *8th Biennial Report, 1897–1898*, 3; *13th Biennial Report, 1907–1908*, 4.

41. U.S. Commission on Industrial Relations, *Report on the Relations and Conditions of Capital and Labor Employed in the Mining Industry* (Washington, D.C.: Government Printing Office, 1901), 12:266; U.S. Commission on Industrial Relations, *Final Report and Testimony*, 7:6738–50; CMI, *12th Biennial Report, 1905–1906*, 142–44; *13th Biennial Report, 1907–1908*, 6; U.S. Congress, House Committee on Mines and Mining, *Investigation of Conditions in the Coal Mines of Colorado*, 2:1782–83; USMI/NM, *Annual Report, 1902*, 354–55; U.S. Commission on Industrial Relations, *Final Report and Testimony*, 7:6759.

42. U.S. Commission on Industrial Relations, *Final Report and Testimony*, 7:6752–53; Colorado Fuel and Iron Company, *Industrial Bulletin* 8, no. 5 (15 December 1923): 9; Colorado Fuel and Iron Company, *Blast*, 15 April 1932, 11.

43. Colorado Fuel and Iron Company, *Blast*, 15 April 1932, 11; CMI, *13th Biennial Report, 1907–1908*, 6; USMI/NM, *Annual Report, 1910*, 493–94; U.S. Congress, House Committee on Mines and Mining, *Investigation of Conditions in the Coal Mines of Colorado*, 1:405.

44. CMI, *13th Biennial Report, 1907–1908*, 6.

45. A. C. Watts, "Features of Coal Mining in Utah, Principally in Carbon

County," Rocky Mountain Coal Mining Institute, *Proceedings, 1915,* 62; Papanikolas, "Utah's Coal Lands," 118.

46. Report of the Governor of New Mexico, 1909, in U.S. Department of the Interior, *Reports of the Department of the Interior for the Fiscal Year Ended June 30, 1909, Administrative Reports,* vol. 2, *Indian Affairs, Territories,* 662; USMI/NM, *Annual Report,* 1909, 691; *Annual Report, 1910,* 483.

47. WMI, *Annual Report,* 1912, 5; George B. Pryde, "The Union Pacific Coal Company, 1868 to August 1952," *Annals of Wyoming* 25, no. 2 (July 1953): 199; ibid., 194; Thomas Gibson, "What the Union Pacific Coal Company Is Doing for Safety First," Rocky Mountain Coal Mining Institute, *Proceedings,* 1917, 125–29; Pryde, "The Union Pacific Coal Company," 196.

48. W. J. Murray to Victor-American superintendents, in U.S. Commission on Industrial Relations, *Final Report and Testimony,* 8:7351.

Chapter 5

1. Colorado Inspector of Coal Mines (hereafter cited as CMI), *13th Biennial Report,* 1907–1908, 7; *Engineering and Mining Journal,* 13 February 1909, 359–61.

2. On the establishment of the U.S. Bureau of Mines, see William Graebner, "The Coal Mine Operator and Safety: A Study of Business Reform in the Progressive Period," *Labor History* 14, no. 4 (Fall 1973): 483–505, and *Coal Mining Safety in the Progressive Period: The Political Economy of Reform* (Lexington: University of Kentucky Press, 1976).

3. *Rocky Mountain News,* 1 February 1910, 14; *Denver Post,* 3 February 1910, 16.

4. *United Mine Workers Journal,* 15 December 1910, 3; 24 February 1910, 1.

5. *Denver Post,* 19 November 1910, 16.

6. *Denver Post,* 11 October 1910, 3, 14.

7. Colorado Bureau of Labor Statistics, *12th Biennial Report, 1909–1910,* 26.

8. *United Mine Workers Journal,* 27 October 1910, 1.

9. Ibid., 17 November 1910, 4.

10. Ibid., 24 November 1910, 1.

11. *Rocky Mountain News,* 11 November 1910, 14.

12. *Denver Post,* 2 February 1911, 2.

13. House Bill 542, in CMI, *14th Biennial Report, 1909–1910,* 182–215. John B. Ekeley discussed the Alderson Commission and summarized the proposed law in "The New Proposed Coal Mining Law for Colorado," *University of Colorado Journal of Engineering,* no. 7 (1910–11), 26–35.

14. Draft of the senate version of House Bill 542 in Colorado Archives,

Governor John Franklin Shafroth, Box 26727, and in Colorado General Assembly, *House Journal,* 1911, 1069–2067.

15. *United Labor Bulletin,* 6 June 1911, in Colorado Historical Society, Shafroth Collection, Scrapbooks, 2:446; Smith, Lawson, McLennan, and Hickey to Shafroth, 27 May 1911, in Colorado Archives, Governor John Franklin Shafroth, Box 26727. *Engineering and Mining Journal,* 17 June 1911, 1223, also attributed the senate changes to the operators. James Dalrymple likewise believed that the changes were the work of the operators. See *The Miners Advocate,* 1 February 1914, clipping in Denver Public Library, Western History Department, Edward Lawrence Doyle Papers, scrapbook. Edward L. Doyle to Shafroth, 18 May 1911, in Colorado Archives, Governor John Franklin Shafroth, Box 26727; *Denver Times,* 5 June 1911, clipping in Colorado Historical Society, Shafroth Collection, Scrapbooks 2:446.

16. *Denver Post,* 5 June 1911, clipping in Colorado Historical Society, Shafroth Collection, Scrapbooks, 2:445.

17. U.S. Congress, House Committee on Mines and Mining, *Investigation of Conditions in the Coal Mines of Colorado,* 63d Cong., 2d sess., 1914, 1:405, 1805.

18. Ibid., 1:405.

19. Rocky Mountain Coal Mining Institute, *Proceedings; Organizational Meeting, November 12 & 13, 1912,* 1, 4, 7.

20. Ibid., 17.

21. Ibid., 18–19.

22. Colorado General Assembly, *Senate Journal,* 1913, 936.

23. Colorado, *Session Laws, 1913,* 178.

24. Ibid., 167–68.

25. *Rocky Mountain News,* 23 March 1913, clipping in Denver Public Library, Lawson Scrapbooks, 1:20; *Denver Express,* 25 March 1913, clipping, ibid.; *Rocky Mountain News,* 23 March 1913, clipping, ibid.

26. U.S. Congress, House Committee on Mines and Mining, *Investigation of Conditions in the Coal Mines of Colorado,* 1:405; U.S. Commission on Industrial Relations, *Final Report and Testimony,* S. Doc. 415, 64th Cong., 1st sess., 1916, 8:8411; see also ibid., 8437; U.S. Congress, House Committee on Mines and Mining, *Investigation of Conditions in the Coal Mines of Colorado,* 2:1781.

27. U.S. Commission on Industrial Relations, *Final Report and Testimony,* 7:6549; U.S. Congress, House Committee on Mines and Mining, *Investigation of Conditions in the Coal Mines of Colorado,* 2:1787.

28. U.S. Commission on Industrial Relations, *Final Report and Testimony,* 7:6409.

29. James Dalrymple noted that "in enumerating mines opened and closed, these apply usually to very small country banks which come and go

under different names in different localities, probably as a demand for a wagon load of coal prompts some enterprising miner or farmer to get a lease on some old mine and work it for a short time and then give it up or sublease it. This accounts for so many new names of mines that open and close during the course of each year." CMI, *4th Annual Report, 1916,* 5.

30. New Mexico, *Laws, 1912,* 149.

31. Ibid., 154.

32. Montana, *Revised Codes of Montana of 1907,* "Political Code," sec. 1679, 1682, pp. 479–80.

33. Montana, *Revised Codes of Montana of 1907, 1915 Supplement,* "Political Code," sec. 1679–1710q, pp. 272–305.

34. See Robert W. Larson, "The Profile of a New Mexico Progressive," *New Mexico Historical Review* 45, no. 3 (July 1970): 233–44.

Chapter 6

1. *Denver Republican,* 5 May 1913, clipping in Denver Public Library, Western History Department, John R. Lawson Scrapbooks, 1:92.

2. U.S. Congress, Senate, *Report of the United States Coal Commission,* S. Doc. 195, 68th Cong., 2d sess., 1925, pt. 1:151, 155–60, 272.

3. Data on production and employment are derived from the reports of the state coal-mine inspectors.

4. U.S. Commission on Industrial Relations, *Final Report and Testimony,* S. Doc. 415, 64th Cong., 1st sess., 1916, 8:7025–31; Donald Joseph McClurg, "Labor Organization in the Coal Mines of Colorado, 1878–1933" (Ph.D. dissertation, University of California, Berkeley, 1959), 205–6.

5. United Mine Workers of America, District 15, "The Struggle in Colorado for Industrial Freedom," Bulletin No. 2, 20 August 1914, 1, copy in Denver Public Library, Western History Department, Edward Lawrence Doyle Papers, Box 1, Env. 13; United Mine Workers of America, District 15, "The Struggle in Colorado for Industrial Freedom," Bulletin No. 1, 12 August 1914, 1, ibid.

6. Frank E. Gove to editors, 27 September 1913, in Colorado Division of State Archives and Public Records (hereafter cited as Colorado Archives), Governor Elias M. Ammons, Box 26751, "Corres. re Miners Strike, A-O, 1913–1915."

7. *Pueblo Star-Journal,* 16 November 1913, 7.

8. Committee of Coal Mine Managers, *Facts Concerning the Struggle in Colorado for Industrial Freedom* (Denver, 1914), 8, 9, 15.

9. U.S. Congress, House Committee on Mines and Mining, *Investigation of Conditions in the Coal Mines of Colorado,* 63d Cong., 2d sess., 1914, 2:2232.

10. Ibid., 1:497.

11. Ibid., 1:405.

12. Ibid., 1:435, 452.

13. Ibid., 1:470.

14. U.S. Commission on Industrial Relations, *Final Report and Testimony*, 7:6441, 6454–55.

15. Ibid., 8:7201; 7:6954.

16. Ibid., 7:6530–31; 8:8012–13.

17. Ibid., 8:8006.

18. Ibid., 8:8688–89; 8:7807.

19. Ibid., 8:8689.

20. Ibid., 8:7767.

21. Ben F. Selekman and Mary Van Kleeck, *Employes' Representation in Coal Mines: A Study of the Industrial Representation Plan of the Colorado Fuel and Iron Company* (New York: Russell Sage Foundation, 1924); John D. Rockefeller, Jr., *The Colorado Industrial Plan* (n.p., 1916). Employees in CF&I's steel mills and other operations adopted the plan later.

22. Rockefeller, *Colorado Industrial Plan*, 72.

23. Selekman and Van Kleeck, *Employes' Representation in Coal Mines*, 137–38.

24. Ibid., 182, 190.

25. Colorado Industrial Commission, *The United Mine Workers of America, District No. 15, Employees of the Colorado Fuel and Iron Company vs. The Colorado Fuel and Iron Company. Findings and Award* (20 October 1917), 15.

26. Colorado Fuel and Iron Company, *Industrial Bulletin* 4, no. 3 (30 April 1919): 6; Federal Council of Churches of Christ in America, Department of Research and Information, "Industrial Relations in the Coal Industry of Colorado," *Information Service* 10, no. 11 (14 March 1931), copy in Colorado Archives, Governor William H. Adams, Correspondence, 1930, Box 26839, ff. 60, "Industrial Commission."

27. F. C. Miller, "Safety Measures, Fuel Department, The Colorado Fuel and Iron Company," Rocky Mountain Coal Mining Institute, *Proceedings, 1925*, 1:40–44; Colorado Fuel and Iron Company, *Industrial Bulletin* 11, no. 2 (15 April 1926): 17.

28. *Denver Post*, 31 October 1933, 1. CF&I steel-mill workers remained under the Industrial Representation Plan until 1942.

29. Charles Bostwick Friday, "Government Intervention in the Settlement of Industrial Disputes in Colorado" (M.A. thesis, University of Colorado, 1947), 22–25; U.S. Congress, House, Colorado Coal Commission, *Labor Difficulties in the Coal Fields of Colorado, 1914–1915*, H. Doc. 859, 64th Cong., 1st sess., 1916, 4.

30. Hazel Alice Glenny, "A History of Labor Disputes in the Northern Colorado Coal Mining Fields with Emphasis on the 1927–1928 Strike" (M.A. thesis, University of Colorado, 1938), 55–57.

31. Colorado Industrial Commission, *2d Biennial Report, 1917–1918*, 8; A. F. Desau [?] to John Shuler, 9 February 1945, letter in Colorado Archives, Department of Natural Resources, Division of Mines, Administrative Files, 1883–1972 (1947), Box 43919; Thomas Allen to Governor Edwin C. Johnson, 18 December 1934, letter in Colorado Archives, Governor Edwin C. Johnson, Correspondence, 1934, "Coal Mine Inspector," Box 26880, ff. 29.

32. University of Colorado, Institute of Behavioral Science, Western Coal Project, "The Life of the Western Coal Miner: Part I, Toil and Rage in a New Land," videotape, 1982. Workers' compensation originally provided benefits only for workers injured or killed as a result of accidents on the job. Occupational diseases were excluded from coverage. One of the Colorado Industrial Commission's earliest rulings denied benefits to a coal miner because his disability "arose from asthma and fibrosis of the lungs," not accident-related injury. Colorado Industrial Commission, "Steve Vehos, Claimant vs. The Frederick Fuel Co., Employer and the Employers' Mutual Insurance Co., Insurer," Claim #3532, *1st Biennial Report, 1915–1917*, 13–14.

33. U.S. Commission on Industrial Relations, *Final Report and Testimony* 7:6455; Colorado, *Session Laws, 1911*, 680–81; U.S. Commission on Industrial Relations, *Final Report and Testimony*, 7:6619, 6618.

34. U.S. Commission on Industrial Relations, *Final Report and Testimony*, 7:6542, 6468.

35. U.S. Congress, House, *Labor Difficulties in the Coal Fields of Colorado*, 15.

36. Livoda to B. T. Poxson, 6 November 1927, letter in Colorado Archives, Governor William H. Adams, Correspondence, 1927–1928, "Coal Strike," Box 26828, ff. 157.

37. Testimony of John Lueras, Colorado Industrial Commission hearings, 20 December 1927, typescript in University of Colorado, Western History Collection, Josephine Roche Papers, Box 7, "R.M.F. Co.—Colo. Industrial Hearings—Miners' Wages & Working Conditions, Dec. 19 thru 22, 1927," 141; testimony of Joe Varanek, 19 December 1927, ibid., 39; testimony of James Allender, 20 December 1927, ibid., 120; Colorado Industrial Commission, *10th Biennial Report, 1926–1928*, 55.

38. Testimony of Paul Damas, Colorado Industrial Commission hearings, 20 December 1927, typescript in University of Colorado, Western History Collection, Josephine Roche Papers, Box 7, "RMF Co.—Colo. Industrial Hearings—Miners' Wages & Working Conditions, Dec. 19 thru 22, 1927," 285; testimony of James Allender, 20 December 1927, ibid., 218.

39. "Schedule of Grievances and Demands of Colorado Coal Miners," typescript, ibid., "Demands of Strikers—1927"; "Demands of the I.W.W. in the Coal Mines of Colorado," flyer, ibid.; Donald Joseph McClurg, "The

Colorado Strike of 1927: Tactical Leadership of the I.W.W.," *Labor History* 4, no. 1 (Winter 1963): 73–74.

40. Colorado Industrial Commission, *10th Biennial Report*, 1926–1928, 54.

41. "Declaration of principles and agreement by and between the Rocky Mountain Fuel Company and the United Mine Workers of America, District No. 15, For Period Beginning September 1, 1930 And Ending August 31, 1932," in Mary Van Kleeck, *Miners and Management: A Study of the Collective Agreement Between the United Mine Workers of America and the Rocky Mountain Fuel Company and an Analysis of the Problem of Coal in the U.S.* (New York: Russell Sage Foundation, 1934), 248–73. This document renews the original agreement signed 16 August 1928.

42. National fatality rates for the period 1913–33 are derived from data in U.S. Department of the Interior, Geological Survey, *Mineral Resources of the United States*; U.S. Department of Commerce, Bureau of Mines, *Mineral Resources of the United States*; U.S. Department of the Interior, Bureau of Mines, *Minerals Yearbook*; U.S. Department of the Interior, Bureau of Mines, *Status of Safety in Mining*, Information Circular #7181 (1941); U.S. Department of the Interior, Bureau of Mines, *Safety in the Mining Industry*, Information Circular #7458 (1949); and U.S. Department of the Interior, Mine Enforcement and Safety Administration, *Injury Experience in Coal Mining, 1975*, Information Report 1077 (1978).

Chapter 7

1. Utah Mine Inspector (hereafter cited as UMI), *Annual Report*, 1914, 102; Alex Bisulco, Aguilar, Colorado, interview, 27 June 1978, University of Colorado, Institute of Behavioral Science, Coal Project.

2. O. G. Shearer, quoted in Anna Rochester, *Labor and Coal* (New York: International Publishers, 1931), 150.

3. U.S. Department of the Interior, Bureau of Mines, *Coal Mine Fatalities in the United States, 1870–1914 with Statistics of Coal Production, Labor, and Mining Methods, by States and Calendar Years*, Bulletin #115 (1916), 117; Edward Eyre Hunt, Jr., *What the Coal Commission Found: An Authoritative Summary by the Staff* (Baltimore: Williams and Wilkins, 1925), 256; D. K. Wilson, "Prevention and Reduction of Accidents in Wyoming," Rocky Mountain Coal Mining Institute (hereafter cited as RMCMI), *Proceedings, 1934*, 27.

4. Ben F. Selekman and Mary Van Kleeck, *Employes' Representation in Coal Mines: A Study of the Industrial Representation Plan of the Colorado Fuel and Iron Company* (New York: Russell Sage Foundation, 1924), 45; testimony of E. H. Weitzel, Colorado Industrial Commission Hearings, 10 February 1928, typescript in University of Colorado, Western History Collection, Josephine Roche Papers, Box 7, "RMF Co.—Colo. Industrial Hear-

ings—Miners' Wages & Working Conditions—Strike—Feb. 2 thru Feb. 17, 1928," 9.

5. Wyoming Inspector of Coal Mines (hereafter cited as WMI), *Annual Report, 1914* (District I), 3.

6. New Mexico Inspector of Mines (hereafter cited as NMMI), *20th Annual Report, 1931*, 5.

7. Colorado Industrial Commission, *10th Biennial Report, 1926–1928*, 54; testimony of Joe Varanek, 19 December 1927, Colorado Industrial Commission Hearings, typescript in University of Colorado, Western History Collection, Josephine Roche Papers, Box 7, "RMF Co.—Colo. Industrial Hearings—Miners' Wages & Working Conditions—Strike—Dec. 19 thru 22, 1927," 33.

8. "Agreement By and Between the Northern Colorado Coal Producers' Association and the United Mine Workers of America, District No. 15" (9 October 1933), copy in Colorado Historical Society, Bear Canon Coal Company Collection, Box 10, ff. 4.

9. WMI, *Annual Report, 1914*, 5.

10. J. F. Pettit, "Accidents in Utah Mines and Some Problems To Be Met," RMCMI, *Proceedings, 1916*, 101; Utah Industrial Commission (hereafter cited as UIC), *Biennial Report, 1918–1920*, 272–73.

11. NMMI, *Annual Report, 1918*, 61; *Annual Report, 1919*, 15.

12. U.S. Congress, Senate, *Report of the United States Coal Commission*, S. Doc. 195, 68th Cong., 2d sess., 1925, pt. 3:1684.

13. U.S. Congress, House Committee on Mines and Mining, *Investigation of Conditions in the Coal Mines of Colorado*, 63d Cong., 2d sess., 1914, 2:1784. See also Rochester, *Labor and Coal*, 154–55; *Rocky Mountain News*, 18 July 1920, 5.

14. WMI, *Annual Report, 1915*, 5.

15. U.S. Commission on Industrial Relations, *Final Report and Testimony*, S. Doc. 415, 64th Cong., 1st sess., 1916, 7:6469; Colorado State Inspector of Coal Mines (hereafter cited as CMI), *3d Annual Report, 1915*, 11.

16. Pettit, "Accidents in Utah Mines," 98; NMMI, *18th Annual Report, 1929*, 6.

17. CMI, *5th Annual Report, 1917*, 9; *6th Annual Report, 1918*, 6, 45.

18. CMI, *5th Annual Report, 1917*, 9.

19. *United Mine Workers Journal*, 6 November 1913, 4; 17 December 1914, 4; 28 May 1914, 4.

20. See testimony of Samuel Tencher, National Fuel Co.; P. M. Peltier, Boulder Valley Coal Co.; W. W. Cowden, Crown Fuel Co.; Charles Liley, Liley Coal Mining Co.; Stanley Blose, Consolidated Coal Co., and others in Colorado Industrial Commission Hearings, 28–29 December 1927, typescript in University of Colorado, Western History Collection, Josephine

Roche Papers, Box 7, "RMF Co.—Colo. Industrial Hearings—Miners' Wages & Working Conditions—Strike—Dec. 23 thru Dec. 31, 1927," 627–741; E. H. Weitzel, "The Foreman in Industry," RMCMI, *Proceedings, 1918*, 48–49.

21. U.S. Congress, Senate, *Report of the United States Coal Commission*, pt. 3:1913, 1915.

22. "Report of the Safety Committee," RMCMI, *Proceedings, 1924*, vol. 2, supplement no. 1. See also *Proceedings, 1926*, 2:41–44.

23. Helen Z. Papanikolas, "Utah's Coal Lands: A Vital Example of How America Became a Great Nation," *Utah Historical Quarterly* 43, no. 2 (Spring 1975): 119; A. C. Watts, "Features of Coal Mining in Utah, Principally in Carbon County," RMCMI, *Proceedings, 1915*, 61–64, 66; UIC, *Biennial Report, 1924–1926*, Bulletin #4, 16, 36.

24. B. W. Dyer, "The New General Coal Mine Safety Orders of the State of Utah," RMCMI, *Proceedings, 1925*, 1:90.

25. UIC, *Biennial Report, 1928–1930*, Bulletin #4, 5.

26. NMMI, *Annual Report, 1925*, 8; *Annual Report, 1914*, 31. W. C. Holman, "Minimizing and Localizing Coal Mine Explosions," *Coal Age*, 1 May 1924, 627; NMMI, *Annual Report, 1925*, 21; *Annual Report, 1928*, 5; Gilbert C. Davis, "Ten Year Campaign for Safety at Phelps Dodge Mines Yields Worth-While Results," *Coal Age*, April 1934, 123–24, 134.

27. George B. Pryde, "The Union Pacific Coal Company, 1868 to August 1952," *Annals of Wyoming* 25, no. 2 (July 1953): 196; Thomas Gibson, "What the Union Pacific Coal Company Is Doing for Safety First," RMCMI, *Proceedings, 1917*, 127; WMI, *Annual Report, 1922*, 6.

28. Pryde, "The Union Pacific Coal Company," 196; V. O. Murray, "Rules and Methods of the Safety Department of the Union Pacific Coal Company," RMCMI, *Proceedings, 1932*, 74–77.

29. CMI, *7th Annual Report, 1919*, 8; *11th Annual Report, 1923*, 12.

30. CMI, *1st Annual Report, 1913*, 8; *2d Annual Report, 1914*, 11.

31. CMI, *1st Annual Report, 1913*, 7–8; Colorado, *Session Laws, 1913*, 203. See also *Rocky Mountain News*, 4 December 1914, clipping in Denver Public Library, Western History Department, Edward L. Doyle Papers, Box 1, Env. 16, U.S. Commission on Industrial Relations, *Final Report and Testimony*, 7:6464; U.S. Congress, House Committee on Mines and Mining, *Investigation of Conditions in the Coal Mines of Colorado*, 1:24.

32. Dalrymple to deputy inspectors, 7 March 1928, in Colorado Division of State Archives and Public Records (hereafter cited as Colorado Archives), Governor William H. Adams, Correspondence, 1927–28, box 26815, ff. 29, "Coal Mine Inspector."

33. Federal Council of Churches of Christ in America, Department of Research, "Industrial Relations in the Coal Industry of Colorado," *Information Service* 10, no. 11 (14 March 1934): 10.

34. Dalrymple to Governor William H. Adams, 28 April 1932, in Colorado Archives, Governor William H. Adams, Correspondence, 1932, box 26844, ff.29, "Coal Mine Inspector." See also "Temporary 19th Annual Report, 1931," mimeo, ibid. James Dalrymple, "Coal Mining and Coal Mine Inspection," RMCMI, *Proceedings, 1934,* 61.

35. U.S. Commission on Industrial Relations, *Final Report and Testimony,* 7:6463; CMI, *11th Annual Report, 1923,* 11.

36. Colorado, *Session Laws, 1921,* 158; *Session Laws, 1925,* 361.

37. William D. Tudor to Governor Morley, 5 November 1925, in Colorado Archives, Governor Clarence Morley, Correspondence, 1925–26, box 26810, "Coal Mine Inspector, 1925"; Governor Morley to H. M. Graves, 28 December 1925, ibid.

38. Dalrymple to Governor Morley, 5 October 1925 and 20 October 1925, ibid.

39. Dalrymple to Governor Morley, 20 October 1925, ibid.

40. *Pueblo Star-Journal,* 18 February 1926, clipping, ibid.; CMI, *14th Annual Report, 1926,* 15.

41. *Dalrymple v. Sevcik,* 80 *Colorado* 297 (1926), p.303.

42. CMI, *14th Annual Report, 1926,* 15–16. Colorado, *Session Laws, 1927,* 485, 487.

43. Dalrymple to C. E. Williamson, 7 September 1927, in Colorado Archives, Governor William H. Adams, Correspondence, 1927–28, box 26815, ff. 29, "Coal Mine Inspector"; Colorado Attorney General, *Biennial Report, 1927–28,* opinion #178, 18 August 1927, 138; opinion #501, 16 November 1928, 255.

44. Sanders to Elliot, 14 June 1927, in Colorado Archives, Governor William H. Adams, Correspondence, 1934, box 26844, ff. 29, "Coal Mine Inspector"; Elliot to Governor Adams, 16 June 1927, ibid.

45. Colorado, *Session Laws, 1929,* 259; CMI, *17th Annual Report, 1929,* 12, 24.

46. Colorado, *Session Laws, 1931,* 196–98, 194; *Session Laws, 1937,* 835.

47. Colorado, *Session Laws, 1917,* 142; *Session Laws, 1925,* 366; *Session Laws, 1929,* 257; *Session Laws, 1931,* 200; *Session Laws, 1921,* 158; *Session Laws, 1925,* 361–62.

48. Wyoming, *Session Laws, 1925,* 55; *Session Laws, 1919,* 16–17; *Session Laws, 1925,* 51, 56–57; *Session Laws, 1927,* 124–25, 116; *Session Laws, 1923,* 81–82; *Session Laws, 1925,* 54; *Session Laws, 1929,* 42.

49. Wyoming, *Session Laws, 1925,* 81; *Session Laws, 1933,* 63; *Session Laws, 1925,* 242–44.

50. UIC, *Biennial Report, 1918–1920,* 272, 271.

51. *Coal Age,* 13 March 1924, 395; 20 March 1924, 431.

11. U.S. Congress, Senate Committee on Mines and Mining, *Inspections and Investigations in Coal Mines,* 76th Cong., 1st sess., 1939, 6.

12. *United Mine Workers Journal,* 1 February 1939, 12–13; 1 November 1939, 13.

13. U.S. Congress, House Committee on Mines and Mining, *Inspections and Investigations in Coal Mines,* 76th Cong., 3d sess., 1940, 173.

14. John B. Andrews, "What Is Wrong with Mine Safety Legislation," *American Labor Legislation Review* 27, no. 2 (June 1937): 74–75; U.S. Congress, House, *Inspections and Investigations in Coal Mines* (1940), 165.

15. B. A. McWilliams, in *United Mine Workers Journal,* 1 July 1940, 10.

16. Circular letter in Colorado Archives, Department of Natural Resources, Division of Mines, Administrative Files, 1883–1972, Box 43919, "1942."

17. New Mexico Inspector of Mines (hereafter cited as NMMI), *31st Annual Report,* 1942, 7; Utah Industrial Commission (hereafter cited as UIC), *Report, 1940–1942,* Bulletin #4, 76.

18. Safety Circular, September 1944; Safety Circular, December 1944, in Colorado Archives, Department of Natural Resources, Division of Mines, Administrative Files, 1883–1972, Box 43919, "1944"; "Important Paper to be Read and Discussed By All Officials' Institutes," ibid.

19. Safety Circular, 23 November 1942, in Colorado Archives, Governor Ralph L. Carr, Correspondence, 1942, Box 27025, ff. 33; Safety Circular, 25 June 1942, ibid.

20. "Courses for Study—Officials, Complete Sets by Thomas Allen," in Colorado Archives, Department of Natural Resources, Division of Mines, Administrative Files, 1883–1972, Box 43919; CMI, *Combined Annual Reports, 1941–1943,* 3.

21. U.S. Department of Labor, Bureau of Labor Statistics, *Handbook of Labor Statistics, 1950 Edition* (Bulletin #1016, 1951), 178; UIC, *Report, 1940–1942,* Bulletin #4, 62.

22. U.S. Congress, H. Rept. 168, *Investigations in Coal Mines,* 77th Cong., 1st sess., 1941, 4; U.S. Congress, House, *Inspections and Investigations in Coal Mines* (1940), 4.

23. National Coal Association, letter, 7 February 1940, in Colorado Archives, Governor Ralph L. Carr, Correspondence, 1940, Box 27007, ff. 33; U.S. Congress, Senate, *Inspections and Investigations in Coal Mines* (1939), 56, 66–68, 62–63.

24. Resolution by the Rocky Mountain Coal Mining Institute, in U.S. Congress, Senate, *Inspections and Investigations in Coal Mines* (1939), 88. See the views of operators' groups in U.S. Congress, House, *Inspections and Investigations in Coal Mines* (1940), 142–43, 546–48, 128–30. See also letter of the Colorado and New Mexico Coal Operators Association to Governor

52. UIC, *Biennial Report, 1922–1924*, Bulletin #4, 10; B. W. D
"The New General Coal Mine Safety Orders of the State of Utah," 90

53. William Monay, "Comment on Utah Mining Law," RMCMI,
ceedings, 1925, 1:104.

54. NMMI, *13th Annual Report, 1924*, 5–9; *14th Annual Report, 192*

55. New Mexico, *Laws, 1933*, 303–52.

Chapter 8

1. Thomas Allen, "Address," Rocky Mountain Coal Mining Inst
(hereafter cited as RMCMI), *Proceedings, 1935*, 102.

2. RMCMI resolution, 5 March 1934, in Colorado Division of
Archives and Public Records (hereafter cited as Colorado Archives), G
nor Edwin C. Johnson, Correspondence, 1934, Box 26880, ff. 29a, "Boa
Examiners of Coal Mine Inspection"; Colorado Attorney General, *Bie
Report, 1933–1934*, Opinion #258, 5 March 1934, 156.

3. Allen to Johnson (no date), in Colorado Archives, Governor Edw
Johnson, Correspondence, 1934, box 26880, ff. 29, "Coal Mine Inspec
Homer A. Feller to Johnson, 14 November 1934; Johnson to Felle
November 1934, ibid.

4. Allen to Johnson, 5 December 1934; Johnson to Allen, 6 Dece
1934, ibid.

5. "Statement of Charges," and "Second Amended Stateme
Charges," in Colorado Archives, Governor Teller Ammons, Corre
dence, 1937–39, Box 26918, ff. 29a, "Coal Mine Inspector"; *Rocky M
tain News*, 16 November 1937, 1, 2.

6. Letter in Colorado Archives, Governor William H. Adams, Box 2
ff. 29, "Coal Mine Inspector"; Johnson to Dalrymple, 13 June 1933, me
Colorado Archives, Governor Edwin C. Johnson, Correspondence,
Box 26862, ff. 29, "Coal Mine Inspector"; C. McCallum to Ammo
August 1938, in Colorado Archives, Governor Teller Ammons, Corre
dence, 1937–39, Box 26918, ff. 29a.

7. *Pueblo Daily Chieftain*, 19 November 1937, 4.

8. Fatality rates are derived from state coal-mine inspectors' repor
from U.S. Department of the Interior, Bureau of Mines, annual bullet
Coal Mine Accidents in the United States, Bulletins 397, 409, 420, 430
444, 448, 456, 462; and U.S. Department of the Interior, Mine Enforce
and Safety Administration, *Injury Experience in Coal Mining, 1975*,
mation Report 1077 (1978).

9. Henry J. Finch, "Trend of Accident Frequency and Severity Ra
Utah Coal Mines," RMCMI, *Proceedings, 1942*, 102.

10. U.S. Department of the Interior, Bureau of Mines, *Are Neu
ards Being Introduced in Coal Mines Faster Than Existing Hazaro
Eliminated?* Information Circular #7140 (1940).

Subcommittee on Labor, *Amending the Coal Mine Safety Act*, 86th Cong., 1st sess., 1959, 55, 56.

30. U.S. Department of the Interior, *Report of Task Force on Coal Mine Safety* (August 1963), in U.S. Congress, Senate Committee on Labor and Public Welfare, Subcommittee on Labor, *Amendments to the Federal Coal Mine Safety Act*, 89th Cong., 1st sess., 1965, 180–88.

31. Data in U.S. Congress, Senate Committee on Labor and Public Welfare, Subcommittee on Labor, *Amendments to the Federal Coal Mine Safety Act* (1965), 27, show that in the period from 1953 through 1964 mines employing fewer than fifteen workers had an average fatality rate of 2.28 per million man-hours, whereas larger mines averaged 1.22 per million man-hours. U.S. Congress, House Committee on Education and Labor, General Subcommittee on Labor, *Coal Mine Health and Safety*, 91st Cong., 1st sess., 1969, 149.

32. Bituminous Coal Operators Association, *Report of the 1967 Special Study Commission of the Bituminous Coal Operators Association on the Bureau of Mines' Special Study to Determine the Sufficiency of the Present Safety Requirements of the Federal Coal Mine Safety Act, as Amended, July, 1967*, reprinted in U.S. Congress, House Committee on Education and Labor, General Subcommittee on Labor, *Coal Mine Health and Safety*, 91st Cong., 1st sess., 1969, 146–58.

33. Fatality data are derived from the annual reports of state coal-mine inspectors and from U.S. Department of the Interior, Mine Enforcement and Safety Administration, *Injury Experience in Coal Mining, 1975*, Informational Report 1077 (1978).

34. U.S. Congress, House, *Coal Mine Health and Safety* (1969), 56, 62.

35. Ibid., 58, 61.

36. Ibid., 50, 52.

37. RMCMI, *Proceedings*, 1969, 45.

38. U.S. Congress, House, *Federal Coal Mine Health and Safety Act of 1969*, H. Rept. 563, 91st Cong., 1st sess., 1969, 6–59; *Coal Age*, March 1970, 73–74.

39. *Denver Post*, 23 April 1970, 40.

40. Colorado State Inspector of Coal Mines (hereafter cited as CMI), *Annual Report, 1970*, 1; Donald Haske, "Impact of the Federal Coal Mine Inspection Law on Colorado Coal Mines," RMCMI, *Proceedings, 1971*, 61, 63.

41. *Denver Post*, 23 April 1970, 35.

42. Ibid., 2 June 1971, 50.

43. *Rocky Mountain News*, 27 August 1971, 5–6.

44. *Denver Post*, 23 April 1970, 40; Norman R. Blake, "Coal Mine Health and Safety—State vs. Federal," RMCMI, *Proceedings, 1973*, 27, 28.

45. U.S. Congress, Senate Committee on Labor and Public Welfare,

Subcommittee on Labor, *Implementation of the Federal Coal Mine Health and Safety Act of 1969*, 92d Cong., 2d sess., 1972, 1–3, 38–39, 55, 64–65, 75–76; Orrin B. Conaway, "Coal Mining: New Efforts in an Old Field," *Annals of the American Academy of Political and Social Science* 400 (March 1972): 95; J. Davitt McAteer, *Coal Mine Health and Safety: The Case of West Virginia* (New York: Praeger Publishers, 1973), 190–202.

46. Committee on Underground Coal Mine Safety, Commission on Engineering and Technical Systems, National Research Council, *Toward Safer Underground Coal Mines* (Washington, D.C.: National Academy Press, 1982), 54–58.

47. Fatality data for the period 1970–80 are derived from the annual reports of state coal-mine inspectors; U.S. Department of the Interior, Mine Enforcement and Safety Administration, *Injury Experience in Coal Mining, 1975* (1978); and U.S. Department of Labor, Mine Safety and Health Administration, annual reports in *Injury Experience in Coal Mining*, Informational Reports 1097 (1978), 1108 (1979), 1112 (1979), 1122 (1980), 1133 (1981), 1138 (1983), and 1143 (1985).

48. Conaway, "Coal Mining: New Efforts in an Old Field," 99.

49. Colorado, *Session Laws, 1971*, 1041–42.

50. NMMI, *60th Annual Report, 1972*, 8; *66th Annual Report, 1978*, 7.

51. Wyoming Inspector of Coal Mines, *Annual Report, 1969*, 4; *Annual Report, 1972*, 4; CMI, *Annual Report, 1969*, 19; *Annual Report, 1970*, 13; Colorado Department of Natural Resources, Division of Mines, *Coal* (hereafter cited as Colorado, *Coal*) *1980*, 20; Colorado, *Session Laws, 1981*, 1660; Montana, *Session Laws, 1981*, 1:25.

52. Colorado, *Session Laws, 1971*, 1041; Colorado, *Coal, 1975*, 9; *Coal, 1976*, 8–9.

53. Colorado, *Coal, 1975*, 2; *Coal, 1978*, 9.

Chapter 10

1. *Rocky Mountain News*, 21 December 1984, 1; 24 December 1984, 18.

2. Ibid., 25 March 1987, 37; *Denver Post*, 25 March 1987, 37.

3. *Denver Post*, 27 December 1984, 20a.

4. U.S. Congress, House Committee on Mines and Mining, *Investigation of Conditions in the Coal Mines of Colorado*, 63d Cong., 2d sess., 1914, 1781–82; U.S. Commission on Industrial Relations, *Final Report and Testimony*, S. Doc. 415, 64th Cong., 1st sess., 1916, 7:6729; Daniel Harrington, "Accident Record in Western Coal Mining States," Rocky Mountain Coal Mining Institute, *Proceedings*, 1927, 2:11–16.

5. Mark Wyman, *Hard Rock Epic: Western Miners and the Industrial Revolution, 1860–1910* (Berkeley and Los Angeles: University of California Press, 1979), 115.

6. Ibid., 115.

7. Ibid., 104–7, 113; Ronald C. Brown, *Hard-Rock Miners: The Intermountain West, 1860–1920* (College Station and London: Texas A&M University Press, 1979), 76–78, 175.

8. Wyman, *Hard Rock Epic*, 84–117; Brown, *Hard-Rock Miners*, 82.

9. Wyman, *Hard Rock Epic*, 114. See also Brown, *Hard-Rock Miners*, 129–31.

10. Wyman, *Hard Rock Epic*, 190.

11. *United Mine Workers Journal*, 15 January 1952, 3.

12. U.S. Congress, House Committee on Education and Labor, Subcommittee on Labor, *Coal Mine Health and Safety*, 91st Cong., 1st sess., 1969, 61.

13. Colorado State Inspector of Coal Mines, *2d Biennial Report, 1885–1886*, 28; Colorado Department of Natural Resources, Division of Mines, *Coal, 1978*, 9; John C. Osgood, quoted in *Pueblo Star-Journal*, 16 November 1913, 7.

Bibliographical Essay

Until the 1970s, mining historians treated coal mining in the West as something of a poor relation compared to the supposedly more glamorous hard-rock mining industry. That attitude has changed somewhat as concern over energy resources and shortages has stirred new interest in America's vast coal reserves. Furthermore, new historical methodologies and emphases, such as those developed in social and labor history, have led some scholars to notice the research potential in the coal camps of the West. Scholars beginning to study the Rocky Mountain coal industry will find at their disposal substantial resources for research and a growing body of literature.

Two useful guides to the literature and primary sources are George Parkinson, *Guide to Coal Mining Collections in the United States* (Morgantown: West Virginia University Library, 1978), with references to more than nine hundred archival and manuscript collections, and Robert F. Munn, *The Coal Industry in America: A Bibliography and Guide to Studies*, 2d ed. (Morgantown: West Virginia University Library, 1977), which includes nearly three thousand references to books and articles on various aspects of coal mining and its history. Two industry publications, *Coal Age* and *Engineering and Mining Journal*, contain a wealth of information on coal mining from the nineteenth century to the present.

Important sources for research on the Rocky Mountain coal-mining industry are the annual and biennial reports of state and territorial coal-mine inspectors. These contain information not only on safety conditions and casualties, but also on the development of the industry. Typically, they include data on production, sales and shipping, economic conditions, employment, and mechanization. The annual *Proceedings* of the Rocky Mountain Coal Mining Institute contain valuable material on industrial conditions, coal-mine technology, and safety issues. Also useful are the U.S. Department of the Interior, Bureau of Mines, *Minerals Yearbook*, and the U.S. Geological Survey, *Mineral Resources of the United States*.

Regional studies of coal mining in the West include H. Lee Scamehorn, "Coal Mining in the Rocky Mountains: Boom, Bust, and Boom," in Thomas G. Alexander and John F. Bluth, eds., *The Twentieth Century American West* (Provo, Utah: Brigham Young University, Charles Redd Center for Western Studies, 1983), 29–55; Duane A. Smith, "Boom to Bust and Back Again: Mining in the Central Rockies, 1920–1981," *Journal of the West* 31, no. 4 (October 1982), 3–10; William S. Bryans, "A History of Transcontinental Railroads and Coal Mining on the Northern Plains to 1920" (Ph.D. dissertation, University of Wyoming, 1987); and James M. Link and Albert M. Keenan, "A Review of the Coal Industry in the Western United States," Colorado School of Mines Research Foundation, Inc., *Mineral Industries Bulletin* 2, no. 5 (September 1968), 1–22.

There is a growing list of books and articles dealing with various aspects of coal mining in the Rocky Mountain West. On the development of Colorado's first coal-mining giant, the Colorado Fuel and Iron Company, see H. Lee Scamehorn, *Pioneer Steelmaker in the West: The Colorado Fuel and Iron Company, 1872–1903* (Boulder: Pruett Publishing Co., 1976), and "John C. Osgood and the Western Steel Industry," *Arizona and the West* 15, no. 2 (Summer 1973), 133–48. Duane A. Smith, *When Coal Was King: A History of Crested Butte, Colorado, 1880–1952* (Golden: Colorado School of Mines Press, 1984), studies one of CF&I's coal camps. Sylvia Ruland's *The Lion of Redstone* (Boulder: Johnson Books, 1981) is a biography of John C. Osgood. Another important personality in Colorado coal is profiled in Marjorie Hornbein, "Josephine Roche: Social Worker and Coal Miner," *Colorado Magazine* 53, no. 3 (Summer 1976), 243–60. Dolores Plested, "Where Coal Was Once King," *Colorado Heritage*, 1987 (Issue 2), 30–43, recalls the trials of a small operator.

Most studies of the development of coal mining in New Mexico focus on the Raton area. See Richard H. Kesel, "The Raton Coal Field: An Evolving Landscape," *New Mexico Historical Review* 41, no. 3 (July 1966), 231–50; Vesta Kiker, "The Kingdom of Colfax," *New Mexico Magazine* 15, no. 6 (June 1937), 22–23, 45; and E. R. Harrington, "King Coal," *New Mexico Magazine* 22, no. 10 (October 1944), 9–11. Robert Glass Cleland's *A History of Phelps-Dodge, 1834–1950* concerns one of New Mexico's prominent operators. Richard Melzer, "A Death in Dawson: The Demise of a Southwestern Company Town," *New Mexico Historical Review* 55, no. 4 (October 1980), 309–30, deals with the life and death of one of the Raton area's most important coal camps.

A useful source for the growth of coal mining in Utah to the mid-1930s is Utah Investigating Committee of Governmental Units, Subcommittee on Coal Resources, *Economic Study of the Development of Utah Coal Resources* (1936). Guy M. Bishop, "More Than One Coal Road to Zion: The Utah Territory's Efforts to Ease Dependency on Wyoming Coal," *Annals of Wyoming* 60 (Spring 1988), 8–16, examines the Mormon colony's early coal-mining efforts and its struggle to break the Union Pacific's coal monopoly in Utah. On the role of the Denver and Rio Grande Western Railroad in Utah see Robert G. Athearn, *Rebel of the Rockies: A History of the Denver and Rio Grande Western Railroad* (New Haven: Yale University Press, 1962), and "Utah and the Coming of the Denver and Rio Grande Railroad," *Utah Historical Quarterly* 27, no. 2 (April 1959), 128–42. More general studies of coal mining in Utah include Thomas G. Alexander, "From Death to Deluge: Utah's Coal Industry," *Utah Historical Quarterly* 31, no. 3 (Summer 1963), 235–47; Helen Z. Papanikolas, "Utah's Coal Lands: A Vital Example of How America Became a Great Nation," *Utah Historical Quarterly* 43, no. 2 (Spring 1975), 104–24; and Floyd O'Neil, "Victims of Demand: The Vagaries of the Carbon County Coal Industry," in Philip F. Notarianni, ed., *Carbon County: Eastern Utah's Industrialized Island* (Salt Lake City: Utah State Historical Society, 1981), 23–39. A. Philip Cederlof, "The Peerless Coal Mines," *Utah Historical Quarterly* 53, no. 4 (Fall 1985), 336–56, is the reminiscence of a small Utah coal operator active from the 1930s to the early 1950s. Especially interesting is Cederlof's account of the stages of mechanization.

The history of coal mining in Wyoming is bound closely to that of the Union Pacific Railroad. See Union Pacific Coal Co., *History of the Union Pacific Coal Mines* (Omaha: Colonial Press, 1940); George B. Pryde, "The Union Pacific Coal Company, 1868 to August 1952," *Annals of Wyoming* 25, no. 2 (July 1953), 191–205; Robert G. Athearn, *Union Pacific Country* (Lincoln and London: University of Nebraska Press, Bison Books, 1971); and William S. Bryans, "A History of Transcontinental Railroads and Coal Mining on the Northern Plains to 1920" (Ph.D. dissertation, University of Wyoming, 1987). More general is Bryans's "Coal Mining in Twentieth Century Wyoming: A Brief History," *Journal of the West* 31, no. 4 (October 1982), 24–35. See also Wyoming Geological Survey, *Review of Wyoming Coal Fields* (1972).

On the history of coal mining in Montana see Robert A. Chadwick, "Coal: Montana's Prosaic Treasure," *Montana: The Magazine of Western History* 23, no. 4 (October 1973), 18–31, and William S. Bryans, "A History of Transcontinental Railroads and Coal Mining on the Northern Plains to 1920" (Ph.D. dissertation, University of Wyoming, 1987). See also Thomas Morgan, "History of Coal Mining in Montana," *Proceedings of the First Montana Coal Resources Symposium* (Butte: Montana Bureau of Mines and Geology, Special Publication 36, 1966), 3–4. Rita McDonald and Merrill G. Burlingame study the history of the Chestnut Mine in "Montana's First Commercial Coal Mine," *Pacific Northwest Quarterly* 47, no. 1 (July 1956), 23–28. William B. Evans and Robert L. Peterson discuss the Northern Pacific's shift from underground to surface mining in the 1920s in "Decision at Colstrip: The Northern Pacific Railway's Open Pit Mining Operation," *Pacific Northwest Quarterly* 61, no. 3 (July 1970), 129–36. In addition to examining Montana's worst coal-mine disaster, Paul Anderson's "'There Is Something Wrong Down Here': The Smith Mine Disaster, Bearcreek, Montana, 1943," *Montana: The Magazine of Western History* 38, no. 2 (Spring 1988), 2–13, discusses the development of coal mining in the Red Lodge area and the history of the Montana Coal and Iron Company.

Historians have paid more attention to labor conflicts in the western coal industry than to the industry itself. This is especially true of the 1913–14 strike in Colorado. Basic sources on the strike include the papers of Governor Elias Ammons in the Colorado Division of State Archives and Public Records; the papers of United Mine Workers leaders John R. Lawson and Edward L. Doyle in the Denver Public Library, Western History Department; and the papers of Edward P. Costigan in the Western History Collections at the University of Colorado, Boulder. Also important are congressional and U.S. Industrial Commission hearings and the report of a presidential commission on the strike. See U.S. Congress, House Committee on Mines and Mining, *Investigation of Conditions in the Coal Mines of Colorado* (63rd Cong., 2d sess., 1914); and U.S. Commission on Industrial Relations, *Final Report and Testimony* (S. Doc. 415, 64th Cong., 1st sess., 1916). The report of the commission named by President Wilson to study the strike is in U.S. Congress, House, Colorado Coal Commission, *Labor Difficulties in the Coal Fields of Colorado* (H. Doc. 859, 64th Cong., 1st sess., 1916). Colorado's coal operators spelled out their case during the strike with a series of pamphlets. See Committee of Coal Mine Managers, *Facts Concerning the Struggle in Colorado for Industrial Freedom*, Series 1 (Denver, 1914). For organized labor's views see the *United Mine Workers Journal.*

Labor conflict in the Colorado coalfields has produced an extensive literature. One of the best studies is Donald J. McClurg, "Labor Organization in the Coal Mines of Colorado, 1878–1933" (Ph.D. dissertation, University of California, Berkeley, 1959). On the strike of 1901 see Colorado General Assembly, Senate Committee to Investigate Conditions in Relation to Coal Strike, *Report*, in *Senate Journal of the General Assembly of the State of Colorado, 13th Session, 1901.* On the strike of 1903–4 see George G. Suggs, Jr., "The Colorado Coal Miners' Strike, 1903–1904: A Prelude to Ludlow?" *Journal of the West* 12 (January 1973), 36–52. The strike of 1913–14 is the subject of George S. McGovern and Leonard F. Guttridge's *The Great Coalfield War* (Boston: Houghton Mifflin, 1972) and McGovern's Ph.D. dissertation, "The Colorado Coal Strike, 1913–1914" (Northwestern

University, 1953). See also Eugene Porter, "The Colorado Coal Strike of 1913: An Interpretation," *Historian* 12 (1949), 3–27. Barron B. Beshoar's *Out of the Depths: The Story of John R. Lawson* (Denver: Colorado Labor Historical Committee of the Denver Trades and Labor Assembly, 1942, 1957) deals with Lawson's role in the strike and his subsequent legal troubles. The life and death of another UMWA organizer is the topic of Zeese Papanikolas's *Buried Unsung: Louis Tikas and the Ludlow Massacre* (Salt Lake City: University of Utah Press, 1982). Manfred F. Boemke, "The Wilson Administration, Organized Labor, and the Colorado Strike, 1913–1914" (Ph.D. dissertation, Princeton University, 1983), examines the federal government's response to the strike.

Even though the 1913–14 strike was a failure for the union, it did result in important changes in the industrial environment, the most notable of which was the Colorado Industrial Plan of John D. Rockefeller, Jr. The Rockefeller Plan still awaits full treatment by a historian. The best study to date is Howard M. Gitelman's *Legacy of the Ludlow Massacre: A Chapter in American Industrial Relations* (Philadelphia: University of Pennsylvania Press, 1988), which examines the work of Rockefeller and William Lyon MacKenzie King in developing and implementing the plan. In focusing on the corporate politics of the plan, Gitelman does not study its impact on CF&I employees. Ben F. Selekman and Mary Van Kleeck reported on the plan in operation in their Russell Sage Foundation study, *Employes' Representation in Coal Mines: A Study of the Industrial Representation Plan of the Colorado Fuel and Iron Company* (New York: Russell Sage Foundation, 1924). See also Rockefeller's testimony in U.S. Commission on Industrial Relations, *Final Report and Testimony* (1916), and his description of the plan in *The Colorado Industrial Plan* (n.p., 1916). McClurg, "Labor Organization in the Coal Mines of Colorado, 1878–1933" (1959), also discusses the Rockefeller Plan in some detail.

The Colorado strike of 1927–28 also has drawn some historians' interest. Basic sources for this strike are the Josephine Roche Papers in the University of Colorado, Western History Collections (including voluminous transcripts of hearings by the Colorado Industrial Commission), and the papers of Governor William Adams in the Colorado Division of State Archives and Public Records. The Colorado Industrial Commission reported on the strike in "Coal Mining Conditions in Colorado," *Monthly Labor Review* 26 (1928), 1131–36. Literature on the strike includes Donald J. McClurg, "The Colorado Coal Strike of 1927: Tactical Leadership of the I.W.W.," *Labor History* 4, no. 1 (Winter 1963), 68–92, and "Labor Organization in the Coal Mines of Colorado, 1878–1933" (1959); Charles Bayard, "The 1927–28 Colorado Coal Strike," *Pacific Historical Review* 32, no. 3 (August 1963), 235–50; Marjorie Hornbein, "Josephine Roche: Social Worker and Coal Miner," *Colorado Magazine* 53, no. 3 (Summer 1976), 243–60; Hazel Alice Glenny, "A History of Labor Disputes in the Northern Colorado Coal Mining Fields with Emphasis on the 1927–1928 Strike" (M.A. thesis, University of Colorado, 1938); and Harry O. Lawson, "The Colorado Coal Strike of 1927–1928" (M.A. thesis, University of Colorado, 1950). Bobbalee Shuler examines a neglected area of labor history, the replacement worker, in "Scab Labor in the Colorado Coal Fields: A Statistical Study of Replacement Workers During the Columbine Strike of 1927–1928," *Essays and Monographs in Colorado History*, no. 8 (1988), 55–75. Shuler finds that replacement workers hired by the Rocky Mountain Fuel Company differed little, in terms of ethnicity, literacy, skills, and marital status, from striking mine workers.

Compared to the research on Colorado, relatively little has been done on conflict in the coal mines of New Mexico, Utah, Wyoming, and Montana. On the United Mine Workers in New Mexico see Lucien H. File, "Labor Unions in New Mexico's Non-Ferrous Metal Mining Industry," *New Mexico Business* 17, no.10 (October 1964), 1–14. Two pieces by Harry R. Rubenstein deal with the Gallup strike of 1933. See "The Great Gallup Coal Strike of 1933," *New Mexico Historical Review* 52, no.3 (July 1977), 173–92, and "Political Repression in New Mexico: The Destruction of the National Miners' Union in Gallup," in Robert Kern, ed., *Labor in New Mexico* (Albuquerque: University of New Mexico Press, 1983), 91–140.

The history of the coal miners' movement in Utah has been explored by Alan Kent Powell and Helen Papanikolas. Powell's book, *The Next Time We Strike: Labor in Utah's Coal Fields, 1900–1933* (Logan: Utah State University Press, 1985), covers the crucial period in labor organization. Powell's M.A. thesis and an article focus on the first years of the twentieth century. See "Labor at the Beginning of the 20th Century: The Carbon County, Utah, Coal Fields, 1900–1905" (M.A. thesis, University of Utah, 1972) and "The 'Foreign Element' and the 1903–4 Carbon County Coal Miners' Strike," *Utah Historical Quarterly* 43, no. 2 (Spring 1975), 125–54. Helen Papanikolas focuses on the radical challenge in the early thirties in "Unionism, Communism, and the Great Depression: The Carbon County Coal Strike of 1933," *Utah Historical Quarterly* 41, no. 3 (Summer 1973), 254–300.

The coal miners' movement in Wyoming and Montana is virtually unstudied. See Bill Bryans, "Coal Mining in Twentieth Century Wyoming: A Brief History," *Journal of the West* 31, no. 4 (October 1982), 24–35; George B. Pryde, "The Union Pacific Coal Company, 1868 to August 1952," *Annals of Wyoming* 25, no. 2 (July 1953), 191–205; and Union Pacific Coal Company, *History of the Union Pacific Coal Mines* (1940). Other than brief references in the literature already mentioned, nothing has been done on the Montana coal miners' movement.

Allen Kent Powell surveys the major episodes of labor conflict in the coalfields of the American West and Canada to 1933 in "Labor's Fight for

Recognition in the Western Coalfields," *Journal of the West* 25, no. 2 (April 1986), 20–26.

In addition to the history of labor conflict, there is growing interest in who the miners were and how they lived in the coal camps. An early study of the foreign-born in the mines was U.S. Commission on Industrial Relations, *The Foreign Born in Coal Mines, Reports*, vol. 15 (Washington, D.C.: Government Printing Office, 1901). The Industrial Commission and congressional hearings on the 1913–14 strike in Colorado explored camp life extensively. The U.S. Coal Commission studied the camps in the 1920s. See U.S. Congress, Senate, *Report of the United States Coal Commission* (S. Doc. 195, 68th Cong., 2d sess., 1925).

A useful and colorful source on the life of the western coal miners is found in interviews by Eric Margolis for the University of Colorado Institute of Behavior Science's Coal Project. Transcripts of these interviews with miners, labor leaders, and others are available at the University of Colorado, Boulder, Western History Collections. The Coal Project produced a videotape, including interviews and archival film, entitled "The Life of the Western Coal Miner; Part I, Toil and Rage in a New Land." A monograph and a dissertation also are based on the Coal Project interviews. See Eric Margolis, "Western Coal Mining as a Way of Life: An Oral History of the Colorado Coal Miners to 1914," *Journal of the West* 24, no. 3 (July 1985), 5–115, and Ronald Loren McMahon, "Visual Sociology: A Study of the Western Coal Miner" (Ph.D. dissertation, University of Colorado, 1978). Duane A. Smith, *When Coal Was King: A History of Crested Butte, Colorado, 1880–1952* (1984), and Elizabeth M. Uhlig, "Starkville: A Colorado Coal Community" (M.A. thesis, University of Colorado, Colorado Springs, 1985), discuss life in two Colorado Fuel and Iron Company's camps. Also useful is the CF&I publication, *Camp and Plant*.

Joe Drasler, *Yugoslav People in Colorado* (n.p., 1980, available in the Genealogy Department, Denver Public Library), and James M. Kedro, "Czechs and Slovaks in Colorado, 1860–1920," *Colorado Magazine* 54, no. 2 (Spring 1977), 93–125, discuss the experiences of important immigrant groups in Colorado. Stanley L. Cuba, "Polish Impressions of Colorado: Letters, Diaries, and Reminiscences of Polish Visitors and Immigrants, 1894–1934," *Essays and Monographs in Colorado History*, Essays, no. 7 (1987), 49–109, includes letters by Polish-born coal miners and labor organizers.

On camp life and ethnicity in New Mexico see Frederick G. Bohme, "The Italians in New Mexico," *New Mexico Historical Review* 34, no. 2 (April 1959), 98–116; Richard H. Kesel, "The Raton Coal Field: An Evolving Landscape," *New Mexico Historical Review* 41, no. 3 (July 1966), 231–50; and two works by Richard Melzer, "A Death in Dawson: The Demise of a

Southwestern Company Town," *New Mexico Historical Review* 55, no. 4 (October 1980), 309–30, and *Madrid Revisited: Life and Labor in a New Mexican Mining Camp in the Years of the Great Depression* (Santa Fe: Lightning Tree, 1976).

On Utah miners and camps see Helen Papanikolas, "The Greeks of Carbon County," *Utah Historical Quarterly* 22, no. 2 (April 1954), 143–64, and "Utah's Coal Lands: A Vital Example of How America Became a Great Nation," *Utah Historical Quarterly* 43, no. 2 (Spring 1975), 104–24; Alan Kent Powell, "The 'Foreign Element' and the 1903–4 Carbon County Coal Miners' Strike," *Utah Historical Quarterly* 43, no. 2 (Spring 1975), 125–54; and Thomas G. Alexander, "From Dearth to Deluge: Utah's Coal Industry," *Utah Historical Quarterly* 31, no. 3 (Summer 1963), 235–47. In "A Struggle for Survival and Identity: Families in the Aftermath of the Castle Gate Mine Disaster," *Utah Historical Quarterly* 56, no. 3 (Summer 1988), 279–92, Janeen Arnold Costa examines how different ethnic groups' cultural traditions and immigration experiences influenced the responses of widows and children to a mine disaster.

The best general study of miners and coal camps in Wyoming is Bill Bryans's "Coal Mining in Twentieth Century Wyoming: A Brief History," *Journal of the West* 31, no. 4 (October 1982), 24–35. Philip A. Kalisch, "The Woebegone Miners of Wyoming: A History of Coal Mine Disasters in the Equality State," *Annals of Wyoming* 42, no. 2 (October 1970), 237–42, also discusses the camps. Glen Barrett, "P. J. Quealy: Wyoming's Coal Man and Town Builder," *Annals of Wyoming* 47 (Spring 1975), 31–44, studies Kemmerer, an independent operator's camp. See also Mrs. Charles Ellis, "History of Carbon: Wyoming's First Mining Town," *Annals of Wyoming* 8 (April 1932), 633–41. Wyoming's most famous incident involving an ethnic minority in the coal camps, the 1882 massacre of Chinese workers at Rock Springs, has been treated widely in texts, surveys, and periodical literature, but has received no detailed study. See Paul Crane and Alfred Larson, "The Chinese Massacre," *Annals of Wyoming* 12 (January 1940), 47–55, and (April 1940), 153–60. Yuji Ichioka, "Asian Immigrant Coal Miners and the United Mine Workers of America: Race and Class at Rock Springs, Wyoming, 1907," *Amerasia Journal* 6 (November 1979), 1–23, studies Japanese miners and how they came to be accepted by the union. See also the same author's *The Issei: The World of the First Generation of Japanese Immigrants* (New York: Free Press, 1988).

The study of work relations is a product of the "new" labor history with its emphasis on workers and work, rather than the "institutional" history of labor unions and industrial conflict. David Montgomery pioneered in the area of "shop floor" studies with "Workers Control of Machine Production in the Nineteenth Century," *Labor History* 17 (Fall 1969), 485–509. Montgomery incorporates the shop-floor approach in *Fall of the House of Labor* (New

York: Cambridge University Press, 1987). Interest in work and work relations in industrial manufacturing may be new, but it is surprisingly old in
coal mining. In 1911 a young man named Joseph Husband wrote his memoir,
A Year in a Coal Mine (Boston and New York: Houghton Mifflin Co, 1911),
with descriptions of the mine environment, work, and hazards. More formal
studies appeared in the 1920s with Selekman and Van Kleeck's *Employes'
Representation in Coal Mines* (1924) and Carter Goodrich's *The Miner's
Freedom* (Boston: Marshall Jones Co., 1925). Labor leader John Brophy
included vivid descriptions of the coal miner's work in his memoir, *A Miner's
Life*, ed. by J. O. P. Hall (Madison: University of Wisconsin Press, 1964).

More recent studies of work and work relations in coal mining include
Keith Dix, *Work Relations in the Coal Industry: The Hand Loading Era,
1880–1930* (Morgantown: West Virginia University, Institute for Labor Studies, 1977); David Allan Corbin, *Life, Work, and Rebellion in the Coal Fields:
The Southern West Virginia Miners, 1880–1922* (1981); Ronald Loren McMahon, "Visual Sociology: A Study of the Western Coal Miner" (Ph.D. dissertation, University of Colorado, 1978); and Eric Margolis, "Western Coal Mining as a Way of Life," *Journal of the West* 24, no. 3 (July 1985), 5–115.

Valuable sources for research in this area include the *Report of the United
States Coal Commission*, congressional and U.S. Industrial Commission
hearings on the 1913–14 strike; the hearings of the Colorado Industrial
Commission during the 1927–28 strike; and the interviews by the University
of Colorado, Institute of Behavior Science, Coal Project.

For the history of coal-mining legislation in the United States see Alex
Trachtenberg, *History of Legislation for the Protection of Coal Miners in
Pennsylvania* (New York: International Publishers, 1942); J. Davitt McAteer,
Coal Mine Health and Safety: The Case of West Virginia (New York: Praeger
Publishers, 1973); Robert E. Barrett, "The Effects of Disasters on Mine
Safety Legislation," Rocky Mountain Coal Mining Institute, *Proceedings*,
1975, 41–42; K. Austin Kerr, "The Movement for Coal Mine Safety in
Nineteenth Century Ohio," *Ohio History* (Winter 1977), 3–18, and "The
Movement for State Regulation of Coal Mines in the Nineteenth Century,"
in Paul Uselding, ed., *Business and Economic History: Papers Presented at
the Twenty-first Annual Meeting of the Business History Conference* (Ur-
bana: Bureau of Economic and Business Research, College of Commerce
and Business Administration, University of Illinois, 1975), 82–97; Glenn F.
Massay, "Legislators, Lobbyists, and Loopholes: Coal Mining Legislation in
West Virginia, 1875–1901," *West Virginia History* 32, no. 2 (April 1971),
135–70; Walter R. Jones, "Coal Mine Explosions at Almy, Wyoming: Their
Influence on Wyoming's First Coal Mining Laws," *Annals of Wyoming* 56,
no. 1 (Spring 1984), 54–65; and two articles by James Whiteside, "Protecting
the Life and Limb of Our Workmen: Coal Mining Regulation in Colorado,
1880–1920," *Essays and Monographs in Colorado History*, Issue 4 (1986),

1–24, and "Coal Mining, Safety, and Regulation in New Mexico, 1882–1933," *New Mexico Historical Review* 64, no. 2 (April 1989), 159–84. William S. Graebner's *Coal Mining Safety in the Progressive Period: The Political Economy of Reform* (Lexington: University of Kentucky Press, 1976) and "The Coal Mine Operator and Safety: A Study of Business Reform in the Progressive Period," *Labor History* 14, no. 4 (Fall 1973), 483–505, deal with the creation of the U.S. Bureau of Mines.

The annual and biennial reports of state and territorial coal-mine inspection agencies are the basic source on coal-mine safety and regulation. Bulletins, information circulars, miners circulars, reports of investigations, and technical papers published by the U.S. Bureau of Mines contain extensive information on mine-safety problems and issues, research, and injury and fatality data. See U.S. Department of the Interior, Bureau of Mines, *List of Publications Issued by the Bureau of Mines from July 1, 1910 to January 1, 1960* (1968), and subsequent editions, for a guide to these publications.

Useful, too, are the numerous congressional hearings on federal coal-mine legislation. See especially U.S. Congress, Senate Committee on Mines and Mining, *Inspections and Investigations in Coal Mines* (76th Cong., 1st sess., 1939); U.S. Congress, House Committee on Mines and Mining, *Inspections and Investigations in Coal Mines* (76th Cong., 3d sess., 1940); U.S. Congress, House Committee on Education and Labor, *Prevention of Major Disasters in Coal Mines: Hearings* (82d Cong., 2d sess., 1952); U.S. Congress, House Committee on Education and Labor, *Coal Mine Safety: Hearings* (82d Cong., 2d sess., 1952); U.S. Congress, Senate Committee on Labor and Public Welfare, Subcommittee on Mine Safety, *Providing for the Welfare of Coal Miners: Hearings* (82d Cong., 2d sess., 1952); U.S. Congress, Senate Committee on Labor and Public Welfare, Subcommittee on Labor, *Amendments to the Federal Coal Mine Safety Act* (89th Cong., 1st sess., 1965); U.S. Congress, House Committee on Education and Labor, *Coal Mine Health and Safety: Hearings* (91st Cong., 1st sess., 1969); and U.S. Congress, Senate Committee on Labor and Public Welfare, Subcommittee on Labor, *Coal Mine Health and Safety: Hearings* (91st Cong., 1st sess., 1969).

On personal injury law and workers' compensation see Gordon M. Bakken, *The Development of Law on the Rocky Mountain Frontier: Civil Law and Society, 1850–1912* (Westport, Conn.: Greenwood Press, 1983), and "The Development of Law in Colorado, 1861–1912," *Colorado Magazine* 53, no. 1 (1976), 63–78; James Weinstein, "Big Business and the Origins of Workmen's Compensation," *Labor History* 8 (Spring 1967), 156–74; and U.S. Department of Labor, *Growth of Labor Law in the United States* (Washington, D.C.: Government Printing Office, 1962, 1967).

For work and safety in hard-rock mining see Ronald C. Brown, *Hard-Rock Miners: The Intermountain West, 1860–1920* (College Station and

London: Texas A&M University Press, 1979); Mark Wyman, "Industrial Revolution in the West: Hard-Rock Miners and the New Technology," *Western Historical Quarterly* 5, no. 1 (January 1974), 39–58, and *Hard Rock Epic: Western Miners and the Industrial Revolution, 1860–1910* (Berkeley and Los Angeles: University of California Press, 1979); David Emmons, "Immigrant Workers and Industrial Hazards: The Irish Miners of Butte, 1880–1919," *Journal of American Ethnic History* 5 (Fall 1985), 41–64; and Brian Shovers, "The Perils of Working in the Butte Underground: Industrial Fatalities in the Copper Mines, 1880–1920," *Montana: The Magazine of Western History* 37, no. 2 (Spring 1987), 26–39.

Index